"This is the most profound—and the most elegantly written—meditation on the historical genealogy, constitutive difficulties, and vexed political meanings of the cluster of ideas and practices that go under the sign of multi-culturalism. By relating multi-culturalism not only to liberalism in the abstract, but also to the knot formed by American exceptionalism and its disavowed alterity, Edmund Fong is able to explore not only the dissimulation and limitations, but also the value and the challenges, of efforts to conceive cultural difference in politically generative ways. In prose that is keenly incisive, finely nuanced, and rigorously argued, Fong helps critics of liberal individualism and of American nationalism get beyond the reactive politics of merely remembering of alterity, to instead think creatively about how to forge emergent political possibilities out of the resistant residues of our vexed history."

—*George Shulman, New York University*

"Edmund Fong argues passionately and eloquently that the dream of optimistic American exceptionalism and the nightmare of racial hierarchy are not opposing forces. Rather, their codependent relationship has persisted throughout and shaped American history, rendering them inseparable. Race—even after its elimination as a structural feature of state institutions—has thus remained as a residual factor that silently shapes contemporary initiatives around multiculturalism and pluralism. Casting a critical eye on how triumphal memorializations of racial struggle strip away any potential for radical transformation, Fong calls for a deeper consideration of how racial ordering has always provided the foundation for America's liberal ideals. A pathbreaking contribution to American political thought!"

—*Julie Novkov, SUNY-Albany*

American Exceptionalism and the Remains of Race

In contemporary American political culture, claims of American exceptionalism and anxieties over its prospects have resurged as an overarching theme in national political discourse. Yet never very far from such debates lie animating fears associated with race. Fears about the loss of national unity and trust often draw attention to looming changes in the racial demographics of the body politic. Lost amid these debates are often the more complex legacies of racial hybridity. Those who are anxious about the disintegration of the fabric of American national identity likewise forget not just how these concerns echo past fears of subversive racial and cultural difference but also exorcise as well the changing nature of work and social interaction.

Edmund Fong's book examines the rise and resurgence of contemporary forms of American exceptionalism as they have emerged out of contentious debates over cultural pluralism and multicultural diversity in the past two decades. For a brief time, serious considerations of the force of multiculturalism entered into a variety of philosophical and policy debates. But in the American context, these debates often led to a reaffirmation of some variant of American exceptionalism with the consequent exorcism of race within the avowed norms and policy goals of American politics. Fong explores how this "multicultural exorcism" revitalizing American exceptionalism is not simply a novel feature of our contemporary political moment, but is instead a recurrent dynamic across the history of American political discourse.

By situating contemporary discourse on cultural pluralism within the larger frame of American history, this book yields insight into the production of hegemonic forms of American exceptionalism and how race continues to haunt the contours of American national identity.

Edmund Fong is Assistant Professor of Political Science and Ethnic Studies at the University of Utah. His research interests occupy the nexus between critical race studies, American political thought and development, and contemporary political theory.

Routledge Series on Identity Politics

Series Editor: Alvin B. Tillery, Jr., *Rutgers University*

Group identities have been an important part of political life in America since the founding of the republic. For most of this long history, the central challenge for activists, politicians, and scholars concerned with the quality of U.S. democracy was the struggle to bring the treatment of ethnic and racial minorities and women in line with the creedal values spelled out in the nation's charters of freedom. In the midst of many positive changes, however, glaring inequalities between groups persist. Indeed, ethnic and racial minorities remain far more likely to be undereducated, unemployed, and incarcerated than their counterparts who identify as white. Similarly, both violence and work place discrimination against women remain rampant in U.S. society. The Routledge series on identity politics features works that seek to understand the tension between the great strides our society has made in promoting equality between groups and the residual effects of the ascriptive hierarchies in which the old order was rooted.

Black Politics Today
The Era of Socioeconomic Transition
Theodore J. Davis Jr.

Jim Crow Citizenship
Liberalism and the Southern Defense of Racial Hierarchy
Marek Steedman

The Politics of Race in Latino Communities
Walking the Color Line
Atiya Kai Stokes-Brown

Conservatism in the Black Community
To the Right and Misunderstood
Angela K. Lewis

The Post-Racial Society is Here
Recognition, Critics and the Nation State
Wilbur C. Rich

Race and the Politics of the Exception
Equality, Sovereignty, and American Democracy
Utz McKnight

Barack Obama and the Myth of a Post-Racial America
Edited by Kevern Verney, Mark Ledwidge, and Inderjeet Parmar

American Identity in the Age of Obama
Edited by Amílcar Antonio Barreto and Richard L. O'Bryant

New Body Politics
Narrating Arab and Black Identity in the Contemporary United States
Therí A. Pickens

American Exceptionalism and the Remains of Race
Multicultural Exorcisms
Edmund Fong

American Exceptionalism and the Remains of Race

Multicultural Exorcisms

Edmund Fong

NEW YORK AND LONDON

First published 2015
by Routledge
711 Third Avenue, New York, NY 10017

and by Routledge
2 Park Square, Milton Park, Abingdon, Oxon OX14 4RN

Routledge is an imprint of the Taylor & Francis Group, an informa business

First issued in paperback 2016

Library of Congress Cataloging-in-Publication Data

Fong, Edmund.
American exceptionalism and the remains of race : multicultural exorcisms / by Edmund Fong.
pages cm. — (Routledge series on identity politics)
1. Political culture—United States. 2. Exceptionalism—United States. 3. Race—Political aspects—United States. 4. National characteristics, American—Political aspects. 5. Cultural pluralism—Political aspects—United States. 6. Multiculturalism—Political aspects—United States. 7. United States—Politics and government—1989– I. Title.
JK1726.F65 2014
306.20973—dc23 2014008844

ISBN13: 978-1-138-79400-9 (hbk)
ISBN13: 978-1-138-68702-8 (pbk)

Typeset in Sabon
by Apex CoVantage, LLC

Contents

Acknowledgments

This book has traveled a long road, and it surely would have lost its way at numerous points if not for the mentorship of many. I would first like to thank Victoria Hattam for her untiring support and intellectual guidance. She has been this book's main creditor despite my many defaults, and I have learned much from her over the years about the rigors and joys of intellectual inquiry. I owe a great debt to the late Victor Wolfenstein as well; without him I would never have set foot on the path of political inquiry. He will always be the model for me of the fearless scholar and capacious teacher. Special and enduring thanks go to George Shulman, Julie Novkov, and Uday Mehta, who helped guide and push this project along at key moments. They gave me the confidence that perhaps I did have something small to say about political theory, race, and American politics. I have also been fortunate to encounter new mentors here at the University of Utah who have helped push this project through its final hurdles. In particular, I owe a debt of gratitude to Peregrine Schwartz-Shea, Daniel Levin, and Brent Steele.

I would also like to thank the University of Utah and my colleagues in the Department of Political Science and the Ethnic Studies Program for providing the institutional support without which this project could never have been completed. I have benefited much from the examples set by my colleagues, and I am thankful for the support they have shown me. I extend thanks to my students over the years as well, who have inspired me and unwittingly served in the refinement of my thoughts. In particular, I thank Neil Gong, Matthew Dell, Rose Blanshei, Nina Pick, Whitney Benns, Esther Kim, Tillie McInnis, Lauren Howells, Rondell Nelson, and Kehaulani Folau.

Special thanks go to the staff at Routledge for the warm and expeditious interest it has shown to this project. In particular, I would like to thank Natalja Mortensen, Michael Kerns, and the anonymous reviewers for Routledge in their generous feedback and hospitable support.

Many friends and colleagues have helped fertilize this book throughout its many stages. Their friendship and camaraderie have provided me a sense of intellectual community over the years, and I am forever thankful for their sustenance both in and outside academia. Special thanks go to my New School crew: Kevin Bruyneel, Catherine Celebrezze, Jennifer Gaboury,

Joseph Lowndes, Nancy Wadsworth, Priscilla Yamin, and honorary member Dan Skinner. I would also like to thank a number of my fellow travelers who have certainly enlivened this work through their conversations and confidences, from diapers to Derrida, disciplinary constraints to advanced Dungeons and Dragons (yes, I confess it): Lourdes Alberto, Dolores Calderon, Willie Gin, Walter Hergt, Albert Lowe, Ella Myers, Megan Obourn, and Clayton Pierce.

Finally, I owe an immeasurable gratitude and infinite responsibility to my parents and loved ones. My father, Benson Fong, and mother, Yuk Ling Fong, have always shown a boundless encouragement toward me, despite their hardscrabble origins. I will never forget that I am one generation removed from peasantry and indentured servitude. I have certainly asked of them more than they bargained for in supporting my drive all these long years. Thanks also to my sister, Eva Fong, and my brother, Alan Fong, who have mentally and physically shaped me in ways that I will leave unsaid. Without a doubt, this book would not have been possible but for the love of my wife, Regina Kim. I still remember that day sitting on the steps of the Brooklyn Academy of Music when I faced a turning point and you guided me through with confidence and assurance. You have always been a friend of my mind. For my parents and siblings, for Regina, and now for my dear dear Oscar, these words are only a beginning.

1 American Exceptionalism's Unfinished Business

Of hope bereft, there's nothing left/But wearing of the black.

—*Hamlet's Lament*[1]

In June 1997, President Bill Clinton launched his "One America in the 21st Century" initiative. In the aftermath of contentious changes to welfare, controversies over his "mend it, don't end it" approach to affirmative action, and the longer shadow cast by the Los Angeles riots of 1992, Clinton auspiciously began his second term with an effort to call attention to the nation's diversity and to encourage dialogue across racial and ethnic divisions. Speaking before the graduating class at the University of California San Diego, President Clinton called attention to the "problem of race" as "the greatest challenge we face" and also "our greatest opportunity," as both the "oldest" question of discrimination and prejudice as well the "newest." Posing the question "can we become one America in the 21st century?" Clinton ambivalently answered:

> Our hearts long to answer yes, but our history reminds us that it will be hard. The ideals that bind us together are as old as our nation, but so are the forces that pull us apart. Our founders sought to form a more perfect union; the humility and hope of that phrase is the story of America and it is our mission today. . . . To be sure, there is old, unfinished business between black and white Americans, but the classic American dilemma has now become many dilemmas of race and ethnicity.[2]

Hoping to lead the country in a "great unprecedented conversation about race," Clinton announced the creation of an advisory panel that would promote dialogue across racial divides "in every community" while recommending "concrete solutions" that would "lift the burden of race and redeem the promise of America." Noting potential skepticism about what he hoped to achieve, Clinton averred that though "nothing more than talk" would not be enough, so to would "disconnected acts of policy." "But if ten years from now," he continued, "people can look back and see that this year of honest dialogue and concerted action helped to lift the heavy burden of race from our children's future, we will have given a precious gift to America." Of course, despite the recommendations of the advisory board and the brief flurry of "dialogue" in communities across the country, the nation's attention would soon shift when news of the Monica Lewinsky scandal first broke in January 1998.

Roughly a decade later, another major public speech on race captured the nation's attention when then-presidential candidate Barack Obama delivered his widely noted speech "A More Perfect Union" at the National Constitution Center in Philadelphia on March 18, 2008.[3] The occasion for the speech was a response to the growing controversy surrounding Obama's association with his longtime pastor Reverend Jeremiah Wright. Video clips of Reverend Wright delivering sermons harshly criticizing the United States government for crimes against people of color went viral, calling into question Obama's association with his pastor's views and directly jeopardizing the optimistic postpartisan image that had first catapulted Obama to national fame during the 2004 Democratic National Convention. Sensing what he would later describe to be a "teachable moment,"[4] Obama moved beyond simply distancing himself from Reverend Wright and spoke at length about the "racial stalemate we've been stuck in for years." The controversies surrounding Reverend Wright's sermons, he argued, "reflect the complexities of race in this country that we've never really worked through—a part of our union that we have yet to perfect." In one of the distinctive moves of the speech, Obama would depict a polarized landscape of intertwined but opposed black and white resentments—the former in response to the contemporary legacies of racial discrimination, the latter in response to the perception that "in an era of stagnant wages and global competition, opportunity comes to be seen as a zero-sum game" particularly with regard to issues like affirmative action. The scandal over Reverend Wright's views, in particular his phrase "no no no, not God bless America, God damn America," played to these resentments and reflected a politics of "division, and conflict, and cynicism" where race served only to incite an endless political spectacle.

Instead, as if channeling Walt Whitman's "Song of Myself," Obama invoked an image of the democratic multitude and called attention to the "choice" offered by this occasion:

> at this moment, in this election, we can come together and say, "Not this time." This time we want to talk about the crumbling schools that are stealing the future of black children and white children and Asian children and Hispanic children and Native American children. This time we want to reject the cynicism that tells us that these kids can't learn; that those kids who don't look like us are somebody else's problem.

Earlier, Obama had repeated his signature move to call attention to the unique circumstances of his own American story. He was the "son of a black man from Kenya and a white woman from Kansas," had attended "some of the best schools in America and lived in one of the world's poorest nations," was married to a "black American who carries within her the blood of slaves and slaveowners," and had an extended family "of every race and every hue, scattered across three continents." He could no more disown Reverend Wright than he could his own white grandmother, "who on more than one occasion has uttered racial and ethnic stereotypes that made me cringe." This decidedly mottled, multiracial, and multicultural heritage was as much a legacy of America as it was of his own background. Binding himself and his candidacy as a vitiation of American exceptionalism, Obama would repeat the line he had used back in 2004: "I will never forget that in no other country on Earth is my story even possible."

These two speeches on race, separated by roughly a decade, encapsulate the tensions that surround the discourses of American exceptionalism, race, and multicultural diversity in contemporary America. They evoke the constellation of arguments that define the larger scope of this book and have structured our understanding of American national identity and its contemporary trajectories. What defines America today? What unites its citizens? What makes it special? Is it living up to its promise? Or is it in decline? Both speeches evoke an image of American national identity and unity as both in question but also prefigured. Clinton spoke of "ideals that bind us together as old as our nation." Obama began and ended his speech with the signing of the Constitution, "where the perfection [or our union] begins." Both speeches as well position race and racial identity as an obstacle to the realization of American exceptionalism and national unity. "To be sure, there is old, unfinished business between black and white Americans," Clinton warned, just as Obama would describe a polarized landscape of racial resentments that would keep us fractured and distracted, unable to bind "our particular grievances" to the "larger aspirations of all Americans." In short, both speeches repeat an opposition between American exceptionalism and its racial divides. The promise of a more perfect union, the realization of American exceptionalism as a nation uniquely devoted to individual liberty, opportunity, and freedom, is both set down in advance and dependent upon transcending the country's racial divides and its racial history.

Of course, that American exceptionalism and race have been opposed and intertwined is as old as the nation itself. Even as Obama called forth the signing of the Constitution "where the perfection" of a more perfect union begins, he also spoke of it as "unfinished" and "stained" by the "original sin of slavery." One might say Clinton and Obama both were merely drawing attention to the unfinished business of American exceptionalism and its ongoing struggle for racial justice. But the repetitive rhetorical structure of the American dilemma should give us pause. Thomas Jefferson, himself hoping to describe and showcase the unique characteristics of the new nation in his *Notes on the State of Virginia*, wondered aloud what would follow upon his own bill to emancipate all slaves born after a certain date:

> It will probably be asked, Why not retain and incorporate the blacks into the state? . . . Deep rooted prejudices entertained by whites; ten thousand recollections, by the blacks, of the injuries they have sustained; new provocations; the real distinctions which nature has made . . . will divide us into parties, and produce convulsions which will probably never end. . . .[5]

Even if slavery were to end, Jefferson seems to conclude, race would continue to divide the nation and foreclose its exceptional promise. It is not just the unfinished struggle for racial equality and racial justice that stands as an obstacle to the realization of American exceptionalism but perhaps the remains of race itself and its ongoing identifications. In particular, it may be that the project of revitalizing and reaffirming American exceptionalism rhetorically *depends* upon continually disavowing race in its material remains and identifications. If so, then race is not just the unfinished remainder in the nation's realization of its exceptional promise but is endlessly deployed in order to conjure the very meaning of American exceptionalism. Not just unfinished, it may perhaps be impossible to resolve given the way American exceptionalism has been conceived and configured.

In fact, despite the sense of paralysis, amnesia, and recursive repetition of these two speeches a decade apart, the belief in American exceptionalism has not waned or lessened in importance. Instead, the climate of American political culture finds itself all the more drawn to and embroiled in the resurgence of anxious and harried forms of American exceptionalism set against endless provocations of race and cultural difference. Amid anti-immigrant hysteria, resolutions against the infiltration of sharia law, or perhaps concern over Newt Gingrich's charge that a "black Kenyan anti-colonial" mentality secretly informs President Obama's worldview, the specters of race have kept pace with claims of American exceptionalism.[6] On the other hand, those who believed that the election of Barack Obama might usher in a postracial era might find an unexpected vitiation of that belief. With a few high-profile exceptions, President Obama has largely steered clear of foregrounding issues of race, even allegedly talking less about race in his first two years of office than any Democratic president since 1961.[7] If President Obama has largely avoided the politically divisive "stalemate" of race, one can chart the evolution of his own relationship to American exceptionalism. President Obama's meteoric rise has always been bound to his self-avowed claim that "in no other country on Earth is my story even possible." He has, as well, invoked the phrase "American exceptionalism" more than any president in the past eighty-two years.[8] But at least in the context of American foreign policy, President Obama early on attempted to qualify his embrace of American exceptionalism. Asked in 2009 at a press conference in Strasbourg, France, whether he subscribed to the "school of American exceptionalism," President Obama responded, "I believe in American exceptionalism, just as I suspect that the Brits believe in British exceptionalism and the Greeks believe in Greek exceptionalism."[9] In his rise to prominence and in his early forays in foreign policy, such statements indicate that Obama had tried to form a more culturally plural conception of American exceptionalism.

Since then one can read his subsequent State of the Union addresses as progressively more strident and less nuanced evocations of American exceptionalism. In 2011 he observed, "We are the first nation to be founded for the sake of an idea—the idea that each of us deserves the chance to shape our own destiny." In 2012, "America remains the one indispensable nation in world affairs." In 2013, over growing concern about the Syrian civil war and possible U.S. intervention, President Obama and Russian President Vladimir Putin engaged in a public dust-up about American exceptionalism, with President Putin stating in a *New York Times* op-ed that "it is extremely dangerous to encourage people to see themselves as exceptional, whatever the motivation."[10] In a speech before the United Nations General Assembly later that month, President Obama dismissed concerns about American empire as "useful propaganda" and reaffirmed that "I believe that America is exceptional . . . to stand up not only for our narrow self-interest, but for the interests of all."[11] Finally, in his 2014 State of the Union address, President Obama concluded his speech by reaffirming that "for more than two hundred years, we have put those things aside and placed our collective shoulder to the wheel of progress," emphatically ending with the simple words "Believe it." What were those "things" put aside? Not the "original sin of slavery" or the history of various exclusions and oppressions that have accompanied the singular "wheel of progress" but stumbles, mistakes, frustrations, and discouragements.

If the larger meaning of American exceptionalism has been symptomatically tied to the disavowals of the remains of race, the thematic focus of this book lies in the role of cultural difference and multiculturalism in leveraging that "old" dilemma for contemporary times. Recall that both Clinton and Obama explicitly drew attention to the nation's diversity in calling for new dialogue on the country's racial divides. Clinton spoke of the need to attend to "many dilemmas of race and ethnicity" and went on to cite as an example "the tension between black and Hispanic customers and their Korean or Arab grocers." Obama repeatedly drew attention to himself as the embodiment of the nation's cultural hybridity, providing him a unique leverage as the heir of many legacies of the American multicultural multitude to bridge the "racial stalemate" of contemporary times. Both speeches therefore frame the country's unavoidable diversity as offering new challenges and opportunities, as connecting its "oldest" problem to its "newest."

Despite their embrace of the new openness toward cultural pluralism and diversity in forging a new American national identity, both men tether that prospect conditionally between the old dilemmas of race and a revitalized American exceptionalism. "In no other country in the world is my story even possible," proclaimed Obama, highlighting his decidedly multiracial and multicultural upbringing. Indeed, the Obama administration has continually showcased unconventional multicultural paragons of American hard work, sacrifice, and responsibility. And yet paradoxically, the new attention to cultural diversity and hybridity is constantly displaced, by him but also in his reception. Critics on the right persistently scrutinize him through the lens of blackness and question his authenticity and patriotism. Meanwhile, even supporters view him singularly as "our first Black president," potentially putting to rest any racial demons through his far-from-radical liberal pragmatism. Our multicultural moment seems to have gone quietly in the night unnoticed, bound for opposed shores, offering no transformative destination of its own. Either denuded in American exceptionalist garb or reduced to the binaries of the American dilemma, the multicultural turn of the past two decades has merely served to vitiate what Clinton called "success in the American Way" while keeping in place the haunting residues of race.

It would be one thing to focus solely on the political maneuverings of these two presidents as I have largely sketched so far. If that were the only arena, one might simply reduce the tensions examined among American exceptionalism, race, and multiculturalism as part of the tumult of our politically partisan present. But the attention to issues of multicultural diversity and cultural pluralism has been a larger phenomenon throughout liberal Western democracies for the past three decades. With the fall of the Soviet Union and the pressures of migration back to the metropoles of an ascendant capitalist world order, the 1990s in particular witnessed an explosion of reflection and commentary on the challenge of how to accommodate and include minority cultural groups in liberal democratic societies. Collectively, this discourse by a broad array of scholars and pundits encompassed a burgeoning set of reflections, proposals, and dilemmas that came to possess a surprising degree of coherence. For instance, the challenge raised by cultural pluralism was persistently framed as a *novel* development on the horizon of late-twentieth-century liberal democracies—as if to say, *now* we are confronting the issue of group difference, *now* we must consider the plurality of national identity. Moreover, the problematizing object—variously formulated as a politics of recognition, a politics of presence, multicultural citizenship, the politics of difference or diversity, or, more simply, the demand for marginalized groups to be included qua their marginalized identity[12]—was persistently framed as a *new* set of demands. And it was axiomatic of this discursive production that the point of contention centered on its tensions with a privileged and stable reference point in the form of a liberal commitment to individual rights and autonomy.

In question throughout this field of multicultural discourse was therefore the formation of new liberal norms of cultural pluralism and how they would bridge new dilemmas of difference—not just race or ethnicity, but also religion, sexuality, and gender. Curiously, many treatments would find their limit in the American case. For every Charles Taylor arguing for the necessity of engaging the politics of recognition, there was a Michael Walzer who argued that this might be salient for some societies but not for an immigrant society like the United States.[13] For every Will Kymlicka who argued that cultural recognition was consistent with and was necessitated by liberal principles of toleration, there was a Brian Barry or a Susan Moller Okin who argued that such recognition was incompatible or in strong tension with equality and autonomy.[14] For every Iris Marion Young or Anne Phillips who sought to devise formal mechanisms for the inclusion of marginalized groups, others, like David Hollinger or Walter Benn Michaels, argued that enshrining group difference fundamentally distorted a core American ethos.[15] In the hands of these and other commentators, multiculturalism became the collective occasion for reimagining the *coherence* and boundaries not just of liberal societies but of American exceptionalism as its most peculiarly insulated instance.

"In the beginning all the world was America," claimed John Locke in the *Second Treatise of Government*, and in that statement lay the mythic foundations of both American exceptionalism and the emergent liberal world system of settler colonialism alike.[16] If at the end of the twentieth century leading into the twenty-first century we find the elaboration of the limits of cultural pluralism revitalizing a discourse of liberal hegemony and American exceptionalism, we ought to pause and consider whether we are dealing with a subterranean grammar that has very deep roots indeed. After all, it was not simply racial conservatives, demagogues, or ethnic nationalists who opposed and sharply questioned the impact of cultural pluralism but predominantly liberals who debated and progressively found their way to a rediscovery of American national identity or of liberalism as a "fighting creed."[17] If we are to understand the roots of how the *new* problem of multicultural diversity could nevertheless repeat a *liberal* American exceptionalism set against the *old* remains of race, we must thus begin with how questions of cultural diversity and multicultural pluralism have been framed and configured within the wider backdrop of a hegemonic liberal discourse. We must thus draw upon critical resources that can give us leverage on the workings of liberalism as a hegemonic and historicist discourse. Elements of Marxist, postcolonial, and poststructuralist theory have long confronted the challenge of grasping the embodiment of a seemingly neutral and universalist Liberal tradition and it is in developing such a critical framework that I now turn.

LIBERAL MULTICULTURAL HISTORICISM

> They cannot represent themselves, they must be represented.
>
> —Karl Marx[18]

Karl Marx's famously elusive line, rendered even more haunting through Gayatri Spivak's postcolonial extension to the subaltern subject,[19] speaks to the dilemmas of representation inherent in what was for Marx a discourse of liberal capitalist historicism. For Spivak, the subaltern could never speak for itself in any transparent way outside the mediation of "power, desire and interest." By definition an excluded remainder caught in the demand for representation yet never fully contemporaneous with itself, the subaltern presence was always at risk over its subjection and appropriation by others. Or, as Marx continued, speaking of Napoleon, "their representative must at the same time appear as their master, as an authority over them, as an unlimited governmental power that protects them against the other classes and sends them the rain and the sunshine from above."[20] Hence, the question of transubstantiating the haunting presence of the subaltern, of giving it a representative political presence, always passed through the filter of an ideological network that "dissimulates the choice of and need for 'heroes,' paternal proxies, agents of power."[21]

Certainly the possibility of group rights and the recognition of cultural difference—that carrot dangled and debated in liberal multicultural discourse—must have occurred to some as a powerful compensatory form of political representation and inclusion for excluded groups. Indeed, many commentators within this discourse sought to foster that inclusionary opening by favorably reworking the normative basis through which racial-ethnic groups could gain a more durable political presence within Western liberal democracies. Multicultural discourse during this period therefore seemed to signal a timely progress, a progressive development in Western liberal democracies wherein the final frontiers of long-standing exclusions were being torn down, just as the Berlin Wall was torn down, paving the way for "full" democracy and the end of history. Liberal commentators seemed willing to acknowledge the tacit white or Eurocentric cultural hegemonies that had for so long shaped the bounds of inclusion and the agendas of its politics; they seemed willing to recognize the internal heterogeneity of their own societies, the undeniable fact of multiculturalism. For Will Kymlicka, the time had come for liberalism to address that blind spot in the tradition over its own "nation-building imperatives," wherein minority groups were marginalized as other in the historical drive for national development.

Multiculturalism was thus increasingly cast in a historicist frame. It was addressed as a novel development in the unfolding trajectory of liberal realization. If historicism is an approach to historical time that privileges a certain vantage point, then the question of the demands raised by excluded racial-ethnic groups and women were transformed into a stage for the ongoing elaboration of liberal norms. If historicism appropriates time by substituting a developmental trajectory for it, then the formulation of cultural group rights around cultural difference would serve as the imagined proxy through which the remains of the racially excluded and others would advance out of their political abjection and enter into the currency of normal politics. Whatever else one might say about cultural pluralism, its extension to the racial and ethnic subaltern sought to transform their claims into a conventional interest. It should be noted that these consequences depend less on the sympathies of liberal commentators than on the very historicist form through which the racial subaltern were assessed, represented, and included. This is necessarily so because privileging the norms of liberalism as the basis for devising the means of inclusive representation severs any mutually constitutive relationship between exclusion and the prior terms of inclusion.[22] It dissimulates that mediating relationship of power, desire, and interest that governs exclusion and representative inclusion alike. Appropriating aspects of the excluded in this manner might lead to alternative future paths in the politics of liberal societies, but this does not address the historically constitutive dynamics that account for exclusion to begin with. For instance, we might come to respect cannibalism or not, as Steven Lukes frames it, but how did we come to see cannibalism as a sign of difference to begin with?[23] It could be said that if this discourse of liberal multicultural historicism offered a timely normative imaginary for the changing demographic makeup in Western liberal democracies, it did so by conflating and appropriating the residual claims of the excluded into a newly emergent problem. Hence the question of reassessing the normative basis for including the subaltern presence may just as well turn out to be the historical repetition of those dividing lines.

To sharpen these contentions, consider the strange fate of race in its peculiar interaction with the historicism of American exceptionalism. Almost from the beginning of liberal multicultural discourse, the proposal to recognize the cultural difference of racial groups encountered fierce criticism and objection. Of course it was evident that in the case of race, recognizing racial difference would be especially problematic given that spurious differences were the very historical basis for the exclusion and domination of blacks and other racialized groups. In addition, not only were such differences prone to essentialist problems, but recognizing them flew in the face of the integrationist consensus that emerged in the United States after the civil rights era. Recognizing racial cultural difference was a nonstarter for a political milieu where recognizing racial classification at all was highly contentious. It seemed to threaten that exceptionalist ideal of American mobility and amalgamation that was reasserting itself at the same time. From a more leftist perspective, sanctioning group difference also betrayed a startling lack of transformative vision. In the eyes of political theorists like Nancy Fraser, drawing a comparison to class stratification, the point was to dissolve group markers that were the result of their subordinate material status, not reaffirm them.[24] When extended to the residual remains of race, this emergent proposal of liberal representation seemed to conflate the two in the worst way possible, naturally inciting a broad reactive backlash.

For critics like David Hollinger and Brian Barry, a liberal revaluation of excluded racial presences became synonymous with residual racial politics altogether. They seemed to view this liberal discursive appropriation of multiculturalism as fully representative of multicultural politics in general.

One would never know from their accounts anything of the heterogeneous political lineage of multiculturalism dating from the 1970s and '80s in specific contexts such as struggles over local school board control or bilingual education or community autonomy or challenges to the disciplinary canons of higher education, none of which possessed any clear-cut demand for the recognition of static cultural difference.[25] Instead, their conflations of an imagined liberal problematizing object became an occasion for exorcizing the haunting remnants of racial politics by repeating the dividing lines that constituted the center of their normative ideals. For Brian Barry, cultural recognition would dissolve the neutrality of the liberal state and fatally compromise its commitment to equality and autonomy.[26] For David Hollinger, multicultural recognition of cultural groups compounded the original corruption of racism. Both racism and the reaffirmation of racial difference lay outside an enduring American ethos of self-transformative possibility. He therefore called for a postethnic politics, considering any form of politicized racial identification to be anachronistic and suspect.[27] In discursive tandem, liberal proponents and critics together conflated emergent political challenges with residual remnants; they forged a renewed liberal imaginary by rehearsing its constitutive problematics; and, in the case of the ghostly remains of race, they exorcized its absent presence as the constitutive limit by conjuring it forth only to drive it away again.

The long legacy of race in the United States thus became the ideal test case for considering the salience, the limits, and the eclipse of this new language of multiculturalism. For liberal multicultural discourse was slowly eclipsed over the challenges raised in the American context. It was eclipsed through the remembrance of the contentious identity politics of the 1970s and 1980s, wherein various left movements in the wake of the eclipse of the civil rights era sought to sustain forms of group identity and insurgent activism. Broadly viewed by conservatives and the liberal mainstream as divisive and "balkanizing," a cultural pluralism that would recognize them seemed to promise a return to the divisiveness of that era.[28] The enthusiasm for cultural pluralism, whether through the politics of recognition, presence, or difference, waned in liberal multicultural discourse, to be surmounted by a new emphasis on cosmopolitanism, wherein trenchant racial identification was the paradigmatic instance to be overcome. Mutatis mutandis, cosmopolitanism, however, was an all-too-predictable outcome of a liberal historicist frame with an all-too-predictable subaltern remainder.

HEGEMONY, ALTERITY, AND CULTURAL DIFFERENCE

For postcolonial scholars like Gayatri Spivak and Dipesh Chakrabarty, thinking through the ideological historicist operations of liberal and Marxist theorizing has been crucial for contesting the lingering hegemony of colonialism as well as for any project of subaltern retrieval. In particular,

Chakrabarty considered both traditions as "indispensable if inadequate" resources for thinking the remainders and residual presences of colonialism in modern politics.[29] If modern politics cannot be thought outside rights, then the critique of its ideological bases could also not be thought outside Marxist categories. Yet both traditions held their own historicist assumptions about the secular transformations of modernity, and both likewise posited subaltern residues that lay hovering on its edges either because they existed in an undeveloped or backward state or because they threatened the coherence of central conceptions in their ideologies. For Chakrabarty, "difference is always the name of a relationship, for it separates just as much as it connects (as, indeed, does a border) . . . subaltern pasts are signposts of this border."[30] Chakrabarty conceived the borders that enable a historicist present to be "time-knots":

> what I have called subaltern pasts and the practice of historicizing is not one of mutual exclusion. It is because we already have experience of that which makes the present non-contemporaneous with itself that we can actually historicize. Thus what allows historians to historicize the medieval or the ancient is the very fact these worlds are never completely lost. We inhabit their fragments even when we classify ourselves as modern and secular. It is because we live in time-knots that we can undertake the exercise of straightening out, as it were, some part of the knot. . . .[31]

The question of subaltern fragments and remainders were, for Chakrabarty, the very condition through which one could historicize at all. But perhaps more important, the trace of these remains revealed not just the noncontemporary and heterogeneous dimensions of the subaltern but a "present" always "out of joint" with itself. What Chakrabarty sought to foster was an approach to the borders and time-knots of modernity that would enable us to reveal not just the limits of historicism but of these limits as the possibility for historicizing differently, in a manner that reworks rather than repeats constitutive borders that seem hard and impermeable but are instead the manifestation of a heterogeneous and noncontemporary present. To "provincialize" European historicist thought was not a project of negating or reversing its universalist pretensions but was, for Chakrabarty, a project and a spur to reconceive these universals through their heterogeneously lived "knots."

But what of hegemony? Chakrabarty's aim was in unsettling the historicist legacies that rendered subaltern beliefs and practices opaque and anachronistic, but Spivak's caution that the workings of "power, desire, and interest" lay at every turn remains in force, as it were. They seem to appear as two ships passing in the night—in the former, a historian urging fellow historians to attend not just to the noncontemporaneity of the present but also to the alterity within the presentisms of the past; in the latter, a caution about the always already presence of ideology in appropriating and speaking for a subaltern remainder. But if hegemony continually dissimulates its own presence, for Spivak, paradigmatically in the appropriation of the subaltern other, then perhaps Chakrabarty calls us to see those hegemonic presences as themselves continually dissimulated, altered in the borders and knots that render it out of joint with itself. The work of Homi Bhabha then might serve to bridge this divide, wherein the cultural encounter between colonial imperial authority and a simultaneously menacing and mimicking colonial subject becomes the scene of "writing" for authority, in the process undermining its own abstract universalist pretensions.[32] Bhabha calls our attention to the constitutive absences in the "presencing" of hegemonic authority: that such authority is never one, that in the scene of making itself a felt presence it has already opened its own alterity, thereby propelling a chain of slippages and disavowals in order to maintain its own illusions. One might put the point in the following way. If the emperor dissimulates his own authority in appearing unclothed, this has salience only in the presence of clothed subjects, thereby opening the alterity of authority and a different register of its power. Hegemony, therefore, is continually shifting—neither an absolute set of authoritative norms or ideas nor an absolute unity of presence but continually reforged in the ambivalent slippages and knots of its scenes of embodiment. All three urge us to "read" catachresis at its origin, not just in the search for alternatives, not just in the search for ulterior motives, but in the alterity of hegemonic norms that continually dissimulate themselves in a double sense—in the representation of an excluded other and in their own authoritative representation. In particular, Homi Bhabha's work calls our attention to the work of culture as occurring on the boundaries, over the liminal space between ideas and presence, within the ambivalences of desire and "presencing." If so, we might begin to consider a different understanding of the cultural demands of our multicultural moment, one wherein cultural difference might be the trace of material struggles, one wherein culture difference, rather than a static identification, marks an arena that allows one to engage the "materialism" of liberal hegemony (always) in formation.

Consider the work of Raymond Williams, who probably coined the phrase "cultural materialism." Himself a critic of the historicist assumptions of Marxist historiography, Williams produced work that continually probed the processes and arenas through which capitalist hegemony and Marxist analysis alike posited discrete periodizations in a developmental logic that admitted no contingent politics but only determining forces and pressures. The dichotomy between a material "base" and an ideological "superstructure" was inadequate not only in examining the lived experiences or "structures of feeling" through which individuals and collectivities negotiated their circumstances but also in accounting for how an ideologically dominant culture changes or asserts itself to begin with. In his classic essay "Base and Superstructure in Marxist Cultural Theory" he dismissed the question begging of Marxist historicism through which problematic formations of capitalist reproduction were explained away by recourse to a language of "time lags" or anachronisms.[33] Even "some of the best Marxist cultural analysis," he argued, were "more at home in what one might call *epochal* questions than in what one has to call *historical* questions" (original emphasis).[34] Drawn to reexamine the notion of hegemony, Williams asserted that "hegemony is not singular; indeed that its own internal structures are highly complex, and have continually to be renewed, recreated and defended; and by the same token, that they can be continually challenged and in certain respects modified."[35]

But what is most interesting for the purposes of the critical framework developed here are his reflections on the "modes of incorporation" through which a dominant culture becomes hegemonic. Calling attention to "educational institutions" as the main agency and arena in the "transmission of an effective dominant culture," Williams emphasized a process of "selective tradition" in which "from a whole possible area of past and present, certain meanings and practices are chosen for emphasis, certain other meanings and practices are neglected and excluded."[36] Yet this "selectivity" is never in itself singular. The line between inclusion and exclusion may be constitutive, but it is, just as well, *ambiguous*. At every moment in the incorporation of a dominant culture, "we have to recognize the alternative meanings and values, the alternative opinions and attitudes, even some alternative senses of the world, which can be accommodated and tolerated within a particular effective and dominant culture."[37] All well and good, one might think; selectivity naturally consists in articulating the line between accepted and alternative associations. Williams, here, however, cautions against a "retreat to an *indifferent* complexity" (emphasis added). Different "alternatives" are not the *product* of selectivity; they are not the *result* of a dominant mode of incorporation; they are the ambiguous condition of possibility for corporation. Williams continues: "But if we are to say this, we have to think again about the sources of that which is not corporate; of those practices, experiences, meanings, values which are not part of the effective dominant culture."[38]

What Williams draws our attention to, I argue, is a conception of cultural alternatives that lie at the very point of contention for hegemony formation, that is to say, the very materiality of hegemony. To be sure, in that process of selectivity, a dominant culture represents alternatives that "can be accommodated and tolerated," but these are overlaid on "sources of that which is not corporate." What he is emphasizing therefore is a notion of alternatives that seem to approach what I've discussed as alterity, that is, a fissure of difference that both propels and problematizes the process of hegemonic "incorporation," existing ontologically prior to its potential incorporation as commodious and tolerable yet itself not quite corporate, not quite corporeal. The point of his approach to culture as a space of alternatives was not to assume their presence from the standpoint of a stable hegemonic and historicist vantage point but to see their dilemmas of corporeality as the very engine internal to hegemony formation. This is why he later drew a distinction between alternative and *oppositional* cultures. Oppositional cultures have already been determined from the standpoint of hegemony; their presence has been stabilized. But, in order to pierce the "epochal" veneer of hegemony, Williams contended that we have to address more "historical" questions, questions contained in culture, questions that probe the very struggles over the "materialism" of hegemony.

Williams further deployed another set of distinctions in his essay, a distinction that has an obvious though ambivalent resonance in engaging the historicist veneer in the hegemony of liberal multicultural discourse. After addressing the distinction between alternative and oppositional cultures, Williams assessed a cross-cutting distinction between residual and emergent cultures. By residual, he meant those "experiences, meanings and values, which cannot be verified or cannot be expressed in terms of the dominant culture, [but] are nevertheless lived and practiced on the basis of the *residue* . . . of some previous social formation" (emphasis added).[39] By emergent, he meant "that new meanings and values, new practices, new significances and experiences, are continually being created."[40] At first glance, his remarks concerning residual and emergent practices seem readily intuitive as operational phases in the development of a more nuanced account of capitalist formation. Capitalist hegemony at any one moment can never colonize all cultural practices; there will always be some that remain as epiphenomenal to it or that have been superseded in their relevance, while there may emerge practices that become of especial concern. Yet to collapse his distinction into the phases of a developmental trajectory seems to go against the spirit of his entire essay. Continually probing the dynamism and instability in the hegemony of a dominant culture while challenging the naturalized inevitability of historicist approaches, his distinctions, I argue, are not merely nominal terms in the unfolding of hegemony, nor are they stable designations in the before and after of hegemonic development. To reify residual and emergent practices from the standpoint of hegemony formation would be to retreat into an "indifferent complexity," with respect not just to the dominant culture but also to these practices themselves that straddle the lines of incorporation.

Certainly, Williams asserted that residual and emergent practices exist in a "temporal relation" to the dominant culture, but this strikes me as the deeper point: their temporality as much as their corporeality is determined from the standpoint of hegemonic materiality.

Part of the complexity in Williams's analysis of residual and emergent practices is that he continually seems to push the two together and thereby threatens his own distinction. For instance, after cautioning against a simple alignment of residual/emergent with alternative/oppositional, Williams states, "it is often a very narrow line, in reality, between alternative and oppositional. A meaning or a practice may be tolerated as a deviation, and yet still be seen only as another particular way to live. But as the necessary area of effective dominance extends, the *same meanings and practices* can be *seen* by the dominant culture, not merely as disregarding or despising it, but as challenging it"[41] (emphasis added). Moreover:

> in the subsequent default of a particular phase of a dominant culture, there is then a *reaching back* to those meanings and values which were created in real societies in the past, and which still seem to have some significance because they *represent* areas of human experience, aspiration and achievement, which the dominant culture under-values or opposes, or even cannot recognize . . . part of our answer to this question bears on the process of the *persistence* of residual practices. [emphasis added][42]

This passage strikes me as very similar to Chakrabarty's discussion of "time-knots." From the standpoint of hegemony, residual and emergent *practices* (which he distinguishes from products) are continually being blurred, associated, conflated, indeed, disavowed on the basis of their commonly associated residues. These residues, moreover, lie not outside the dominant culture as a stable exterior or anterior but constitute a persisting internal alternative that lacks corporeality or a stable materiality. And if it is the case that Williams's concept of alternative is meant to draw attention to an internal kernel of alterity within hegemony formation, then the presence of these residual remains, in both their materiality and their temporality, must be continually represented as of emergent concern, that is, that they constitute the very stakes in the delineation of the normative presence of hegemony itself.

Culture, embodied in the arts and literature, was for Williams the domain that exposed the alternatives of dominant meanings and values. But, far from expressing either a stable set of residual or emergent alternatives, literature itself often blurred those distinctions. What made the analysis of culture so significant for him was not that it contained a stable refuge of cultural difference from hegemonic domination nor obviously that it was the superstructural handmaiden of hegemony but that the materiality of cultural differences constituted the contested crucible of hegemony formation and opposition alike. For Williams, cultural materialism revealed hegemony always in formation but, just as significant, hegemony as never in itself a singular process but as always shifting, always being re-created and represented, always, therefore, other to itself. And perhaps the central dynamic in that contestation concerned the "presencing" of residues and remains, of fragments that call forth the alterity of a dominant cultural set of meanings and values, in both their corporeal and their temporal manifestations.

If multiculturalism became a timely emergent concern for a historicist liberal discourse, then we might see its dilemmas between abstract ideas and embodied presence, its recycling of racial remainders, it contortions over representation, not as a novel development in the realization of liberal norms but as exposing the contested kernels of alterity in the coherence of those very norms. The focus on cultural difference, then, might be given a different basis. Instead of an excluded presence raising the challenge of its inclusion, we might see cultural difference as a contested trace of material and temporal struggles within the very meanings and values of western liberal democratic societies. And, as such, we might see multiculturalism as neither fundamentally oppositional nor ideologically superstructural; instead, by calling forth residues and spectral remnants, multiculturalism necessarily reopens rifts of alterity that allow a different embrace.

UNTIMELY MULTICULTURALISM?

In his various studies of liberal discourse, Michel Foucault sought precisely to engage what one might describe the strange presence of its manifestations.[43] By foregrounding what he called its "lines of fragility," by dwelling on its productive use of interned bodies and spaces, he sought to capture its motivating ideas at the point of their problematization in historical experience, thereby puncturing the veneer of its steadily accumulating truth or of its sensible coherence as a natural and inevitable outcome. Describing his own work as a "history of the present," he was, of course, a fierce critic of historicist discourses, with a particular animus in exposing the productive uses of their dreams and disavowals.

This analysis of liberal multicultural discourse likewise attempts to capture the animus over cultural pluralism during the 1990s by considering its overall scope set against its perceived limits, its patterns of selectivity with regard to its liberalism, its attempts to represent the residues of its racial past as cautions against the future, and, in particular, the strange contortions involved when those residues remain to beckon different understandings of their possibilities. I concentrate on its coalescence in the American context because its proposals were met with the fiercest consideration there and because its own racial remains became the spur for sorting through the limits of cultural pluralism's potential manifestations. It was in the hands of its American commentators that one witnesses what I call the multicultural exorcisms of the remains of race—rites and rituals of remembrance to ward off alternative manifestations of their meanings and associations. In so doing, they reaffirmed a historicist trajectory wherein cultural pluralism would naturally eclipse itself into an affirmation of cosmopolitanism more generally and an American exceptionalism more stridently.

By calling forth and exorcizing remnants of the past over an emergent and timely question, however, these commentators within liberal multicultural discourse draw attention to the alterity of their own invocations. If emergent problems of toleration and pluralism in Western liberal democracies were settled by recourse to residual anxieties of the past, then those same problems could lead to the remembrance of these residues in different ways, opening a different register of their normative implications. At the very least, we might contest the normative chains of memory through which the presences of race are repetitively represented as a constitutive limit. That is to say, we might see in multicultural discourse a spur for what Nietzsche called its *untimely* associations to counter the naturalized inevitability of its historicist embrace.[44] For Nietzsche, human motivation and action were driven by their reactions to the world around them and by the memory of remnants and fragments, "indigestible stones" he called them, through which their lives could be given particular purpose and, most important, *renewed*. What the historicism of his day seemed to disavow were precisely these lived associations in the pursuit of an objectivist form of knowledge. In recalling one's untimeliness, therefore, Nietzsche urged his readers to embrace and meditate upon their fragmented residues—not in their finality or stability but so that they could be remembered differently and thereby open up the possibility of different futures. It was paradoxically in considering oneself as counter to one's time that Nietzsche believed one could change one's time. If we follow Raymond Williams in considering culture as the arena for struggles over the materiality of hegemony, then the dilemmas over the representation and significance of cultural difference—its liminal position with respect to ideas and presence, its ghostly oscillation between past and present—might form the sinews of an untimely embrace that breaks the spell of its hegemonic dissimulations.

In each of the following chapters, therefore, I consider key moments in the discourse of an American liberal multiculturalism in both their timely and their untimely memorial appropriations. Chapter 2 explores the beginnings of the liberal interest in multiculturalism when the demands over excluded racial-ethnic minorities raised a problem of representation. I consider what was then a proposed solution in the formulation of group rights and its liberal legitimation in assigning a normative significance to cultural difference. But these considerations immediately recalled the residues of race in the United States and therefore the elaboration of the limits of representative inclusion. Consequently, I analyze this particular configuration of proposed liberal multicultural norms: in their problematization of racial presences and in their vexed mobilizations of historical memory.

Chapter 3 concentrates on the shift in language from cultural pluralism to cosmopolitanism in liberal multicultural discourse. Accompanying this shift was the reassertion of American exceptionalism over the prospects of racial inclusion. Paradoxically, contesting the feasibility of liberal multiculturalism became the occasion for American commentators to reassert a new brand of exceptionalism in the form of cosmopolitanism. But by mobilizing the exceptional promise of an American ethos in order to fix and exorcize the corruptive manifestation of racial ascription and identification, these commentators expose the lineaments of their own historicist substitutions and anxieties. In reexamining these appropriated remains, I explore a different untimely understanding of the centrality of race to a supposedly enduring and consensual American liberal exceptionalism.

Certainly one of the main "lines of fragility" in the development of liberal multicultural discourse has been the tension between tolerating cultural differences and ensuring the autonomy of women. Chapter 4 explores these tensions through the 1999 publication of Susan Moller Okin's *Is Multiculturalism Bad for Women?* Okin's essay and the comments it spawned highlighted a series of sensational criminal trials in the United States during the late 1980s and '90s, when the proposal for a "cultural defense" gained some limited traction. Culpability for some acts of violence, it was proposed, should be mitigated on the basis of cultural beliefs that might sanction them. These trials seemed to emphasize the dangers to the autonomy of women when such cultural differences around gender and sexuality were sanctioned. But, as is the case overall in this study, much depends upon how such differences are represented and the residual legacies that have come to shape their emergent apprehension. I therefore explore how the "cultural defense" appeared in criminal jurisprudence and the legacies that have shaped its particular manifestation. Though different cultural practices may lie in tension with the autonomy of women, these particular disputes over the "cultural defense" were less a result of these innate differences than of the patriarchal and racialized development of American criminal jurisprudence. Again, what was assessed as an emergent dilemma or threat is upon closer examination the occasion for consolidating a certain hegemonic configuration that disavowed the presence of its own residual alterity.

If the dilemmas over the autonomy of women constituted one central fault line of liberal multicultural debate, then certainly its other main fault lines concerned the relationship between race and ethnicity and race and class. For many commentators on the American scene, these two fault lines were problematically intertwined. On the one hand, a norm of cultural pluralism seemed to transform marginalized and excluded racial groups into ethnic cultural groups possessing conventional interests. On the other hand, these substitutions seemed to evacuate the particular class dimensions of liberal societies overall. From a variety of angles, therefore, the emphasis on cultural pluralism and diversity was critiqued as spawning a diversionary politics inattentive to class inequality. Chapter 5 therefore reexamines these problematizing strands, tracing them to the discursive shifts during the civil rights era, when ethnic culture became an object of governmental interest mediating both the effort to end racial discrimination and the challenge of addressing trenchant inequality in Lyndon Johnson's War on Poverty. If these shifts laid the foundations for later multicultural contestations, they also reveal the patterns of disavowal over the deeper implications of inequality in the American canon. An early advocate of ethnic cultural pluralism, Daniel Patrick Moynihan is a key figure here in conceptualizing and bridging these two projects and in the remainders that would follow shaping the contours of an emergent liberal multiculturalism.

Finally, I conclude with some remarks about the possibilities of challenging this American exceptionalist grammar. My approach to multiculturalism in the course of this book has revolved less on the question of its intrinsic merits than on the uses to which it is put and on the mobilizations of racial residues that, far from being a fixed presence, continually serve to consolidate a certain historicist and hegemonic coherence of its possibilities. But I have tried to show that the very instability called forth in the representation of cultural difference—the continual slippages and disavowals between emergent and residual problematizations of race—reveals the alterity not just of racial difference but also of liberalism as continually other to itself. By following the threads of its dissimulations, we might unshackle the enduring patterns that retain race as the exceptional other for an American liberal exceptionalism. If so, it might free us to better appreciate the hybrid struggles that have come to shape American political identity and culture and might open us to engage the practice and struggle of crafting different untimely futures, rather than one of binding ourselves to some pregiven exceptionalist origin. I examine these possibilities with a concluding discussion of President Obama's Second Inaugural address.

NOTES

1. *Hamlet's Lament* was an early-nineteenth-century era blackface minstrelsy production. Quoted in Ray B. Browne, "Shakespeare in American Vaudeville and Negro Minstrelsy," *American Quarterly* 12, no. 3 (Autumn 1960): 381.
2. Bill Clinton, University of California San Diego Commencement Address, June 14, 1997, accessed February 1, 2014, http://clinton6.nara.gov/1997/06/1997–06–14-president-at-uc-san-diego-commencement.html.
3. Barack Obama, "A More Perfect Union," March 18, 2008, accessed February 1, 2014, http://my.barackobama.com/page/content/hisownwords/.
4. Joe Klein, "Why Barack Obama Is Winning," *Time*, October 22, 2008, accessed January 31, 2014, https://web.archive.org/web/20081026022816/http://www.time.com/time/politics/article/0,8599,1853025-2,00.html.
5. Thomas Jefferson, *Notes on the State of Virginia* (New York: Penguin Books, 1998), 145.
6. Robert Costa, "Gingrich: "Obama's 'Kenyan, Anti-Colonial' Worldview," *National Review*, September 11, 2010, accessed January 31, 2014, www.nationalreview.com/corner/246302/gingrich-obama-s-kenyan-anti-colonial-worldview-robert-costa.
7. Ta-Nehisi Coates, "Fear of a Black President," *The Atlantic*, September 2012, accessed February 1, 2014, www.theatlantic.com/magazine/archive/2012/09/fear-of-a-black-president/309064/.
8. Robert Schlesinger, "Obama Has Mentioned 'American Exceptionalism' More Than Bush," *U.S. News*, January 31, 2011, accessed February 1, 2014, www.usnews.com/opinion/blogs/robert-schlesinger/2011/01/31/obama-has-mentioned-american-exceptionalism-more-than-bush.
9. "New Conference by President Obama," April 4, 2009, accessed February 1, 2014, http://www.whitehouse.gov/the-press-office/news-conference-president-obama-4042009.
10. Vladimir V. Putin, "A Plea for Caution from Russia," *New York Times*, September 11, 2013, accessed February 1, 2014, www.nytimes.com/2013/09/12/opinion/putin-plea-for-caution-from-russia-on-syria.html.
11. Barack Obama, "Remarks by President Obama in Address to the United Nations General Assembly," September 24, 2013, accessed February 1, 2014, www.whitehouse.gov/the-press-office/2013/09/24/remarks-president-obama-address-united-nations-general-assembly.

12. Charles Taylor, "The Politics of Recognition," in *Multiculturalism: Examining the Politics of Recognition*, ed. Amy Gutmann (Princeton: Princeton University Press, 1994), 25–73; Anne Phillips, *The Politics of Presence* (Oxford: Oxford University Press, 1995); Will Kymlicka, *Multicultural Citizenship: A Liberal Theory of Minority Rights* (Oxford: Oxford University Press, 1995); Iris Marion Young, *Justice and the Politics of Difference* (Princeton: Princeton University Press, 1990); Brian Barry, *Culture and Equality* (Cambridge: Harvard University Press, 2001), respectively.
13. See Taylor, "The Politics of Recognition," and Michael Walzer, "Comment," in Taylor, *Multiculturalism*, 25–73, 99–103, respectively.
14. See Kymlicka, *Multicultural Citizenship*; Barry, *Culture and Equality*; Susan Moller Okin, "Is Multiculturalism Bad for Women?," in *Is Multiculturalism Bad for Women?*, ed. Joshua Cohen, Matthew Howard, and Martha Nussbaum (Princeton: Princeton University Press, 1999), 9–24.
15. See Young, *Justice and the Politics of Difference*; Phillips, *The Politics of Presence*; David Hollinger, *Postethnic America: Beyond Multiculturalism* (New York: Basic Books, 1995); Walter Benn Michaels, *Our America: Nativism, Modernism, and Pluralism* (Durham: Duke University Press, 1995).
16. Peter Laslett, *Locke's Two Treatises of Government: A Critical Edition with Introduction and Notes*, 2nd ed. (Cambridge: Cambridge University Press, 1970), 319. See also Herman Lebovics, "The Uses of America in Locke's Second Treatise of Government," *Journal of the History of Ideas* 47, no. 4 (Oct.–Dec. 1986): 567–581.
17. Richard Rorty, "The Unpatriotic Academy," *New York Times*, February 13, 1994, accessed February 1, 2014, http://www.nytimes.com/1994/02/13/opinion/the-unpatriotic-academy.html; Taylor, "The Politics of Recognition."
18. Karl Marx, "Eighteenth Brumaire of Louis Bonaparte," in *The Marx-Engels Reader*, ed. Robert C. Tucker (New York: Norton, 1972), 608.
19. Gayatri Spivak, "Can the Subaltern Speak?," in *Marxism and the Interpretation of Culture*, ed. Cary Nelson and Lawrence Grossberg (Chicago: University of Illinois, 1988), 271–313.
20. Marx, "Eighteenth Brumaire of Louis Bonaparte," 608.
21. Spivak, "Can the Subaltern Speak?," 279.
22. Bhikhu Parekh, *Rethinking Multiculturalism: Cultural Diversity and Political Theory* (Cambridge: Harvard University Press, 2002).
23. Steven Lukes, *Liberals and Cannibals: The Implications of Diversity* (London: Verso, 2003).
24. Nancy Fraser, "From Redistribution to Recognition?," *New Left Review* 212 (July/August 1995): 68–93.
25. David Theo Goldberg, ed., *Multiculturalism: A Critical Reader* (Cambridge: Blackwell, 1994); Arthur M. Melzer, Jerry Weinberger, and M. Richard Zinman, eds., *Multiculturalism and American Democracy* (Lawrence: University Press of Kansas, 1998).
26. Barry, *Culture and Equality*.
27. Hollinger, *Postethnic America*.
28. Arthur M. Schlesinger Jr., *The Disuniting of America: Reflections on a Multicultural Society* (New York: Norton, 1998).
29. Dipesh Chakrabarty, *Provincializing Europe: Postcolonial Thought and Historical Difference* (Princeton: Princeton University Press, 2000).
30. Ibid., 110.
31. Ibid., 112.
32. Homi Bhabha, *The Location of Culture* (New York: Routledge, 1994).
33. Raymond Williams, "Base and Superstructure in Marxist Cultural Theory," in Williams, *Problems in Materialism and Culture* (London: Verso, 1980), 32–33.

34. Ibid., 38.
35. Ibid.
36. Ibid., 39.
37. Ibid.
38. Ibid., 40.
39. Ibid.
40. Ibid., 41.
41. Ibid., 42.
42. Ibid.
43. For example, Michel Foucault, *Discipline and Punish* (New York: Vintage, 1977); Foucault, *The History of Sexuality, Volume 1* (New York: Vintage, 1990); and Paul Rabinow and Nikolas Rose, eds., *The Essential Foucault* (New York: New Press, 2003).
44. Friedrich Nietzsche, *Untimely Meditations* (Cambridge: Cambridge University Press, 1997).

2 The American Exception

The Politics of Recognition and Individual Autonomy

> The act of recognition becomes an act of constitution: the address animates the subject into existence.
>
> —Judith Butler[1]

Forty years after the Civil Rights Act of 1964, the United States remains defined by racial stratifications that significantly affect the life chances and opportunities of individuals on a variety of levels. Though racial discrimination is no longer given the overt sanction of law, the will to address structural inequities defined by race has steadily eroded and teeters on the brink of outright elimination. On the level of political discourse, even the attempt to invoke racial realities or propose new efforts at remediation seems to prime charges of divisiveness and partiality. Yet in the midst of this retreat from race, the 1990s witnessed vigorous debates around the concept of multiculturalism, giving new impetus and energy to considerations of the role of difference within liberal societies. Such debates fostered the hope of conceptualizing new ways of accommodating forms of cultural difference for the purpose of rendering these societies more equitable and inclusive while further distancing these societies from the record of genocide and ethnic cleansing so prevalent in the twentieth century. One could say that a prominent subtext of these debates over cultural difference and justice thus lay in attributing a kind of historical accountability and continuity to sovereign states for their past deeds with respect not simply to the historical record but also significantly with regard to the recognition and respect of a globalized community.[2]

For those concerned about members of racialized groups in the United States, debates over multiculturalism thus offered a new opening for broaching the subject of race on the register of national politics. The possible affinity between race and these multicultural debates was implicit from the very beginning. Many of the ideas animating the liberal debates over multiculturalism in the mid- to late 1990s were prefigured in the curricular reforms of the 1970s and 1980s that sought to supplement if not decenter traditional

Eurocentric and male accounts of American history.[3] At play within such reforms was an irreducible debate over historical accountability in terms of both historical remembrance and the contemporary inclusion of cultural difference. Such reforms and the more abstract liberal debates of the 1990s thus dovetailed with concerns about rendering Western liberal democracies more inclusive with respect to cultural minorities around dimensions of race and ethnicity.

Yet, in the encounter between these debates over multiculturalism and the concept of race, the results have been less fruitful and more troublesomely portentous. In general, two trends have emerged. Insofar as multicultural norms of inclusiveness and toleration of cultural difference are accepted in the wider political discourse, race is seen as a form of ethnicity, as another variant of a hyphenated identity. Hence, an equivalence is drawn between "African-American and, say, Polish-American heritages."[4] The significance of this assimilation primarily revolves around the voluntary and symbolic nature of ethnic identity. White ethnics, for example, may or may not choose to emphasize their ethnic identification, and such identification plays only a symbolic role. For many racialized individuals, such a voluntary conception of their racial identification might prove desirable and attractive if not for the fact that such an assimilation seriously undermines any claims about the involuntary and discriminatory constraints of race. Indeed, such arguments that African Americans are simply another ethnic group like Italian Americans are often deployed to undermine the justification for preferential programs such as affirmative action. Hence, rather than drawing attention to racial injustice, the price of multicultural inclusion under this trend renders the material and symbolic roots of racial identity opaque.

The second trend pertains more specifically to liberal treatments of multiculturalism among those who are committed to cultural pluralism and inclusiveness for reasons of justice. Given an explicit concern over rectifying the exclusion and forms of harm around categories of cultural difference, particularly mindful of the legacy of race, this trend views the category of race as too corrupted a "language" to be positively recuperated within any new multicultural accommodation. Under this view, any redeployment of race invites unacceptable forms of essentialism, either on the part of the dominant culture or between the members of the racial group itself. Further, since the legacy of race is one of fictive and invidious distinctions, efforts at addressing racial stratification and discrimination often involve efforts at eradicating the basis of racial groupings.[5] The dilemma here is that if the first trend allows racial groups "a seat at the table" of cultural pluralism at the expense of emptying what makes it distinctive and gives it social meaning, the second trend seems to deprive racialized individuals and groups of any kind of normative recognition as other than the victims of racial discrimination and structural inequity. If racial identity is emptied of any distinctive meaning in the first, racial identity in the second accords something of a pariah status.

With the widespread view among the public at large that race is declining in significance, coupled with the unyielding if not increasing presence of racial inequality, these two trends in the "encounter" between multiculturalism and race generate perversities that seem to take us farther and farther away from productive means of addressing racial equality and of expanding the autonomy and participation of racial minorities. Either the recognition of race is gutted of any distinctive claim upon the society at large, or else the inability to conceptualize a normative role for racialized individuals leaves them in a limbo of exceptionalism. No matter the resolve and commitment to eradicating the unjust stratifications underlying race, there seems to me something fundamentally wrong with envisioning racial justice as involving only specifically targeted policies aimed at class stratifications while problematizing any recourse on the part of racialized individuals and groups to advance normative aims on the basis of their identities. Most important, this vision conceives the problem of race as one of unintended outcomes subject to state management. It depoliticizes race by eviscerating inquiries into its causes as a matter subject to democratic action.

As a result of these trends, one might conclude that multiculturalism either obfuscates our understanding of race or else is of little worth in illuminating and addressing racial oppression and domination. Though multiculturalism surely does have aspects that obfuscate our ability to address racial injustice, I shall argue in this chapter that it also provides resources for engaging racial injustice in a normatively productive manner and, perhaps just as important, creates spaces for racialized individuals to contest the meanings of race not solely as a matter of symbolic recognition but also as tied to ideological constructs with material consequences. Simultaneously, by examining the roots of this exceptionalism around race within the literature of multiculturalism, I shall argue that we can nuance our understanding of multiculturalism and the matrices through which cultural differences gain political significance.

Identity politics looms large within the arguments of this and other chapters. There is a political and polemical subtext for this. Given the steadily increasing loss of political will for ameliorating specifically racial forms of injustice, many arguments among those predisposed toward addressing racial injustice advance the claim that "identity politics"—meaning those efforts on the part of racial and other culturally marginalized groups such as women and homosexuals to politicize aspects of their identities—has had a fragmenting effect on building political consensus with little or no productive gain.[6] In the course of developing my arguments about race and multiculturalism, I hope to show that the signal contribution of multiculturalism to our understanding of race ought to be the ways in which we are always situated within the politicization of certain identifications if not identities and that what makes certain cultural identifications or differences more politically salient at certain times can be understood only within a field of intersubjective elaboration of national identity, which is to say on a normative level around notions of civic propriety and valorized citizenship.[7] To maintain multiculturalism's focus on the level of civic identity is thus importantly to forestall its reprivatization into discrete acceptable identities, a trend that is common in liberal treatments of multiculturalism. Hence, against the polemical charge that identity politics among the culturally marginalized fosters fragmentation, I argue that we need to widen our understanding of identity politics, that racial discrimination and racial stratification are always already implicated in a form of identity politics, and that however we imagine the terms of our coalitions, identity politics remains an irreducible component of our politics, helping us both understand the causes and postulate normative futures. If my arguments are convincing at all, it should be clear that we need more proliferation of identity politics or at least spaces in which different groups can come to the fore to politicize their identities—not in any isolated or discrete manner but as part of an inclusive and thoroughly dialogic approach to national identity.

RACE AND THE REMAINDERS OF IDENTITY POLITICS

As the discourse of liberal multiculturalism evolved, a language of cosmopolitanism increasingly attracted adherents.[8] Surely one of the indications of this new upsurge, David Hollinger noted, was the proliferation of cosmopolitan modifiers.[9] There are "vernacular cosmopolitans, rooted cosmopolitans, critical cosmopolitans, . . . actually existing cosmopolitanism," all of whom seek to mediate in various ways the origins and normative scope of classic conceptions of cosmopolitanism.[10] Hollinger goes on to argue that the proliferation of cosmopolitan modifiers involves not just an indication of the critical mass of cosmopolitan concerns but also something of the substantive connections between these treatments. One dimension of this connection involves a critical presupposition, and the other concerns what we might call a normative promise and ethical imperative. Whereas classic cosmopolitanism, rooted in the Stoic tradition, appeals to the universal in humanity, the new cosmopolitanism begins with a critical premise—that we are bounded by the social and communal particulars marking our location. But if we are bounded, limited, even constrained by these particulars of location, we are not determined by them. And, given the dangers of absolutist forms of national and subnational forms of identity, we have an ethical imperative to resist overdetermining conceptions of collective identity and an urgent need to substantiate the promise of cosmopolitan affinity. Hence, the contemporary modifiers of cosmopolitanism, Hollinger argues, evince a concern to relate its normative promise and ethical imperatives to existing realities and concrete particulars. It is the productive and timely tension between these two that accounts for the resurgence of cosmopolitan discourse over the past five years.

To speak of the normative promise and ethical imperative underlying contemporary cosmopolitan discourse thus implies a futural orientation. It involves various attempts at analyzing the sources of and building the categories for an as yet unrealized cosmopolitan affinity between different cultures, different nations, even different groups straddling the boundaries of nations. But this futural orientation is likewise timely. Which is to say that the future promise and future imperative underneath cosmopolitan concerns are tied to the present as the scope of the present-future. The promissory note encompassing the normative dimensions of cosmopolitanism is itself constituted in the present. What is this scope of the present-future that propels the discourse of cosmopolitanism? Clearly, the growing interconnections and processes of globalization provide one indisputable context for new treatments of how groups of people bounded by national, cultural, class, gender, sexual, racial, and ethnic identifications are and ought to be related to one another. But the context of proliferating networks of globalization do not alone account for the normative promise and ethical imperative of cosmopolitan discourse. In addition there is the reality that, despite the lessons learned about the dangers of ethnic and racialized nationalisms of the twentieth century and in reaction to the system imperatives of economic and technological forces under globalization, these forms of particular and provincial identifications are both resurging and retrenching, particularly in developing and underdeveloped nations. Hence, the present-future of cosmopolitanism derives from the attempt to transcend and move beyond absolutist and exclusive forms of identification. It is an attempt at reimagining the normative boundaries of the civic subject, one that is more attuned to the pressing realities of our time.

But there is another derivation of the present-future of cosmopolitanism, one more rooted in the transformations of another pressing if not timely discourse. Hollinger himself poses the question of what accounts for the sudden emergence of "new cosmopolitanism" in the second half of the 1990s. In addition to the processes of globalization and the pressing dangers of ethnoreligious nationalisms, he also attributes the rise of cosmopolitan concerns to "the dead-ends reached by identity politics within the United States."[11] In addition, he cites an article arguing that the concept of cosmopolitanism is now replacing multiculturalism as both methodologically and ideologically superior in the work of literary scholars.[12] I take these two contentions to imply that the development of "new cosmopolitanism" is partly connected to the attempt to move beyond the limitations of both identity politics in the United States and those theories of multiculturalism that remain anchored to them. But how does cosmopolitanism ostensibly supersede the limitations of multiculturalism?

We may find some resource in considering first the common lineages that shape them before turning to cosmopolitanism's departure point. As I indicated, the contemporary discourse of cosmopolitanism proceeds from the critical premise that we are bound by the shared social and communal particulars of our location. These social and communal particulars together form the cultural and political bonds that importantly provide the contexts of meaning through which selfhood and group solidarities are generated. In contrast to the universalism of classic cosmopolitanism, the "new cosmopolitanism" asserts that appeals to the universal cosmopolitan "we" must occur in and through these particular constituents.[13] The actualization of a cosmopolitan solidarity can be generated only through the interaction, perhaps dialogue, of rooted individuals in particular cultural locations. This stress on the constitutive role of cultural group membership alone of course does not separate cosmopolitanism from multiculturalism or even identity politics. All three discourses share the recognition that our cultural markers constitute in important ways the normative dimensions of our individual and group identifications. If identity politics posited too great an epistemological and political connection between individuals and their group identities, multiculturalism expanded the issue to include questions of intercultural politics within the nation-state frame. And with cosmopolitanism, the concern over the genesis of solidarity between diverse cultural groups becomes further expanded to encompass the possibility of solidarities stretching across nations, indeed, species-wide solidarities. As Kwame Anthony Appiah notes in "Cosmopolitan Patriots":

> The cosmopolitan patriot can entertain the possibility of a world in which everyone is a rooted cosmopolitan, attached to a home of his or her own, with its own cultural particularities, but taking pleasure from the presence of other, different, places that are home to other, different, people. . . . [Through human movement] cultural practices would travel also. The result would be a world in which each local form of human life was the result of long term and persistent processes of cultural hybridization: a world, in that respect, much like the world we live in now.[14]

If we were to situate the theoretical development of identity politics, multiculturalism, and cosmopolitanism on a single path, one minimal connection would thus be the normative situatedness of individuals within certain cultural group affiliations.

But what of the lineaments of departure? It is here where the futural orientation of cosmopolitanism guides the way. The overwhelming emphasis within Appiah's treatment is in maintaining the open possibility of cross-cutting, cross-pollinating forms of solidarity. Despite the recognition that we are irreducibly rooted, we must keep open the normative promise of solidarities across national boundaries. Conversely stated, we must not let our normative horizons become determined by our particular locations. If identity politics raised the specter of irreducible fragmentation within the nation-state, multiculturalism raised the normative possibility of the toleration and inclusion of difference within the nation-state through the adjudication of cultural group claims of recognition. Liberal treatments of multiculturalism thus developed into normative arguments over the principles that would guide the liberal state's management of difference. Given the core liberal values of autonomy and toleration, it followed that the accommodation of difference worked best with cultural forms of affiliation that were largely voluntary (at least within liberal Western democracies) and did not substantively conflict with these core liberal values—a model best described as a paradigm of ethnicity where individuals may or may not choose to retain some form of ethnic identification.[15]

Another way of stating the matter is that the most vexing challenges to the liberal state in its accommodation of difference lay in ascriptive or so-called illiberal cultures. Such challenges pointed to the limits of toleration and the sense that liberalism itself is a "fighting creed," a bounded culture solidifying the norms of the liberal state. If this boundedness of liberalism itself is unavoidable, indeed if it is necessary for the cohesion of liberal democratic societies, then the cosmopolitan departure point concerns the ethical imperative not to engage in a liberal insularity. A liberal patriotism, yes, Appiah argues, but, as cosmopolitans, we should "defend the right of others to live in democratic states with rich possibilities of association within and across borders, states of which they can be patriotic citizens."[16] This is a laudable normative ideal, rooted in the fundamental diversity of cultural affiliation. The "rich possibilities of association" thus represent the normative culmination of a certain trajectory: first, from the "dead ends" of identity politics to the limits of the liberal nation-state accommodation of difference and second, toward a cosmopolitan normative and ethical imperative to transcend our situatedness in the boundaries of the liberal nation-state.

Anchored in a recognition of the constitutive dimensions of normative cultures, including liberal ones, this trajectory thus gains its force in part out of an imperative to avoid the "dead ends" of identity politics, what we might categorize as the totalizing and essentializing claims of racial, sexual, and gender identities or any of their multiple configurations. On its face, the future horizon of a cosmopolitan respect for diversity as theorized by Hollinger and others lies in building a language of diversity constituted out of a polemical rejection of the language of identity politics. But I wonder whether the stress on the normative ideals of multicultural inclusion (bounded by the nation-state) and the cosmopolitan promise of transcendence has truly provided the categories in which we can leave identity politics behind. Has the present-future of cosmopolitanism located in the limits of liberal multiculturalism truly reconciled the dilemmas of the present-past of identity politics? After all, the "dead ends" of identity politics can signify not just its future unproductiveness as a salient approach to markers of cultural identity but also the sense in which the "dead ends" of identity politics signify the intractability of its dimensions.

When we consider race as a prime category of identity politics, particularly in the United States, does the polarity between the "dead ends" of identity politics and the futural promise of "rich possibilities of association" lead to better resolutions of the paradoxes of racial identity? Will the consignment of race as a cultural identity to the dustbins of history within liberal multiculturalist and cosmopolitical concerns render it less or more salient as a category constitutive of the demands of cultural recognition? The central concern of this chapter is thus shaped by the critical paradoxes that race poses for the liberal theory of culture that undergirds both liberal normative treatments of multiculturalism and its present-future of cosmopolitanism. My purpose in exploring the dilemmas of race in relationship to liberal presuppositions within multiculturalism is not to argue that liberal multicultural theorists of recognition somehow neglect to include race. The relationship between liberal treatments of multiculturalism and race is far more tangled. And if we are to accept the arguments of Hollinger, the future of multicultural recognition must be built in part out of a transcendence of its languages.

On a general level, this imperative is surely correct. The history of race is the history of a language of hard division justifying domination and exploitation. But the polarity between the excluded remainders of race and the valuation of cultural identifications that are somehow thinner and more voluntary may actually obscure not only the ways in which race, like gender and sexuality, is the product not simply of ascribed identities legitimating continuing injustice but also the ways in which they provide the contexts for arguments over public reason, competing meanings over civic membership, salient forms of political participation—in short, contexts for public autonomy and agency. Race unites as well as divides. Like any other marker of cultural group identity, it has provided the background for understanding and enabling the agency of group members. If the inclusion and participation of all members in the struggle to define the cultural community of norms is the ultimate goal of multiculturalism, then it ought to matter how we recognize the background contexts of the agency of its members. In terms of cultural markers like race, it is this dual legacy and contemporary double bind that animates my treatment of liberal debates of multiculturalism.

THE THEORY OF NORMATIVE CULTURE

The publication in 1992 of Charles Taylor's "The Politics of Recognition" signaled a shift in the discourse of multiculturalism, for it animated a discourse and debate around the relationship of multiculturalism to liberal theories of the state.[17] Issues of pluralism had already become increasingly prominent within liberal debates primarily through the communitarian debates of the 1980s,[18] but Taylor's arguments illuminating the claims of injury around recognition struggles gave multiculturalism a new emphasis within liberal principles. Taylor's essay is rightly seen as seminal because it provided philosophical arguments through which a set of issues within multiculturalism could be productively debated within the liberal tradition. Part of the influence of Taylor's essay is based on the richness of its scope. Taylor is neither the most systematic nor the most sustained commentator within liberal multicultural debates. He has chosen not to follow up on his arguments with a more comprehensive treatise as others, such as Will Kymlicka, have done. Nor does the essay's force lie within a programmatic and prescriptive theory of multiculturalism. Rather, the essay is best described as a phenomenological and genealogical exploration of the sources of multicultural issues within contemporary Western culture. Some of these sources are philosophical, others are about the ontological conditions of identity formation, and still others are about the historical developments through which the needs and demands for recognition appear on the political horizon. As he puts it, "In order to examine some of the issues that have arisen here, I'd like to take a step back, achieve a little distance, and look first at how this discourse of recognition and identity came to seem familiar, or at least readily understandable, to us."[19] The diversity of sources through which Taylor attempts to render intelligible the various facets of multicultural recognition thus provides a rich palette for the contributions of subsequent commentators. These interlocutors have found Taylor's essay productive precisely because it is less concerned with providing answers than with uncovering a world of connected questions.

But the connective tissue within Taylor's essay and within the liberal debates over multiculturalism more generally lies within a conception of culture that gives it operative significance within the radar of liberal concerns. Since liberalism is paradigmatically a theory of rights-bearing individuals guided by principles of autonomy and toleration, among others, such a conception of culture lies primarily in its links to the autonomy of individuals. Again, through the communitarian debates of the 1980s but also more stridently within the second wave feminism of the 1970s, the notion of the unencumbered atomistic individual as the primary unit of political deliberation had already come under attack. The famous shift in John Rawls's position with the publication of *Political Liberalism* signaled a greater recognition and appreciation of the significance of citizens' embeddedness within particular communities that differed greatly from one another in their moral and cultural orientations.[20] Moreover, this significance is not just descriptive. It is not just that actual individuals are always situated within a particular community or stream of cultural orientations, but, more significant, that this situatedness matters for how we understand the individual's actions and how we value their choices. As Joseph Raz has argued, if autonomous freedom is one of the central values of liberalism, an individual's culture is important as "a precondition for, and a factor which gives shape and content to, individual freedom."[21] Will Kymlicka adds, "We decide how to lead our lives by situating ourselves in these cultural narratives, by adopting roles that have struck us as worthwhile ones."[22] Properly recognizing and enhancing the autonomy of individuals depend in some measure, then, on the sustenance of a range of cultural sources.

There is some tension here whether it matters which culture an individual's agency is situated in or whether it is enough from the perspective of the liberal state that a range of diverse cultural options be made available—in effect, whether it is sufficient that individuals have a choice among interchangeable cultural options.[23] Another way of stating this ambiguity is whether we should see the import of culture for individual autonomy in purely functionalist terms as confined to a fuller theory of individual autonomy or whether properly recognizing the autonomy of situated individuals depends on a qualitative recognition of their background culture, a thicker conception of collective autonomy that surrenders the operational unit of the atomistic individual. One consequence of this ambiguity lies in whether it is sufficient for autonomy that a liberal society offer a diverse range of cultural options or whether the recognition of the role of cultures for autonomy depends on something more qualitative and perhaps more definitive. In the first instance, a proper range of cultural diversity secures the autonomy of its citizens because they are not coerced or confined to any one background culture. The second shifts the stress on autonomy from a range of choices to a set of *given* background cultures. Concern over autonomy in this instance revolves upon specific background cultures that are already operative. I want to set this issue aside for the moment and return to it later since it is implicated in the issue of what recognition consists in. For now, suffice it to say that the starting points for liberal debates around multiculturalism all share this notion of the connection between culture and autonomy. Autonomy is enabled and shaped by its situatedness within a particular cultural stream. Cultures provide the contexts through which individuals constitute and distinguish their agency. They are thus the indispensable background of normative agency.

Hence, the significance for liberalism of multiculturalism reposes on this understanding of the integral role cultures play for enabling and enhancing individual autonomy. But more needs to be said about what cultures *are* or, at any rate, what is significant about cultures for liberal concerns. Defining culture is notoriously difficult partly because the content given to any specific definition determines to a large extent the nature of claims that can be advanced upon it. For example, Jeremy Waldron argues that it is mistaken to see "meaningful options" arising from any one given set of cultural sources when in fact they arise from a variety of cultural sources. Alternatively, because of the differences in type, Kymlicka has progressively narrowed his definition of culture to one of "societal cultures" that "provides its members with meaningful ways of life across the full range of human activities, including social, educational, religious, recreational, and economic life, encompassing both public and private spheres."[24] Of course, this does not seem to be a narrowing of his definition until one takes into account the following line: "these cultures tend to be territorially concentrated, and based on a shared language." Kymlicka is primarily concerned with articulating rights claims for national minorities, and hence his definition of culture is meant to insulate his arguments from an undifferentiated extension to other forms of cultural groupings such as "lifestyle" cultures, by which he means more voluntaristic groupings such as around sexuality or other subnational forms of cultural identification.

Despite the fact that definitions of culture determine to a large extent the scope and nature of multicultural arguments, what is common to liberal theories of multiculturalism lies in what cultural practices, discourses, and meanings—however we bound them—provide for individuals and groups. Taylor speaks of an "ideal of authenticity"—that there is a way of being, a sense of identity that feels "true" or "original" to each individual or group. Traced to Herder, Taylor's arguments about authenticity have often been criticized for relying upon some notion of cultural essentialism.[25] But it is also critical to recognize that Taylor's conception of authenticity is also shot through with tension and even contradiction. This is so because our sense of identity, far from being inwardly generated, depends upon its "fundamentally *dialogical* character. We become full human agents, capable of understanding ourselves, and hence of defining our identity, through our acquisition of rich human languages of expression" (original emphasis).[26] Such rich languages of expression thus constitute for Taylor the cultural medium through which identity is developed and secured. As such, our sense of identity can be harmed by "demeaning or contemptible" pictures of these cultural mediums.[27]

Authenticity for Taylor is thus less a preexisting standard than a process of negotiation with others fraught with peril or, alternatively, conducive to solace. The goal of this process is the attempt to articulate distinctions of worth between things we find more significant and true about ourselves and more trivial aspects of who we are. But again, for Taylor, this struggle for authenticity is not a process of discovering some preexisting essence. He states:

> Our attempts to formulate what we hold important must, like descriptions, strive to be faithful to something. But what they strive to be faithful to is not an independent object with a fixed degree and manner of evidence, but rather a largely inarticulate sense of what is of decisive importance. An articulation of this "object" tends to make it something different from what it was before.[28]

As an articulation, our attempt to define what is of authentic importance to who we are reworks the set of circumstances and experiences in which we find ourselves. It is out of this process of articulation, situated in a cultural web, that the search for authenticity generates a congealed identity. But why should identity matter so much?

The significance of identity depends upon his conception of what is distinctive about our philosophical anthropology and what this reveals about human agency. For Taylor, what is distinctive about persons is that they are "self-interpreting animals" whose self-interpretations are constituted by "evaluative distinctions of worth." References to one's identity are always bound up with evaluative discriminations of value about aspects of ourselves or ideals to which we aspire. He states, "the notion of identity refers us to certain evaluations which are essential because they are the indispensable horizon or foundation out of which we reflect and evaluate as persons."[29] We are beings for whom things matter, and these evaluative distinctions are built out of constitutive background contexts. Identity for Taylor thus inescapably involves a moral and normative dimension.

This theory of strong evaluation thus gains constitutive significance for Taylor in linking identity with agency precisely because the evaluations we formulate render our agency meaningful and intelligible.[30] As he argues, "our identity is therefore defined by certain evaluations that are inseparable from ourselves as agents."[31] Moreover, ". . . our ability to adhere as persons to certain evaluations, would be impossible outside the horizon of these essential evaluations, that we would break down as persons, be incapable of being persons in the full sense."[32] Since cultures provide the contexts through which these evaluations are constituted, identity or, more specifically, our identifications represents the intermediary process of human agency. Our choices and actions are intelligible through the cultural contexts from which they arise, and through these actions we come to sediment and define our sense of who we are, whether on an individual or a collective level. It is precisely because there is no one-to-one correspondence between our autonomy and our cultural contexts, precisely because our sense of identity is both the product of human "choice" and of given cultural contexts, that the process of identity formation and of its connections to autonomy gains salience.

BETWEEN IDENTITY FORMATION AND AUTONOMY: THE TENSIONS OF RECOGNITION

Taylor characterizes the struggle for authenticity, the attempt to formulate core evaluations of one's identity as a lifelong process, one often replete with ambivalence and tension. Yet this process is even more complicated when we factor in the dialogic component, namely the role of recognition in shepherding the link between such evaluations and our autonomy. In order for our agency to be intelligible, not just to ourselves but to others, these links must be recognized. And such recognition reposes on the encounter between our own self-interpretations and the understandings of those around us and the society at large. No matter how we understand our own actions and the cultural webs in which they germinate, they will be rendered opaque if those around us and society in general significantly misrecognize the intentions and understandings underlying our actions or else fail to provide recognition altogether. It is on this societal level that multiculturalism embodies a politics of recognition. But it is not just a matter of adding societal recognition to an already preformulated sense of identity. Rather, taking Taylor at his most nuanced conception of identity formation and recognition demonstrates both as integral aspects of the same process. Nor does misrecognition entail simply a short-circuit of this process, for the process of misrecognition is likewise implicated in the process of someone else's identity formation. If we adhere fully to the dialogic component of Taylor's understanding, then the formulation of our identities and the sense of autonomy thus generated are always situated in a web of mutual processes of recognition. The recognition we formulate for others is also often the basis through which we fashion our own sense of autonomy. Or, stated alternatively, the misrecognition one receives is a constitutive feature in the economy of someone else's self-understanding.

Yet often, liberal treatments of multiculturalism fail to maintain these tensions in two respects. First, the strong constitutive connection between autonomy and cultural contexts is often flattened and uncoupled. This is primarily the result of viewing such background cultures as static and, more important, of viewing the process of identity formation as a simple access to or affirmation of such contexts. But, as discussed in the previous section, for Taylor such formulations or articulations bring about something new. They transform such background circumstances, giving them a particular and distinctive evaluative meaning. Second, discussions of group rights within a multicultural framework often address the consequences and remedies of recognition in one-sided terms. The focus is often upon the needs of minority groups without addressing the ways in which such forms of recognition, in particular preexisting forms of misrecognition, have come to form the basis upon which recognition is adjudicated. Such treatments thus fail to implicate the larger webs and discursive understandings within which misrecognitions serve a vital constitutive role. Both of these dimensions often result when liberal treatments of multiculturalism respond to charges of essentialism and are implicated greatly when we turn to the distinctive challenge of race.

For example, wanting to avoid any charges of essentialism, Kymlicka refers to his conception of "societal cultures" as "contexts of choice." For Kymlicka, there is wide latitude within "societal cultures" from which autonomy can be fashioned while still representing an indispensable "context."[33] Because cultures provide the medium in which individuals make their choices and because societal cultures are sufficiently broad to offer a wide scope of choices, protecting autonomy ought thus to include sustaining these societal cultures. In this manner, Kymlicka can still argue for rights claims based on culture without endangering autonomy. But, despite his intentions, it seems to me that this move polarizes individual autonomy against cultural context, severing the complex relationship between the meaning of our choices and of the cultural contexts in which they emerge. It is not that what we draw from cultural contexts is predetermined or fixed, but neither is it the case that autonomy simply reposes upon a range of choices and options. Decoupling culture and autonomy runs the risk of opposing on the one hand a static sense of cultural context and on the other a thin and free-floating conception of individual autonomy. What is lost is the mediated space in which our identifications are forged and in which our agency gains a force and a weight that belie its "choice."

This polarization between culture and autonomy has in fact become the tendency within liberal debates over multiculturalism, particularly in arguments considering group rights for "illiberal" cultures. Whether we are speaking of head scarves in France or female genital forms of mutilation or the fatwah on Salman Rushdie, the lines of debate considering these issues often polarize into an opposition between individual autonomy and a flattened and remarkably unsubtle conception of culture.[34] Let me be clear. As a matter of state policy, there are certainly very hard and difficult cases that force the recognition that there are limits to toleration. Addressing such cases is helpful and illuminating in clarifying the implications of multicultural arguments. In addition, one should note that such debates follow classic liberal predispositions, configuring autonomy as largely freedom from constraint. But the consequences of formulating the debate over "illiberal cultures" as a stark choice between protecting individual autonomy and toleration of a fixed set of cultural practices ironically surrenders the very connection between culture and autonomy stipulated to begin with. What is lost is the very issue of why certain cultural practices become bound up with the exercise of autonomy as something more complex than the subordination to a cultural tradition. Exploring these difficult issues would lead one into examining the contexts of politicization in which certain cultural practices and meanings become expressed as a firm source of identity and as an act of autonomy.[35] It would lead one, I contend, to engage the realm of identity politics.

A related issue regarding the polarization between culture context and individual autonomy is evidenced in regard to the recognition of religious groups, particularly conservative ones that do not privilege autonomy. Jeff Spinner-Halev has argued that "religious conservatives are especially troublesome because they do not have a place in the new, increasingly influential arguments for recognizing cultural diversity and difference."[36] This is so because arguments like those advanced by Kymlicka and Joseph Raz support cultural diversity insofar as doing so maximizes autonomy. The religious conservative who rejects the autonomy of mainstream liberal life can thus appear only highly suspicious from this standpoint. Since cultures are valuable for Kymlicka as "contexts of choice," those that reject individual choice exist outside the scope of liberal protection; potentially subjecting their practices to revision. For Spinner-Halev, however, the religious conservative may be exercising autonomy even if it may lead to "a life of minimal autonomy, a life guided by one main choice."[37] He argues that the account of culture and autonomy found in Kymlicka and Raz is backwards: "Instead of supporting cultural communities or cultural structure because they support autonomy—something that is only sometimes true—liberals should support people's autonomy."[38] As long as there exists a right of exit, Spinner-Halev argues that we ought to recognize the decision among religious conservatives to lead a life with minimal choice. Such a decision appears counterintuitive as an act of autonomy only if we conceptualize autonomy as involving a sense of free-floating choice.[39] The intelligibility of the religious conservative's autonomy is eclipsed when we confine our understanding of autonomy to one of maximal choice. Often it is the rejection of the values of mainstream liberal society, based on depictions of a cultural life revolving around morally devoid consumerist choice that form the basis for the meaning of their autonomy. Unfortunately, Spinner-Halev is not willing to extend this analysis to groups defined through experiences of inequality and oppression. For him, like other liberals who define such groups as aggregates of systemic inequality, the recognition of the bases of group difference can result only in programs of eventual dissolution.

Nevertheless, the conceptualization of culture as possessing normative force within liberal theories of multiculturalism gains significance to the degree that it is theorized as a necessary dimension of individual autonomy. But construing such autonomy as a matter of choice free from constraint flattens the relationship between culture and autonomy where certain forms of autonomy emerge out of cultural identifications that are not perceived or experienced as matters of choice. At the very least, this significantly narrows our ability to comprehend other understandings of autonomy. If issues of multiculturalism were only about group rights and the adjudication of cultural difference in liberal state policy, perhaps a reliance on a principle of choice defining autonomy would be sufficient. In that sense, it would be sufficient for a liberal society to offer a diverse range of cultural options without any specific privileging of one or another. At any rate, this has been the trajectory of Kymlicka's theory, which now defends calls for group rights only in the cases of national minorities. But such a theory provides very little in the way of comprehending movements that politicize cultural identity or of the ways in which such attempts at politicization involve efforts at formulating alternative conceptions of autonomy and, in the case of racialized groups, contesting and challenging prevailing conceptions of their autonomy. Hence, in the next section, I examine more closely the status of race within liberal multiculturalism and the dimensions of autonomy involved in racial identity politics.

RACE AS A NORMATIVE CULTURE?

Since Kymlicka has devoted his efforts primarily toward defending group rights for national minorities, his conception of multiculturalism offers little in the way of sustained reflection about what a multiculturalism surrounding race might entail. But this is not to say that race is of peripheral concern for his theory. Analyzing different sources for cultural diversity and hence different claims for group recognition, Kymlicka sets as his main axis for such claims one that revolves around the distinction between immigrant societies or what he calls "polyethnic states" and national minorities within multination states. Much of the rationale for his defense of rights, which seek to ensure the flourishing of the culture of national minorities, lies in the sense that they are preexisting at the time of their incorporation into a larger state. As stated earlier, such minorities are marked by geographical territoriality and a shared language. This stands in contrast to immigrant societies like the United States where immigration is largely voluntary. Hence, part of the cost of immigrating to a new country involves forgoing strong attachments to their previous culture and integrating within the culture of destination.[40] Though Kymlicka asserts that even immigrants ought to have certain "polyethnic rights"—particularly in cases where their integration into the host country is either resistant or unfair—they are considerably less expansive than those Kymlicka defends for national minorities. But Kymlicka concedes that the situation of African Americans "is very unusual" and lies outside the distinction between voluntary immigrants and national minorities.[41] This is so because "they were not allowed to integrate into the mainstream culture; nor were they allowed to maintain their earlier languages and cultures, or to create new cultural associations and institutions. They did not have their own homeland or territory, yet they were physically segregated."[42] Kymlicka goes on to argue that in response to the uniqueness of the situation of African Americans, many "American liberals have hoped that the immigrant model of integration can be made to work for African-Americans," though Kymlicka concludes that this has proven unrealistic and that any policies appropriate in the case of African Americans will likely be different from those for either voluntary immigrants or national minorities.[43]

If the difficulty with race—and, for Kymlicka, the paradigmatic case of African Americans—were only a question of classification, then it would seem peripheral to his theory. But arguments over how to treat race continue to cloud his case for minority rights. Kymlicka argues that modern liberals often reject minority rights on grounds of justice primarily through the legacy of the *Brown v. Board of Education* decision.[44] If separate is inherently unequal, if it is inherently stigmatizing, then the call for separate institutions or for a status recognizing minority cultures can only appear suspect. In essence, Kymlicka argues that race and, more generally, issues of cultural difference appear on the register of American liberal justice in terms of an equation between inequality and separation, paradigmatically from the decision of *Brown v. Board*. More sharply, the recognition of race as involving unequal separation within liberal justice creates a liberal inability to *recognize* what for Kymlicka are more legitimate markers of cultural distinction. Indeed, this seems to be the case as Kymlicka has more recently argued that "American multiculturalism" has often been exported to other contexts to the detriment of issues of minority nationalism.[45]

This American form of multiculturalism seems to be the product of an emerging consensus around three claims. First, some form of multiculturalism is now unavoidable. Second, "the appropriate form of multiculturalism must be fluid in its conception of groups and group boundaries . . .; voluntary in its conception of group affiliation . . .; and nonexclusive in its conception of group identity [allowing overlapping forms of affiliation]. . . ."[46] And third, "the greatest challenge to creating such a fluid conception of multiculturalism remains the disadvantaged and stigmatized status of African Americans."[47] Kymlicka concludes that the "main challenge for American multiculturalism, therefore, is to reduce the ascriptive, stigmatizing, and segregating elements of 'black' identity, so that being black can come to resemble other ethnic identities in America."[48] Kymlicka accepts these three claims as a matter of American multiculturalism, but he argues that this form of multiculturalism is having a "pernicious influence in other countries, inhibiting efforts to understand and accommodate minority nationalism."[49] The reason for this ostensibly is that the phenotypical and culturalist legacies of racial ascription are so thoroughly corrupted that any attempt to assert harder claims based on cultural identity must endanger autonomy and are politically pernicious. The natural recourse is thus to hinge toleration and recognition upon cultural groups that are fluid and voluntary. Yet, for Kymlicka, "Too often, this open, fluid, and voluntary conception of American multiculturalism has been explained and defended *in contrast to minority nationalism*" (original emphasis).[50]

Whatever the case may be for minority nationalism, it seems clear that race and its legacies continue to be a determining unsettling presence for theories of multiculturalism while existing themselves in an ambiguous position of exceptionalism. Clearly, the infamy of what we would now call the culturalist dimensions of racial ascription renders any claims based on these grounds in the public domain highly suspect even ostensibly in positive characterizations or appeals. This seems entirely correct for a spurious category of difference such as race. This is the sense in which Kymlicka argues that the situation of African Americans constitutes the "deepest challenge" for a fluid conception of multiculturalism, and, in a manner, Kymlicka laments, it also represents the deepest obstacle for how we recognize the rights of minority cultures. Yet it also determines the shape and appeal of an ethnic conception of group difference. Because racial ascription and exclusion depended upon constructing a fixed and involuntary sense of group distinctiveness grounded in morphological characteristics, the ultimate promise of multiculturalism must lie in a conception of groups that is fluid, voluntary, and nonexclusive. As an ideal, this formulation seems unobjectionable for race. Indeed, we might hope that racial identity as we understand it now might fade to extinction. But how are we to arrive there? And what of the individuals figured under its boundaries?

Virtually all of the commentators discussed here support various redistributive and affirmative action schemes as a means of ameliorating racial inequality and injustice, but very little is discussed concerning the means through which racialized individuals and groups come to fashion their own autonomy, an autonomy that may derive and as such become intelligible only upon the basis of claims that refer to a racialized legacy that is beyond choice. Surely one of the core appeals of multiculturalism lies in the ability to publicly express and assert forms of cultural identifications as an act of political participation, as an agent of civic membership widening and, in some cases, challenging prevailing conceptions of the civic subject. Yet this sense of autonomy is left ambiguous for racialized groups caught between a prescription for a voluntarist sense of ethnic identity and a suspicion of any normative claims based upon race.

Two aspects of this ambiguity in the relationship between autonomy and racialized groups bear further examination. The first concerns the sense in which the history of the American civic subject has always been substantiated and "fleshed out" through thicker culturalist rationales, rationales that determined what virtuous citizenship involved and the boundaries of inclusion/exclusion that would circumscribe it. There is now a burgeoning literature that explores exactly this question, tracing how liberal notions of self-government, consent, and freedom were often "wedded" in public and official discourse to culturalist rationales that differentiated the capacity for autonomy.[51] Such rationales often depended upon constructions of racial, gender, and class distinctions to define not only the space of exclusion but also the nature of inclusion. Which is to say, such constructions and their implications for notions of autonomy were implicated in discursive webs of recognition and misrecognition. These constructions were engaged thus in the political process of rendering particular conceptions of autonomy *recognizable*, carried out on the basis of distinguishing these various notions from others misrecognized as illegitimate or deviant. The identity politics of dominant and ascendant groups were tied to the delimiting of the political possibilities, indeed the political *intelligibility* of others. This was true not just for racialized groups but also irreducibly for women, homosexuals, those occupying the lowest levels of the economic order, the disabled, and a host of other more or less salient categories of difference. What some theorists denote as the operations of heteronormativity were consequently secured and sedimented through processes of recognition on the level of identifying abject forms of civic autonomy.[52]

Perhaps more pertinent to the issue of autonomy regarding the inclusion/exclusion of racialized groups lies in the growing literature analyzing the relationship between race and ethnicity at the moment in which ethnicity began to be articulated as an alternative conception of difference during the Progressive era.[53] For example, Victoria Hattam argues that in the work of Horace Kallen, the classic articulator of ethnic difference, we find the articulation of a form of cultural difference that did not threaten loyalty to the nation but "strove to fix race in order to unfix ethnicity."[54] By oppositionally twinning race and ethnicity, figures like Kallen during this period could argue for a form of cultural difference socially voluntary in nature as opposed to being hard-wired in race, civically enhancing as opposed to civically degenerate. And yet, this genealogy resembles quite similarly the rhetorical juxtapositions that have come to define the status of race within multiculturalism. An ethnic model of voluntary and fluid cultural difference is held against the inevitably hard ascriptivism associated with race. We may wonder whether the emergent concern over the normative culture of race replays a long familiar residual pattern.

Of course, liberal multiculturalists and cosmopolitans might object that the valence has rightly changed. After all, the point now is to end the exclusionary manifestations of race. Yet by failing to adequately conceptualize the political autonomy of raced subjects as more than aggregate victims, as more than the targets of government policy, such semantic constructs trade too easily upon older and more pernicious discourses, discourses that delimited and constrained the space of autonomy for African Americans and others. Indeed, we find cultural arguments prevalent today that oppose the "success" of older European immigrants and newer Asian immigrants against the situation of African Americans. Though such rationales may no longer appeal to physical differences, culturalist arguments such as the enduring "culture of poverty" thesis continue to bound the sense of the civic subject, not just against racialized groups but also by privileging more dominant and ascendant ones. Contesting these understandings of the civic subject and of the sense of autonomy they entail need not necessarily take the form of providing alternative cultural formulations as in affirmations of racial identity, but they may, and as a matter of autonomy we need to conceptualize ways in which such political contestation can invoke the history of race as a background horizon of significance without succumbing to the dangers of essentialism.

Finally, it seems clear that the stark polarity between choice and unchoice in defining autonomy within the theory of normative culture flattens our ability to comprehend the autonomy of racialized groups. The legacy of race as an ascriptive identity has always hinged on the sense in which race implied necessity. To critically reflect upon and draw upon this legacy as a background source of autonomy is often felt as manifestly not a choice. Indeed, given the continuing structural inequities that define life chances for African Americans, it seems profoundly disempowering to reconfigure their appeal to racial identity and its historicity as a matter of voluntary choice. This is disempowering in a double sense: first, as the result of a determination by academic theorists and second, for substantive reasons having fully to do with drawing attention to what are often experienced as decisive and inescapable background contexts of agency. We need a better and more nuanced understanding of the connections between the politicization of cultural identifications and what it means to express one's autonomy. We need in short to reattend to the dilemmas of identity politics.

There is a great deal of irony in the sense that race remains inadequately recognized within the discourse of multiculturalism. Out of a fear of legitimating racial difference as salient to autonomy, attempts to render recognizable acts of autonomy from the standpoint of a racialized background remain opaque and liminal. More important, new understandings of what ought to constitute legitimate and acceptable forms of civic agency (and the cultural referents they spring from) continue to be produced out of a problematic exclusive construal of what race represents. After all, liberal treatments of multiculturalism are not just about bringing liberal theory up to date with the politics of recognition; rhetorically they are themselves engaged already in a politics of recognition. This reinscription of the abjection of race is, as I have tried to argue, a result of an insufficient examination of the links between culture and autonomy and the lack of an explicit engagement with the politically productive history of race in shaping the contours of recognizable autonomy. In the former, a flattened conception of culture and autonomy conceives the category of race as incorrigibly an essentialized context of constraint, one that could never be a source of an autonomy based on choice. In the latter, the manner in which multiculturalism and the politics of recognition are seen as novel demands on the register of liberal justice blinds us to the way in which notions of legitimate civic autonomy have always been secured politically through forms of recognition and misrecognition. This is a central dynamic in the history of race, and, as such, attempts to draw from this history as an act of political autonomy and political contestation remain opaque and consequently are reinscribed as abject.

THE PUBLIC REGISTER OF JUSTICE

The challenge of race to multiculturalism sharpens the ways we imagine political contestation that draws from issues of cultural difference. In responding to the challenge raised by the politics of recognition and the politics of difference, liberal discussions have primarily evolved into efforts at policing the bounds.[55] This is to say not that liberal debates around multiculturalism are hostile but that the challenges raised by cultural difference to liberal understandings of autonomy have been assimilated under notions of group rights, specifically, within a conception of voluntaristic ethnicity. The very notion of group rights signals the subtle manner in which the dimension of political contestation within the politics of recognition is domesticated. *Granting* recognition of cultural difference involves a new schematic of *distribution*. Certain forms of cultural difference are legitimized from the standpoint of the state as primary *goods* to which members may *possess* certain rights. Such language indicates the way in which the distributive paradigm of classic liberal theory has come to find renewed shape in the discourse of multiculturalism.

It is useful in this regard to recall Iris Marion Young's critique of the distributive paradigm in her 1990 book, *Justice and the Politics of Difference*.[56] For Young, the distributive paradigm as a register of justice clouds aspects of social justice that are distorted when we conceive of them as matters subject to distribution. In particular, two problems for Young arise when we consider certain matters of social justice from the standpoint of distributive justice. First, in considering social justice in terms of the allocation of goods, the "social and institutional context that often help determine distributive patterns" tend to be ignored.[57] This is because the focus is placed on the resultant inequality in the outcome of goods, rather than on the processes that cause the inequality. What is of decisive importance for Young in this regard are aspects of these contexts that help explain and determine these patterns, aspects such as "decision-making power and procedures, division of labor, and culture." Second, in extending metaphorically the distribution of material goods to nonmaterial goods, Young argues that the distributive paradigm often treats these nonmaterial "goods" "as though they were static things, instead of a function of social relations and processes."[58] By fetishizing what are the results of social process and relations, notions such as autonomy become discrete, static objects. By extension, whatever supports are established for these notions likewise are rendered as discrete and static.

For Young, these two tendencies within the distributive paradigm obscure many aspects of the claims of social injustice within the politics of difference. The tendency to treat the issues raised by such politics as a form of interest-group politics is a consequence of rendering the issues of cultural difference into one of access to static things. As such, remedies of these claims to social injustice invariably distort or ignore the way in which issues of cultural difference implicate and emerge out of a web of social and institutional contexts. But what undergirds the politics of difference as other than a form of interest-group politics is precisely the attempt to politicize and bring to public awareness such contexts, contexts that shape, constrain, and give meaning to the political agency of subalterns and the claims they advance.

Moving away from the distributive paradigm leads Young to another important point, namely that certain forms of cultural domination and oppression are beyond the realm of law and policy to remedy.[59] This means not that they lie outside the bounds of politics but that the administering of justice through a new redistribution of goods does not capture the distinctive harm nor the roots of these cultural processes. Rather, what is central about them is the inability to contest them on a recognizable public register. All of the various proposals Young advances in the course of her book are united in attempting to pluralize the ability of individuals and groups to politicize and bear testimony to social processes of meaning construction that distort or render invisible their ability to participate within a democratic public. Whether through providing new institutional resources or, more controversially, veto power in decision-making procedures for groups positioned under the sign of difference, such proposals are meant to strengthen the ability of individuals and groups to counteract the processes of cultural elaboration that undergird established norms of civic agency and the prevailing public register of justice.

Nowhere does Young explicitly identify her arguments with those of multiculturalism. Yet her attempt to transform prevailing liberal conceptions of justice according to the demands raised by the politics of difference deepen many of the arguments I have advanced regarding the inadequacy of prevailing liberal trends about the significance of multiculturalism, particularly when the group difference at hand involves race. Despite the controversiality of many of her proposals, a guiding ethos or principle of democratic political participation inspires her work and as such powerfully illuminates what I have attempted to argue should be the connections between multiculturalism and race, a connection that brings race within the concerns of multiculturalism while opening spaces of productive politics around racial identity.

If we take multiculturalism to be centrally tied to questions of cultural difference and their impact upon understandings of what I have called civic autonomy, then explicitly attending to the challenges posed by race deepens our understanding of the links between context and autonomy, between culture and agency. By drawing attention to the normative significance race has served in delineating the scope of civic autonomy, a crucial corrective is advanced when we likewise consider the scope of the politics of recognition in our ongoing acts of recognition within the horizon of multiculturalism. This is especially true of liberal accounts of multiculturalism that proceed by donning the mantle of liberal adjudicators of justice. Certainly, this involves moving beyond a flattened understanding of the link between culture and agency, an understanding that renders our referencing of cultural context into one of access to a discrete and static good. For what is being politicized is precisely these links, links that are often claimed as being of political significance in a dynamic intersubjective sense rather than in a transhistorical or anthropological one. If the concept of race demonstrates the inadequacy of this—in terms not of an inherent essentialism but of pointing to a wider field of political meaning production—then we need to alter our understanding of the challenges raised by multiculturalism. Rather than assign an exceptional normative culture to racial subjects or assimilate them to a category of ethnicity that bears its own fraught and sedimented history with it, any advances in considering the background sources of autonomy and agency must confront and engage the constitutive remains and materiality of race. Constructing a multicultural horizon without racial remainder demands no less.

NOTES

1. Judith Butler, *Excitable Speech: A Politics of the Performative* (New York: Routledge, 1997), 25.
2. See for example Elazan Barkan, *The Guilt of Nations* (New York: Norton, 2000). This strand also moves within the growing attempt to recast the

transformations of the civil rights era in terms of American superpower and Cold War considerations. See Mary Dudziak, *Cold War Civil Rights: Race and the Image of American Democracy* (Princeton: Princeton University Press, 2002), and Rogers M. Smith and Phillip A. Klinkner, *The Unsteady March: The Rise and Decline of Racial Equality in America* (Chicago: University of Chicago, 2002).

3. These curricular reforms emerged, in turn, out of the local, municipal struggles for community defense and self-determination in urban cities during the 1960s and 1970s. For a concrete examination of the fluidity of these emerging languages, see Robert O. Self, *American Babylon* (Princeton: Princeton University Press, 2003).
4. Mary C. Waters, *Ethnic Options: Choosing Identities in America* (Berkeley: University of California Press, 1990), 157–158.
5. See for example, Nancy Fraser, "From Redistribution to Recognition?," in Fraser, *Justice Interruptus: Critical Reflections on the "Postsocialist" Condition* (New York: Routledge, 1997), 11–39, and Jeff Spinner-Halev, *Boundaries of Citizenship: Race, Ethnicity and Nationality in the Liberal State* (Baltimore: Johns Hopkins University Press, 1994).
6. See, for example, Todd Gitlin, *Twilight of Our Common Dreams: Why America Is Wracked by Culture Wars* (New York: Metropolitan Books, 1995); Michael Tomasky, *Left for Dead: The Life, Death and Possible Resurrection of Progressive Politics in America* (New York: Free Press, 1996); or John Higham, "Multiculturalism and Universalism: A History and Critique," *American Quarterly* 45 (June 1993): 195–219.
7. For a similar though ultimately critical account of multiculturalism and the politics of recognition see Patchen Markell, *Bound by Recognition* (Princeton: Princeton University Press, 2003). Markell focuses his analysis on the quest for securing sovereign agency, not in the sense of the state but in the more individual sense of being in command and control of who we are in the face of subjection at the hands of others. For Markell, insofar as recognition involves securing this hope, it is an impossible task, and as such the politics of recognition will always be caught within its own paradox.
8. David A. Hollinger, "Not Universalists, Not Pluralists: The New Cosmopolitans Find Their Own Way," *Constellations* 8, no. 2 (2001): 236–248.
9. Ibid., 237.
10. Ibid.
11. Ibid., 246, n8.
12. Cyrus R.K. Pattell, "Comparative American Studies: Hybridity and Beyond," *American Literary History* (Spring 1999): 166–186. Jeremy Waldron has also endorsed this conception of a cosmopolitan alternative in "Minority Cultures and the Cosmopolitan Alternative," *University of Michigan Journal of Law Reform* 25, no. 3: 751–93.
13. Of course, not all agree that we should limit cosmopolitanism this way. Martha Nussbaum is perhaps the most prominent defender of classical universalist appeals to cosmopolitanism. See her "Patriotism and Cosmopolitanism," in *For the Love of Country: Debating the Limits of Multiculturalism*, ed. Joshua Cohen (Boston: Beacon, 1996), 2–17.
14. Kwame Anthony Appiah, "Cosmopolitan Patriots," in *For Love of Country: Debating the Limits of Multiculturalism*, ed. Joshua Cohen (Boston: Beacon, 1996), 22–23.
15. In this regard, liberal defenders could draw on established strands of cultural pluralism already present within the liberal tradition such as through the arguments of Horace Kallen and Randolph Bourne at the turn of the twentieth century.

16. Appiah, "Cosmopolitan Patriots," 29.
17. Charles Taylor, "The Politics of Recognition," in *Multiculturalism*, ed. Amy Gutmann (Princeton: Princeton University Press, 1992), 25–73.
18. See, for example, Alasdair MacIntyre, *After Virtue: A Study in Moral Theory* (London: Duckworth, 1981); Michael Sandel, *Liberalism and the Limits of Justice* (Cambridge: Cambridge University Press, 1982); Michael Walzer, *Spheres of Justice: A Defense of Pluralism and Equality* (Oxford: Blackwell, 1983).
19. Taylor, "The Politics of Recognition," 26.
20. See especially the introductory remarks for this change: John Rawls, *Political Liberalism* (New York: Columbia University Press, 1993), xvi–xviii.
21. Joseph Raz, *Ethics in the Public Domain: Essays in the Morality of Law and Politics* (Oxford: Oxford University Press, 1994), 178. One can take this in a deeper sense as well; that is, not only does one's cultural background amend the content of our freedom, but also liberal freedom itself involves a process of subjection. See Uday S. Mehta, *The Anxiety of Freedom: Imagination and Individuality in Locke's Political Thought* (Ithaca: Cornell University Press, 1992).
22. Will Kymlicka, *Liberalism, Community, and Culture* (Oxford: Oxford University Press, 1989), 76.
23. As Jeremy Waldron has argued, ". . . that people need cultural materials does not show that what people need is 'a rich and secure cultural structure'. It shows the importance of access to a variety of stories and roles; but does not . . . show the importance of something called membership in a culture." Waldron, "Minority Cultures and the Cosmopolitan Alternative," 783–784.
24. Will Kymlicka, *Multicultural Citizenship* (Oxford: Oxford University Press, 1995),76.
25. Since the essay is in part directed at uncovering the politics of recognition of various "minority or 'sub-altern' groups" as well as the claims of certain strands of feminism, it is entirely appropriate to be concerned over the essentialist implications of Taylor's understanding of authenticity. Yet what is often not noted is that the text of his essay is virtually synonymous with portions of his *The Ethics of Authenticity* (Cambridge: Harvard University Press, 1991). Indeed, the object of his concern there is less the politics of recognition of subaltern groups than an overall "malaise of modernity," in which Taylor is primarily concerned with the eclipse of a certain moral agency. Interestingly, his conception of authenticity there turns on its tensions and contradictions rather than on the recovery of some source of authentic essence. Indeed, there is a sense in which the ideal of authenticity in his analysis results from a tragic encounter with the forces of atomizing modernity. Admittedly, Taylor there focuses on the "slide into subjectivism" as a consequence of the ideal. But the flip side of this is likewise a retreat into the solace afforded by an overdetermining identity.
26. Taylor, "The Politics of Recognition," 32. The full implications of this tension have yet to be explored fully. For if identities depend upon a relationship of recognition for enactment, once we surrender a strong notion of preexisting essence, then identities become less discovered through recognition than produced through it. For an analysis of this tension, see Patchell Markell, "The Recognition of Politics: A Comment on Emcke and Tully,"*Constellations* 7, no. 4 (2000): 496–506, as well as his more developed argument in *Bound by Recognition*.
27. Taylor, "The Politics of Recognition," 36.
28. Charles Taylor, "What Is Human Agency?," in *Human Agency and Language: Philosophical Papers*, vol. 1 (Cambridge: Cambridge University Press, 1985), 38.

29. Ibid., 35.
30. For fuller discussions of Taylor's theory of strong evaluation see Daniel M. Weinstock, "The Political Theory of Strong Evaluation," in *Philosophy in an Age of Pluralism: The Philosophy of Charles Taylor in Question*, ed. James Tully (Cambridge: Cambridge University Press, 1994), 171–193; also, Nicholas H. Smith, *Strong Hermeneutics: Contingency and Moral Identity* (New York: Routledge, 1997), 35–40.
31. Taylor, "What Is Human Agency?," 34.
32. Ibid., 34–5.
33. Kymlicka, *Multicultural Citizenship*, 82–84.
34. See, for example, Susan Moller Okin, "Is Multiculturalism Bad for Women?," in *Is Multiculturalism Bad for Women?*, ed. Joshua Cohen, Matthew Howard, and Martha Nussbaum (Princeton: Princeton University Press, 1999), 9–24.
35. This is as true of cultural practices that we may disavow as it is of those we uphold. That is, understanding autonomy as emerging out of social webs is shot through with valences.
36. Jeff Spinner-Halev, *Surviving Diversity: Religion and Democratic Citizenship* (Baltimore: Johns Hopkins University Press, 2000), 24.
37. Ibid., 54.
38. Ibid., 55.
39. Tariq Modood makes a related point about the difficulties involved in "recognizing" religious groups, particularly when we hold them against an understanding of autonomy based on a context of choice. See "Anti-essentialism, Multiculturalism, and the 'Recognition' of Religious Groups," in *Citizenship in Diverse Societies*, ed. Will Kymlicka and Wayne Norman (Oxford: Oxford University Press, 2000), 175–189.
40. Kymlicka, *Multicultural Citizenship*, 63.
41. Ibid., 24.
42. Ibid.
43. Ibid., 25.
44. Ibid., 58–60.
45. Will Kymlicka, "American Multiculturalism in the International Arena," *Dissent* (Fall 1998): 73–79.
46. Ibid., 73.
47. Ibid.
48. Ibid. Kymlicka then goes on to discuss David Hollinger's *Postethnic America: Beyond Multiculturalism* (New York: Basic Books, 1995) as the most sophisticated articulation of this "consensus" view.
49. Ibid.
50. Ibid.
51. The most well-known example remains the work of Rogers M. Smith in his *Civic Ideals: Conflicting Visions of Citizenship in U.S. History* (New Haven: Yale University Press, 1997). See also the excellent edited collection by David F. Ericson and Louisa Bertch Green, *The Liberal Tradition in American Politics* (New York: Routledge, 1999). For treatments that address more generally the relationship of liberal thought to specific political and cultural contexts, see Carol Pateman, *The Sexual Contract* (Stanford: Stanford University Press, 1988), and Uday S. Mehta, *Liberalism and Empire* (Chicago: University of Chicago Press, 1999).
52. For heteronormativity, see Judith Butler, *Bodies That Matter* (New York: Routledge, 1993), and Michael Warner, *The Trouble with Normal* (Cambridge: Harvard University Press, 1999), among others.

53. See, for example, Victoria Hattam, *In the Shadow of Race: Jews, Latinos, and Immigrant Politics in the United States* (Chicago: University of Chicago Press, 2007). Other treatments include Desmond King, *Making Americans: Immigration, Race, and the Origins of Diverse Democracy* (Cambridge: Harvard University Press, 2000), and Matthew Frye Jacobsen, *Whiteness of a Different Color: European Immigrants and the Alchemy of Race* (Cambridge: Harvard University Press, 1998).
54. Hattam, *In the Shadow of Race*, 75.
55. I am using the term "policing" in the sense Jacques Ranciere employs the term—as a function of administering an already established set of rules, codes, and meanings. See his *Dis-agreement* (Minneapolis: University of Minnesota, 1999).
56. Iris Marion Young, *Justice and the Politics of Difference* (Princeton: Princeton University Press, 1990).
57. Ibid., 14.
58. Ibid., 15.
59. Ibid., 124.

3 Exceptional Remains
Cosmopolitanism's Province in the American Imagination

Unto myself my Selfe my Selfe betray . . . I cannot live, with nor without my Selfe.

—George Goodwin[1]

In *Race and Reunion: The Civil War in American Memory*, historian David W. Blight begins his book with the spectacle of the fiftieth anniversary commemoration of the Battle of Gettysburg, which took place July 1–4, 1913.[2] No typical reenactment or gathering of civil war veterans, the semicentennial commemoration was unprecedented in logistical scope and attendance. "Designed to be a festival of sectional reconciliation and patriotism," some fifty-three thousand surviving veterans, Blue and Gray, attended the event with at least an equal number of spectators and an army of cooks, porters, and other support staff. Fully subsidized by the states and Congress, more than $2 million had been appropriated for the event and for the travel expenses of any Civil War veteran.[3] Over the course of those four days, the speakers at the event—dignitaries, veterans, governors—reinforced again and again the theme of fraternal reconciliation, of a strengthened national union forged in a conflict nobly fought among two equivalent sides fighting for freedom.

As *Race and Reunion* documents, this discourse of fraternal reconciliation had by then been long sown over the preceding three decades. Its political and social context in the deepening Jim Crow system of the South as Reconstruction quickly faded evinced the terms upon which that fraternal reconciliation was secured. For the exorcism of sectional strife became dependent upon the resubordination of blacks and the excision of all traces of the underlying conflicts behind the war, most notably around slavery.[4] The semicentennial of Gettysburg thus became the occasion for the national reaping of this long-simmering harvest. No clear records exist of the presence of black veterans among those veterans who attended; certainly no space was allotted for blacks to speak at the four-day event nor any speakers who dwelled upon either slavery or the failures of racial reconciliation. "The 1913 'Peace Jubilee,' as organizers called it, was a Jim Crow reunion, and white supremacy might be said to have been the silent, invisible master of ceremonies."[5]

On hand to cement this fraternal reconciliation was, of course, the newly elected Woodrow Wilson, the first Southerner to occupy the White House since the Civil War. Having already declared it "an impertinence to discourse upon how the battle went, how it ended," Wilson nonetheless focused his remarks upon the subsequent fifty years and what they had meant in terms of the evolution of "the maturity and might of a great nation."[6] For Wilson the preceding fifty years had witnessed the burgeoning of a great nation that "God has builded [*sic*] by our hands." In keeping with the tradition of America's special providence and in employing the familiar tropes of the jeremiadic tradition, Wilson questioned whether the task of the nation was complete—"has it yet squared itself with its own great standard set up at its birth, when it made that first noble, naïve appeal to the moral judgement of mankind to take notice that a government had now at last been established which was to serve men, not masters?"[7] Wilson's answer was negative. Though the veterans' "task is done . . . they look to us to perfect what they established." Indeed, Wilson proclaimed, "The days of sacrifice and cleansing are not closed." Speaking to the reconciled nation, he exhorted, "Do not put your uniforms by. Put the harness of the present on." Simultaneously invoking a pure founding with binding original commitments and an incomplete present state of affairs, Wilson in his peculiar jeremiadic terms called on the nation to deliver its redemptive promise. What was this promise he invoked?

On this score, Wilson's speech at Gettysburg provides little in the way of substantive content. The son of an oratorically gifted Presbyterian minister, Wilson, for all his martial metaphors, did not match the intensity of his rhetoric with an equal intensity of substance beyond an appeal to a solidarity grounded in freedom. One senses a yearning in the new president for the exercise of statesmanship where "Every day something must be done to push the campaign forward . . . with an eye to some great destiny."[8] Foremost for Wilson seems to be the dream of a sovereign agency, grounded in a communal space of becoming, of a brotherhood of free men acting in unity and concert toward some providential plan of self-making. Certainly, the context of the occasion no doubt limited Wilson in restricting his prescriptions to a reaffirmed vigilance in a brotherly community of freedom. The "host" he hoped to lead were the "great and small, without class or difference of kind or race or origin; and undivided in interest."[9] Yet in sounding the mystic chords of the American nation—a nation defined by core ideals of expansive freedom yet caught in a liminal process of becoming—Wilson was clearly not advancing a "new birth of freedom" in Lincoln's sense:

> We have found one another again as brother and comrades in arms, enemies no longer, generous friends rather, our battles long past, *the quarrel forgotten*—except that we shall not forget the splendid valour, the manly devotion of the men arrayed against one another, now grasping hands and smiling into each other's eyes. How complete the union has become and how dear to all of us, how unquestioned, how benign

> and majestic, as state after state has been added to this *our great family of free men!* [emphasis added][10]

For though Wilson tied the redemptive providence of the American nation to the expansion of "our great family of free men," the completion of that project of fraternal recognition and reconciliation turned upon the performance of a coming together premised on "the quarrel forgotten." What did forgetting mean on this occasion? Certainly it did not mean forgetting the battle and its time-space coordinates. Nor did it mean forgetting the primary belligerents. The Union and Confederate veterans attended the event in full regalia. Indeed, when Wilson spoke, a Union and a Confederate veteran flanked him on either side. Nor even did it literally mean that the quarrel had been forgotten. To say that a conflict is forgotten is to remember it in the act of utterance. To be sure, in the context of the overall event, Wilson's utterance remembers in a particular way. The fraternal strife that threatened the brotherhood of free men, that threatened the redemptive promise of the American nation, was displaced and expelled upon the bodily presence or, rather, absence, of black veterans. For the very presence of black veterans would have raised difficult questions about the war's meaning and about their status within the family of free men fifty years after the event. It would have forced the recognition of a conflict at the heart of that fraternal solidarity rather than one displaced to the peripheries of its social body and in the past of its becoming.

As dramaturgy, Wilson did indeed bind words to deeds on that occasion. Welding future dreams of communal freedom to a past left behind, the "quarrel forgotten" gains its social embodiment in the exclusion of the black presence at the heart of its ritualized and future citational performance.[11] Wilson's rhetorical strategy of calling forth a nation rooted in a "quarrel forgotten" would not be the last time such a strategy was employed.[12] Indeed, one could argue that it has become the rhetorical stock of choice when dealing with race in late-twentieth and early-twenty-first-century America. Perhaps the key to its embodiment and therefore its power as citational performance lies in the liminal space it carves, between normative ideals and a leveragable dead past synchronized with and between the present embodiments of that normative agency. Out of the liminal cohesion of Wilson's performance, a certain communal agency/solidarity was forged, one that depended on the silent identification of black veterans (active participants to the quarrel in question) with a quarrel that must be both left behind and remembered. This latter dimension is significant, and its power lies precisely in its ambiguity. For in exulting the nation to move beyond its "quarrels," in calling forth its immemorial unity, the ambiguity of slavery and more generally of race is positioned outside the community. To bring up the "quarrel" itself becomes tantamount to threatening the community.

As is well known, Wilson did indeed go on to embrace the role of statesman, and in his internationalism and his efforts at creating the League of Nations one can see him as holding a version of Kantian cosmopolitanism.

A community of free *nations* may have been his enduring ideal, underlying his support for struggles over self-determination. Domestically, of course, Wilson saw no contradiction between fashioning communities grounded in freedom and subordinating blacks and other racialized groups or continuing to disenfranchise women. Did he hold merely an ethnic conception of nationalism and self-determination, as one commentator argues?[13] Undoubtedly, this is true. But the paradox remains. For Wilson in his speech at the Gettysburg Reunion did not appeal to a *white* nation. At the very least he did not have to "cite" that "creedal" understanding of the American ethos: the "great and small, without class or difference of kind or race or origin; and undivided in interest." Herein lies the paradox, for Wilson displays not the least amount of irony or resistance in resonating with that sense of American exceptionalism. And this eschatology, if one may call it that, of communal becoming, secured in advance in the origins of the founding, allowed Wilson to refashion the Civil War and "the quarrel" into a national sense of agency, a reconfigured basis for American exceptionalism.

We might pose this paradox differently in terms of the category of ascriptivism. Through Rogers Smith's work, the concept of ascription has powerfully enabled the recovery of racially discriminatory arguments in American political history and the prominent role that they have played in the nation's unfolding.[14]For not only does the concept serve to mark and name those public invocations of racial exclusion and marginalization (as well as other discriminatory signifiers); it also locates them within the ongoing political matrix through which the nation comes to define itself, giving shape and coherence, a ground and a direction for its identity and ideals. Yet how would we reconcile Wilson's speech at Gettysburg with the concept of ascription? For the performance of that event stamped through Wilson's words was most certainly exclusionary. And in echoing the tones of Lincoln, Wilson, likewise, sought to coalesce a ground of communal identity. But what kind of ascriptivism is it that defines itself in the absence of race or, more precisely, in the absent presence of race, since blacks and slavery occupied the margins of the event and the speech?

Perhaps all this shows is that words and deeds are not the same. Yet if history is minimally a record of words and deeds, of words attached to deeds, of deeds inspired by words, then the paradox of race in relation to the American "creed" becomes a central preoccupation if we wish to inquire not just into the history of American ideals of freedom but also into their uses in forging the future of national solidarity and the continuing "deeds" which such ideals sanction. We live in a time wherein the "quarrel forgotten" gains a renewed resurgence, where a perceived crisis of national identity and the supposed erosion of national ideals presses within the transitions of the post–civil rights era, multiculturalism, and rising global attachments. More recently, many variations of cosmopolitanism have sought to respond to these developments, some with the explicit aim of reinvigorating the nation, all with the implicit concern for moving beyond the nation's ascriptive past.

AMERICAN LIBERALISM'S SWOLLEN DREAM

> . . . structure—or rather the structurality of structure—although it has always been at work, has always been neutralized or reduced, and this by a process of giving it a center or of referring it to a point of presence, a fixed origin. The function of this center was not only to orient, balance, and organize the structure . . . but above all to make sure that the organizing principle of the structure would limit what we might call the *play* of the structure. . . . The concept of centered structure is in fact the concept of a play based on a fundamental ground, a play constituted on the basis of a fundamental immobility and a reassuring certitude, which itself is beyond the reach of play. [original emphasis]
>
> —Jacques Derrida[15]

This essay, first presented at the landmark 1966 conference on structuralism at Johns Hopkins University, marked Derrida's intervention into the French structuralist currents then making their way into American academia. What is most notable about Derrida's intervention, however, was his attempt to show that though structuralist theoretical efforts, like that of Claude Levi-Strauss or, earlier, of Ferdinand de Saussure, allowed for advances in comprehending the semiological structures of cultural or philosophical texts—of the way in which the play of meanings or significations was governed by structures that surround and suffuse a text—they inevitably ran up against a limit that could not be brought within the terms of the structure, could not be itself the element of play within the structure. This center, thus, exists paradoxically both "*within* the structure and *outside it*" (original emphasis).[16] It exists within because it governs the play of elements within the structure and yet also remains outside because it cannot itself become the subject of play within the totality. This paradox, for Derrida, thus generates a formidable problematic. Because of his overarching critique of what he calls the "Western metaphysics of presence," structuralist accounts that try to puncture the givenness or transparent self-evident nature of objects or concepts by rooting them within relevant structural relations encounter a limit that because it is both absent and present, outside as well as inside, becomes trapped in a certain "repetition," a repetition that reconfirms as either origin or telos the full presence of a center that is "beyond play."[17] Such attempts that confine themselves to analyzing the play of elements within a structure are forced to confirm the center of a structure as either original presence that has been lost or an absent presence to be found.

Marking perhaps his poststructuralist position, Derrida concludes, "Play is always play of absence and presence, but if it is to be thought radically, play must be conceived of before the alternative of presence and absence. Being must be conceived of as presence or absence on the basis of the possibility of play and not the other way around."[18] Hence, insofar as one is attempting to critique the naturalization or self-evidence of a text's meanings or significations, the attempt to comprehend the structural determinants of a text, to comprehend the play of elements within that text, must envision play not simply as that which follows from a given structure but must as well envision the contingent play out of which the particular oppositions of absence and presence—of a center that is simultaneously inside and outside, *both* an originary foundation *and* an eschatological end—are germinated. It is thus only by reaffirming this contingent play that the nostalgic pessimism of a lost presence or of a utopian absence redeemed can be unhinged. In short, the determinative hold of a structure to restrict the field of play is dependent upon our adherence to the oppositions of absence and presence that constitute the center of a structure.

All of this is of course highly abstract, and one may wonder what any of this has to do with liberalism, race, or multiculturalism. Consider, however, Martin Luther King's "I Have a Dream" speech. There is perhaps no other text short of the Declaration of Independence that commands the center of American political culture today.[19] Not just liberals but conservatives cite it regularly. And within it one finds the paradoxical elements that constitute on the one hand the jeremiadic rhetoric of colonial Puritanism and on the other a triumphalism of the liberal creed. What is paradoxical, however, is the familiar play of absence and presence within its terms. For the context of the speech is of course the pinnacle of the civil-rights-era struggle for most clearly, though not exclusively, an end to Jim Crow segregation and de jure discrimination on racial or other grounds. Culminating the August 28, 1963, March on Washington, King's speech fully proceeds against the backdrop of an emphatic presence of "race" within the nation's capital. And yet the undeniably moral and utopian appeal of King's speech nevertheless operates according to a familiar though nevertheless ambiguous play of absence. Perhaps the most famous quote from his speech, "I have a dream that my four little children will one day live in a nation where they will not be judged by the color of their skin but by the content of their character," appeals to the absence of "race" or at least the absence of skin color as the ultimate instantiation of the nation's "self-evident truths."[20] In addition, the temporal dimension of King's speech likewise plays upon ambiguities of absence and presence. After beginning by noting the "difficulties and frustrations of the moment," King nevertheless asserts, "I still have a dream. It is a dream deeply rooted in the American dream." King thus ties the absence of the reality to a dream fully present not just at that moment but in the "true meaning" of the nation's creed. It is thus a "true meaning" to the nation's founding, a dream fully present within its terms, if only as a dream. And yet, it is a dream that is caught between its failure in the present and its future redemption. King repeatedly juxtaposes realities that confound the dream with the declaration "I have a dream today." It is a powerful mix of absence and presence. Indeed, it is out of those juxtapositions of absence and presence that King's speech opens a space of communal exhortation and therefore a space of communal solidarity for the nation. The realization of the dream gains its moral force precisely through its absence in the present. Suspended between a founding moment (the dream at any rate) and its future awakening, King attaches the power of this dialectic of the nation's creed to that of race and religion.[21]

Its moral force notwithstanding, however, King's speech has moved into the center of American political culture, I would contend, precisely because of the ambiguity of its play on the absence and presence of race. For in a time when the legacies of the civil rights era are increasingly under attack and curtailment, King's speech is ironically often utilized precisely to curtail these "advances." In these appropriations, truly realizing the American creed of which King dreamed would mean the absence of race. Indeed, the "presence" of the American dream can only be threatened by the presence of race. Of course, using King simplistically in this way entails a serious bracketing and erasure of his other commitments, his other speeches. In particular, his continuing attempts to link the "freedom struggle" more explicitly to poverty and opposition to American imperialism are conveniently excised.[22] Hence, the centrality of King's appropriation depends upon the degree in which it accords with and is confined to the ambiguities of the absence or presence of race in the American creed itself. And indeed, given this ambiguity in the founding documents of the country, it is not surprising that the play of its elements should likewise be caught within the polarity of a promise outlined in advance, secured in the founding origin and a future redemption that fully promises its presence.

If multiculturalism is a form of national reconciliation of the transformations on the one hand of the post-1960s civil rights legacies and on the other of the tremendous post-1965 immigration trends, then King's speech as center also engenders a certain ambiguity in the relationship of race to the grafting of immigrant hopes to the "true meaning" of the American dream. Indeed, this is the case as debates over multicultural pluralism have shifted over the past decade to new articulations valorizing more cosmopolitan understandings. For the ideal of cultural pluralism undergirding liberal approaches to multiculturalism has as its implicit boundary line the harder ascriptive associations attached to race. Based on this often unacknowledged grounding in race, the ideal shaping notions of culturally plural tolerance have coalesced around notions of autonomy maximizing choice, albeit a "choice" powerfully inflected by culture. A resurgent cosmopolitanism thus offers the possibility of steering the nation toward that normative ideal while remaining open, indeed, cultivating openness toward the world and its multitudinous diversity. And in amending that ideal to recognize a certain form of cultural pluralism, such cosmopolitan understandings afford the possibility of strengthening the communal bonds of national identity by enlarging the capacities and adherents of its dream.

Yet in what ways does that cosmopolitan imaginary in twenty-first-century America remain conditioned by a structural ambiguity around race? In what ways does the liberal American dream, clothed in cosmopolitan garb, exported to the world as both an open eschatological ideal and a fully present founding origin, rely upon ascriptive categories to ground its space of becoming and vouchsafe its liminal anxieties? That there are such liminal anxieties is evident in these two great transformations of American political culture in the past half-century. The civil rights era's great struggle over race and a host of other ascriptive hierarchies juxtaposed both the failure of the American dream and its potential realization. Likewise, the great transformation of the nation's demography subsequent to the Immigration and Nationality Act of 1965 raised the issue of the bonds that would tie national identity together and the terms within which political culture would be contested. How would these developments intersect?[23] How would the nation sustain itself? Would the predominantly non-European immigrants align themselves with the failure of the American dream? Or would they come to reinvigorate and confirm its founding ideals? Multiculturalism as a highly contentious negotiation of these questions contains both of these possibilities and was always therefore an "impossible" construct. In its arguments against Eurocentrism and assimilation, its prioritizing of cultural groups marked by racial and ethnic categories, multiculturalism seems to hold tightly the failure of the American dream. Yet in its vision of a culturally plural nation marked by moral and political equivalence, united in the pursuit of life, liberty, and happiness, multiculturalism seemed to vitiate the promise of the American dream.

As a consequence of this "impossible" anxiety, cosmopolitan variations of multicultural themes thus seek in the American context to resolve these ambiguities, to reconcile the demands of cultural particularity within the bonds of a liberal national identity. But in its efforts to do so, I argue, such cosmopolitan reconfigurations evince to a greater or lesser degree a structure of liberal ideology that sets in motion a familiar "play" of the absence and presence of race, a play that reconfirms the presence of a core American national identity as founding origin and eschatological end and hence a core that is outside its historical and future corruption. The work of the historian David Hollinger, I will attempt to show, is demonstrative of these tensions. His *Postethnic America; Beyond Multiculturalism*, published in 1995, represented a major intervention in the debates over multiculturalism, and his call for a cosmopolitan alternative heralded a shift toward liberal reaffirmations of autonomy rooted in voluntary choice.[24] Yet, in that text and in other works, Hollinger also explicitly ties this to the strengthening of a distinctively American national culture, indeed, as the recognition and reinvigoration of the exceptionalist character of the American liberal nation-state and its "core" values. Fluctuating between milder and more alarmist language, Hollinger offers an intervention that bespeaks a fundamental anxiety confronting the reproduction of the American liberal nation-state, caught as it is between the "nation's strictly nonethnic ideology" and its "predominantly *ethnic* history" (original emphasis).[25] The current wave of immigration only heightens this anxiety and, as we shall see, the boundary line hinges around racial identification. And, ultimately, the ambiguous absence and presence of race become the possibility for the reaffirmation of national culture and national solidarity.

But before analyzing the tensions and familiar idiomatic oppositions of Hollinger's intervention, I wish to explore in greater depth a structuralist reading of American liberal ideology, if only to heighten the magnetic fields out of which its pathways are continually channeled. Tocqueville is perhaps the originator of structuralist insights into the founding conditions of American political culture. In noting the special conditions of relative equality within the early American polity, Tocqueville identified a number of dynamics and characteristics to which students of American political culture have returned again and again. Yet it is Louis Hartz, I argue, in his classic *The Liberal Tradition in America* who took a structuralist account of liberal *ideology* to its logical and interpretive extreme.[26] But, in the book's insights as well as its tensions and founderings, Hartz provides a window into the functionings of the liberal tradition in America. As a critic of the "irrational Lockianism" that seemed to hold hostage the American political imaginary, Hartz saw his effort as bringing into relief this unacknowledged and implicit constraint. Paradoxically, however, Hartz seemed to fall prey to the very structure of liberal ideology he wished to contest and therefore presented a totalizing historical narrative. This narrative reached a limit in its theorizing of American historical conflicts, most notably around slavery, the Civil War, and, more generally, race.

On the contrary, for Rogers Smith, the role of race or, more broadly, the centrality of ascriptive traditions throughout American history have proven the lie to Hartz's totalizing liberal account of American history. Smith's notion of multiple traditions contesting throughout American history ostensibly provides a more historically accurate portrait of American political culture as well as a counter to liberal celebratory accounts of the nation's historical trajectory. Yet, in positing a contest among multiple *traditions*, Smith's formulation does not escape entirely the elision of race or other ascriptive hierarchies at the root of liberal *ideology*.[27] For, though Smith posits the undeniable presence of racial and ascriptive hierarchies as shaping the political culture of the nation's history, he still effects a triangular split on the level of ideas and traditions among liberal democratic principles, a somewhat puzzling ascriptive *tradition*, and their "play" within the contextual imperatives of history. Despite his intention to render contingent the tapestry of American political culture, this split offers the possibility of reinscribing an ideological core of liberal ideals as against the illegitimate and delinked play of the absence/presence of race.

Taking these ideas together, I argue, we can better comprehend the structural patterns out of which American liberal ideals of universal freedom and equality, of a notion of autonomy that substantiates that imaginary, remain constituted by an exclusionary presupposition of race. Both in some sense seek an escape from the ideological stranglehold of a liberal ideal that obfuscates the possibilities of the American political imaginary. If one renders race fully absent from its narrative, the other places it front and center, yet neither fully escapes or exposes a deeper logic through which a form of American liberal ascription *binds* race to its liberal ideals rather than serving as the marker of their separation. And if the primary concern of this chapter lies in exploring the centrality of the role of race in constituting that imaginary, that space of ascription, then perhaps we should apply Derrida's caution that breaking the illusions of a structure's presence hinges on conceiving the play of race beyond its horizons as the constitutive absence and presence for a liberal Being. The possibilities of working through the tensions embodied in multiculturalism and contemporary American political life seem fully tied to this unshackling of race as supplement in the anxieties of liberal becoming.

OF LIBERALISM'S ILLUSIONS AND ELISIONS

> A hunger has finally appeared for getting outside the national experience.
>
> —Louis Hartz[28]

Of course, the irony of Hartz's sentiment lies in the fact that recent scholarship has sought to "get outside" Hartz himself. On the fiftieth anniversary of the publication of his text, a number of commentators published essays on the enduring question of the value of Hartz's "liberal society analysis." Of the three essays, one argued for the continuing interpretive value of Hartz's concepts, another found incredulous the continuing debate over Hartz, and a third found the filial uses of Hartz somewhat beside the point.[29] What seems common to all three is an identification of Hartz's work with the very notion of a liberal consensus view that he sought to illuminate and move beyond. The legacy of Hartz thus seems to lie in an almost celebratory account of the enduring nature of American political culture qua liberalism. Did it even matter that he bemoaned the state of American political culture at the time that he wrote *The Liberal Tradition in America*, specifically its failure to explore socialist possibilities?

It is an interest in recovering that critical dimension within the text that I believe spurs my structuralist reading of it.[30] One key dimension of such a reading is the issue of whether Hartz saw himself as offering a history of American political culture or instead an ideological structure that shapes and narrates a certain history of American politics, similar to what Foucault calls his own project in *Discipline and Punish*, where he describes it as "writing the history of the present."[31] Like Foucault's text, the significance of its insights lies not primarily with the "historical facts" that it reveals but in the attempt to generate a certain genealogy and raise to awareness a "history" that undergirds the present. Foucault thus offers us an alternative history, one that narrates the rise of a certain disciplinary power/knowledge regime to unsettle the humanist discourse through which we narrate that same historical time frame. Hartz, I argue, is engaged in a similar though not identical project. Frustrated by the "unanimity" and "irrational" hold that a "Lockian liberalism" has upon American political discourse, particularly apparent during the 1950s, when *The Liberal Tradition in America* was written, Hartz sets out to identify the structural features that have accounted for that enduring presence. Yet Hartz narrates a "history" as well, a history that proceeds as the play of these structural features. The key question is how ought we to understand the *purpose* of Hartz's narrative.

Hartz's "liberal society analysis" proceeds from the interaction and consequences of two structural features of the American founding. On one hand, inspired by Tocqueville, Hartz drew consequence from the "relative" way in which the nation was "born equal," relative that is, to Europe.[32] Connected to this was Hartz's notion of the "fragment society." Those who migrated to American shores "left behind" the ideologically fractured divisions of the Old World; in effect, they carried with them only a "fragment" of that past.[33] Together, they combined to set in motion a political dynamic in which Lockian liberal ideals could find widespread material expression and that, perhaps more important for Hartz, did not have to compete with and define itself against an active feudal tradition: "America represents the liberal mechanism of Europe functioning without the European social antagonism."[34] One consequence that Hartz noted repeatedly was that a liberal society, because it had no innate feudal tradition or history, could likewise not imagine a socialist future. Another was the centrality of Horatio Alger myths of economic mobility and opportunity. Because of this structural dynamic surrounding the "absence" of European social antagonism, Hartz believed that the liberal society of America was doomed to a stale repetition of the same.

But we are missing something vital in the text if we see Hartz as merely offering a truthful historical narrative that proceeds from these features. Hartz begins his book with what he calls a "storybook truth about American history; that America was settled by men who fled from the feudal and clerical oppressions of the Old World."[35]And, having fled those oppressions, they found themselves in a virgin land of "atomistic social freedom."[36] This "truth" has a fabulous quality to it. As an origin myth it constitutes the center to which we return again and again for political and moral guidance. In any case, Hartz's analysis, so based, proceeds with the following statement: "*If* there is anything in this view, *then* the outstanding thing about the American community in Western History *ought* to be the non-existence of those oppressions . . . that the American Community *is* a liberal community" (my emphasis).[37] I emphasize here the conditional nature of the statement. Hartz is not simply asserting an historical fact. He is positioning this "storybook truth" as an ambiguous conditional, from which, if true, certain structural dynamics and consequences ought to be set in motion. Calling it the "master assumption," Hartz envisions his role as a "cultural analyst," describing the features of the triumph of the "liberal idea."[38] He does not narrate the rise of the liberal idea; "natural liberalism" is assumed to be fully present at the birth of the nation. Instead, *if true*, then Hartz wishes to hold a mirror to the structure that follows. "Natural liberalism" is thus a "psychological whole"; it represents an "ideological victory," and, as such, it must structure a certain history.[39]

Perhaps the most well-known dynamic that springs forth from Hartz's approach to the functioning of liberalism in America is its depiction of liberal themes and attachments as operating irrationally. For the familiar move in his readings of figures from Andrew Jackson to George Fitzhugh is to show how an irrational or unconscious attachment to liberal myths constrains or, in the latter's case, fatally compromises the political arguments advanced.[40] Efforts that seek to move outside the terrain of liberal ideology are rendered illegible, while efforts that move within its terms remain inflected by an unconscious attachment to a liberal mythology that implicitly warps its possibilities. Yet how is it that such an irrational attachment could exert such a gravitational effect? One could see him as merely claiming that liberal attachments functioned solely on a prereflexive level, that such attachments are simply taken for granted as part of a consensual grammar of political life. On the other hand, irrationality could be taken as the sign of a deeper, highly cathected interior struggle within the realm of the unconscious.

Hartz's sardonic tone does not help clarify the matter, yet it is hard to see a prereflexive liberalism driving the dogmatism he claims to find within such irrational attachments or one that would escape a struggle that "like the slaying of a Freudian father . . . goes on in a sense forever." Such an unconscious attachment would not even be liberalism—properly understood as a set of theoretically linked arguments—instead functioning on the level of an imaginative repetition of liberal myths and symbols.[41] Hence, he argues, "a society which begins with Locke, and *thus transforms him*, stays with Locke, by virtue of an absolute and irrational attachment it develops for him. . . . It has within it, as it were, a kind of self-completing mechanism, which insures the universality of the liberal idea" (my emphasis).[42] Once transposed, the "self-completing mechanism" indicates a kind of policing mechanism that again suggests not an inert prereflexive attachment but a structure that is engaged in its continual maintenance. The "irrational" hold of Lockian ideals thus structures and drives, sets in play, a "dogmatic liberalism" that fails to comprehend itself for what it really is and therefore to raise to the level of conscious contestation its future and potential possibilities: "there has never been a 'liberal movement' or a real 'liberal party' in America; we have only had the American Way of Life, a nationalist articulation of Locke which usually does not know that Locke himself is involved. . . . Ironically, 'liberalism' is a stranger in the land of its greatest realization and fulfillment."[43] If this passage is at all significant, it seems to counter the interpretation that Hartz is claiming a liberal consensualism in American history. Consensualism is not the right word. "Dogmatic" was his modifier, a dogmatism lodged in the imaginative unconscious caught in a repetitive cycle over the symbols and fantasies of an American way of life. Nowhere was this more apparent for Hartz than during the McCarthyite era that immediately preceded the publication of the book and in which the "compulsive power" of this liberal dogmatism of an American way of life could come to pose a "threat to liberty itself."

To take seriously the irrational component of Hartz's liberalism, I argue, takes us from the realm of liberal theory into the realm of the American imagination, into the realm of its imaginative spaces where liberal values are given manifest meaning within the symbols and idioms of the nation. It is the space that I would call ascriptive in the sense of a space through which liberal values and ideals are ascribed and given presence within the contextual imaginary of any particular moment. But if it is the case that this irrationalism was for Hartz patterned more along the lines of an unconscious attachment rather than a prereflexive or assumed one, then why did he not seek to illuminate the forces or conflicts that maintained and drove its hold on the American political imaginary? Why did he choose to gloss over major ideological conflicts such as the Civil War or the prominent role of race in shaping the imaginary of the nation?[44] Why did he fail to explore more fully the deeper logics that might have explained the enduring presence of its liberal myths?

Hence, the question posed earlier remains: how are we to interpret Hartz's historical narrative *without* erasing his critical stance? Or, in more Derridean terms, how might we seek to recover those critical perspectives by putting his own liberal society analysis under erasure? Describing Hartz as advancing a hegemonic liberal "consensus" view, I believe, must elide his critical perspective if we view him as offering merely a historically truthful account of American political culture. Rather, I believe it is better to see his account as holding a mirror to the narrative structure that flows from the "dogmatic" view of America's liberal origins. *If* we believe in the founding myths of America's liberal origins, how must we narrate the trajectory of American political history? This dogmatic view was fully present at the time Hartz wrote. Then as now, a direct line to a certain construction of founding origins remains a powerful evocative force in American political culture. We have come to split the Civil War between a poetic romance of brotherly conflict and a struggle over slavery and the nation's reaffirmation. We hold a sanitized narrative of American history as a model for the world to emulate. We believe that our credentials as "leader of the free world" are ensured by our unique circumstances as being the "land of the free."[45] Hartz's ultimate target was an "American absolutism," and we simplify the paradoxical nature of Hartz's book if we see him as solely making a pious offering on the altar of that same liberal absolutism.

Rather than see him as an historian of American political culture, I believe it is more important to view him within *The Liberal Tradition in*

America as attempting to divine the mythological structure of American liberalism and how it has shaped and constrained the possibilities of the American political imaginary. In this regard, Hartz offered a number of strategies for contesting this structure. Foremost for Hartz was simply the effort of rendering conscious the hold that a liberal mythology has had in shaping the currents of American political thought. Primarily, the distinctiveness of his readings of American political thought lies in the unconscious constraints that have deflected and channeled their possible trajectories. Hence, "what is at stake is nothing less than a new level of consciousness, a transcending of irrational Lockianism, in which an understanding of self and an understanding of others go hand in hand."[46] Describing this as a "dialectic process," Hartz believed the McCarthyite "evil" could yield the challenge of a "*conscious* good."[47] Confronting and contesting the uses of an irrational liberalism could raise to awareness an articulation of liberal or other ideals that could unshackle themselves from American liberalism's ideological myths.

In addition to rendering explicit and conscious the manner in which a liberal dogmatism gains its power through the implicit constraints it places, Hartz also offered a number of cryptic and largely hopeful possibilities that would pluralize and relativize this dogmatism. Hartz believed that the basic "ethical problem of a liberal society" was the danger of unanimity, yet, despite his own analysis of the irrational dogmatism that liberalism held in constraining the political imaginary, Hartz did believe that "counter resources" existed.[48] Most notably, particular articulations of liberal ideals were for Hartz themselves plural, setting in motion the familiar dynamic in which the alterity of liberal ascriptions were continually folded back into the historicism of the same. Lauding the "spirit of Brandeis, Roosevelt, and Stevenson," Hartz believed that the Progressive tradition simply failed to recognize its own reliance on a certain liberal dogmatism.[49] Though that liberal ideology has for Hartz structured the play of political thought, that play has not been univocal or unilinear. Indeed, throughout the text and more prominently in his subsequent *The Founding of New Societies*, Hartz believed that the involvement of the United States in global affairs would force a "sense of relativity" that would shatter "American provincialism abroad as well as at home."[50] Though Hartz viewed his analysis of America's "fragment absolute" as structuring an unconscious play of liberal ideals and liberal mythology, he holds out the possibilities of on the one hand its internal plural possibilities and on the other the ability of Americans to "transcend" its dogmatic "past" through the encounter with "alien cultures."

Yet, ultimately, the legacy of Hartz remains tied to the very structure he wished to identify and transcend.[51] By isolating a central presence from which the play of the liberal imaginary issues forth, Hartz seemed to confirm the very notion of an America "born equal" that he questioned at the very beginning of the book. He could not bring that myth into a deeper, sustained interrogation without unraveling the very imaginative structure he sought to expose. It is telling that he concludes his study:

> Can a people "born equal" ever understand peoples elsewhere that have to become so? Can it ever understand itself? These were the questions which appeared at the beginning of this book: inevitably also they are the questions which appear at the end.[52]

What were conditional questions that probed the mythology at the center of American liberalism have transmogrified into questions fully within its structure. Hartz thus falls prey to the very liberal mythology he attempted to render transparent. Consequently, the "history" he provides consolidates rather than contests the dogmatic hold through which a liberal ideology narrates its hegemony. This is so, I argue, not because there was a conscious consensus for him around liberal theory but because he left intact and failed to demystify those liberal myths that exercised a sovereign hold on the American political imaginary. Despite asserting that "counter resources" existed, Hartz's narrative emphasizes the narrow bandwidth through which the political imaginary is channeled. Despite repeatedly claiming that the American story was "riddled with paradox," he argued that those ruptures and ambiguities are always movements that reconsolidate the center of his structure. Yet, perhaps, in holding a mirror to the structure of American liberal ideology, Hartz nevertheless reveals the ambiguities of race as the inner absent logic within the tapestry he narrates. Hartz was clearly most animated by the failure of a socialist imaginary to gain purchase within American political culture. Race was at best a peripheral and perhaps a future challenge to its idioms. Yet his narrative founders most evidently in its attempts to smooth over the issue of slavery, the "confusions" of the Civil War, the total absence of the Jim Crow system. A deeper recognition of the presence of race within the narrative of American history certainly troubles the "consensus view" of liberal ideology Hartz seems to offer. Alternatively, perhaps the absence of race is the constitutive support for the structure of liberal ideology he failed to fully illuminate.

At any rate, it is the former perspective that shapes Rogers Smith's approach to Hartz's work. The hegemonic liberal view, whether it is derived from Tocqueville, Gunnar Myrdal, or Hartz, inevitably elides and erases the central presence of what he categorizes as "ascriptive traditions." Such ideological rationales of unequal status, whether involving the proper role of women or the inferiority of racialized groups, have always been prevalent within the discourses, legislative actions, and judicial rulings that constitute American political culture. Rather than seeing a monolithic liberal hegemony, Smith thus views the history of American political culture as a contingent combination of a number of *multiple traditions*, most notably involving liberalism, republicanism, and the aforementioned ascriptive traditions. As he argues, "American politics is best seen as expressing the interaction of multiple political traditions, including *liberalism, republicanism,* and *ascriptive forms of Americanism*, which have collectively comprised American political culture, without any constituting it as a whole" (original emphasis).[53] In his later work *Civic Ideals*, Smith thus sought to document the recurring contestations through which ascriptive ideologies had been utilized to give manifest meaning to the nation's civic ideals at any particular moment.[54]

Unlike Hartz, Smith posits race and other ascriptive hierarchies as playing a central presence in the development of American political culture. What is especially noteworthy in Smith's account is the dynamic through which he theorizes the prevalence of such ascriptive graftings. Rather than an unconscious liberal or ascriptive commitment that determines their presence in American history, Smith locates their alchemy within the imperatives of temporal nation building. As he argues, first, such political imperatives involve "first, aspirants to power require a population to lead that imagines itself to be a 'people'; second, they need a people that imagines itself in ways that make leadership by those aspirants appropriate. These needs drive political leaders to offer civic ideologies, or myths of civic identity, that foster the requisite sense of peoplehood. . . ."[55] Ascriptive forms of "peoplehood" then become highly germane in providing thicker accounts from which Americans can identify with liberal or other ideals. Racial forms of ascriptivism have thus powerfully enabled forms of solidarity so that an American identity can be seen as distinctive and of proprietary interest for individuals. It is such imperatives in time and the absence of such thicker rudiments on the level of liberal democratic theory that explain the recurring presence of racial and other ascriptive forms of hierarchy. Indeed, later in *Civic Ideals*, this notion of lacunae plays a prominent role in his critique of pure contractarian forms of Rawlsian liberalism.[56] Calling Rawlsian reformulations a form of "evasive nationalism," Smith argues that the very way in which such theorizations are meant to be agreed upon and adopted by "every liberal democratic society" is precisely what will render them insufficient for being adopted in purified form by any *particular* society. Hence, the door will be perpetually left open for ascriptive supplements to such accounts the moment they are appropriated in time for a particular society.

Smith concludes his study by calling for a reconceptualization of the American nation as the "Party of America." In many ways, Smith's attempt to reformulate how we conceive of American national commitments echoes some of the strategies Hartz suggested in subjecting to conscious contestation a certain "irrational" absolutist sense of American exceptionalism. For Smith, seeing a nation as a political party highlights the contingent basis of its identity. It is an agglomeration of peoples tied together for specific and contingent political purposes without presupposing some original essence or identity. As such, a party must be "achieved" in some sense and is always subject to its constituents at any particular moment. At the very least, this makes it more difficult (though not impossible) to ground ascriptive forms of identification in "civic mythologies" of the nation's origins. Hence, viewing America as a "Party" renders whatever forms of civic identity we deploy as being within time and open to its contingent directions. And, as Smith notes, party membership is often an enduring form of identification, strong enough to hold the allegiance of its members without a necessary basis in ascriptive mythologies.[57]

Having articulated the historical and temporal dynamics through which ascriptive forms of identification have gained purchase and thrived within the history of American political culture, Smith thus, rightly in my view, takes head on the challenge of crafting civic ideals within nation-building imperatives rather than evade the question of national identification. Indeed, for Smith, not to do so merely concedes the field to less savory forms of identification. Hence, Smith advocates that political elites and citizens subject and fashion their liberal and democratic commitments to the challenges of nation building and sustaining national support while being ever mindful of the powerful draw of ascriptive inegalitarianism. In keeping with the view that the nation be seen as a highly contingent construct, one for which we bear responsibility, Smith thus argues, "American liberal democracy thus is not the 'core' meaning, but rather an available meaning, that U.S. citizens can and I believe, should give to their distinctive, highly contested historical collective creation. To do so they should strive not to find and follow a golden past full of mythic heroes. They should try to become architects of a better civic life today."[58]

Yet, despite Smith's emphasis that we view American political history as well as America's political future through the lens of its contingent possibilities, I wonder whether his normative appeals for "an available meaning" of liberal democratic values remain tied to a split between "illiberal ascriptivism" and a liberal democratic tradition that he repeatedly insists is in logical contradiction. I find it puzzling and highly ambiguous that, after exhaustively documenting the graftings of such "illiberal" forms of ascriptivism onto liberal democratic ideals, Smith wishes to purify, on the level of an abstract theoretical plane, a notion of a liberal democratic *tradition* that may reorient and rightly supply the nation's civic identity. Against those who would ostensibly throw the baby out with the bath water, Smith is right to advocate that such liberal values are not a "core" meaning and that we must be willing to reimagine them in better ways. Yet why hold onto some notion of a pure liberal tradition if it is not in some sense a structuring presence meant to condition and constrain the possibility of its play?

The problem lies primarily with Smith's formulation of multiple traditions and the subtle manner in which their combinations in the temporal life of the nation become reconfigured as a contest between illiberal and illegitimate forms of ascriptivism split off in history from their corruption of a purified liberal tradition. At the very least, it is hard to see how Smith's position is fundamentally different from the argument of inadequacy he deploys against Rawls. In Smith's argument, Rawls evades the challenge of fostering a civic sense of identity by locating it outside its temporal and specific contextual life, thereby inadequately meeting the challenge of those imperatives through which ascriptive mythologies thrive. If this reinforces the view that political ideas by themselves are not sufficient in building actual political communities, then what is the significance of appealing to the logical borders of liberal or other ideas? In his own nation-building framework, the framework of political development, the liberal and ascriptive traditions are not structurally equivalent. One occupies the realm of pure ideas and principles; the other points to particular claims of embodiment. And if any such ideas require the need for a people to imagine themselves in their particularity, then severing their connections must take place within the realm of political culture, within the constructions of their explicit and more subtle linkages, rather than in parsing out their differences on a logically idealist level. By holding onto a liberal tradition logically incompatible with such ascriptive formulations, by reinscribing a split between such ideals on the level of tradition and their corrupting play in history, Smith seems to undermine the very contingency of the nation's typology. By appealing to a logically pristine sense of the nation's liberal democratic values outside history, he is thus able to vouchsafe the anxieties of its historical play. To be sure, Smith's final chapter in *Civic Ideals* hardly strikes a triumphalist tone. Fully cognizant of the recurring manner in which ascriptive forms of inegalitarian hierarchy have thrived alongside of the nation's loftiest ideals, Smith does not elide the challenge of redirecting the nation's civic ideals and civic identity toward a more egalitarian future. His tone is one of caution, even perhaps unacknowledged pessimism.

Pessimism and triumphalism, however, are two sides of the same coin, drawn as they are to the same constitutive center. Recall Hartz, who, despite his critical perspective, could not but reaffirm a certain triumphalism of the liberal creed. Hartz at any rate attempted to disclose the structural play of an unconscious liberal *ascriptivism*. For the "fragment" that would condition and constrain the political imaginary of the nation stemmed from a *liberal* ascriptive myth that continuing generations of Americans reaffirmed and reinscribed. Yet, because Hartz remained enthralled by the very liberal ascriptive mythology whose effects he sought to uncover, he could not effectively theorize the presence of other ascriptive myths, most notably around race. And, despite Smith's attempt to debunk the triumphalism of liberal consensus views by accounting for the recurring presence of ascriptivisms like racial hierarchy in American political discourse, his formulation of multiple traditions, between an ascriptive tradition and a liberal tradition, preserves a split that renders opaque the very challenge of theorizing their relation together in a different way. Smith, then, does not go far enough in rendering contingent the structural play of the nation's ideals and sense of identity. For, having disclosed the contingent play in its history, Smith remains tied to a structural opposition outside its history, one in which the central presence of a liberal tradition remains constituted by the logical absence of other ascriptive forms of identification.[59] Smith, I argue, is caught in a symptomatic structural impasse; between the nation-building imperatives of civic ascription and a liberal ideal uneasily situated with any form of ascription. At best, he cautions continued vigilance.

We may never return to a civic identity in which forms of liberal ascription exist in coherence with blatant and explicit forms of racial hierarchy, yet will we continue to engage in the structural play of a liberal ascription that remains tacitly tied to the ambiguous and anxious exclusion of racial and other ascriptions? Recall then Wilson's speech at Gettysburg and his attempt at consolidating what he called "this *our* great family of free men!"As the nation continues its postcolonial moment,[60] will the liminal anxieties of fostering a this-worldly sense of civic identity lead to a renewed "quarrel forgotten"? Will race, those positioned under the sign of race, become subtly identified with the outer boundary of its newly narrativized ascription? How might we instead reimagine the life of racial subjects within liberal democratic inspired ideals of an American civic nation? With these questions in mind, it is to David Hollinger's conception of cosmopolitanism as a new opportunity for Americans to forge a stronger civic national identity that I now turn.

COSMOPOLITANISM'S PROVINCE

> To write the story of the nation demands that we articulate that archaic ambivalence that informs the *time* of modernity.
>
> —Homi Bhabha [61]

Perhaps the most common readily identifiable example of multiculturalism in the American context lies in the call for and inclusion of minority "voices" within the canons of the nation's pedagogical spheres. Embodied in a simple civics class, a nation's pedagogy mediates history and the present and offers narratives that inculcate certain values while generating a process through which participants can come to identify with these narratives and ascribe them to themselves within their own self/social understandings. It is through this ascribing process that a nation's pedagogy can be said to reproduce its communal solidarity. By calling for the inclusion of minority "voices," these instances of multiculturalism seek to mediate the processes of the nation's spaces of ascription by including ascriptions of difference. If so, then these paradigmatic instances of multiculturalism always involve some complicated negotiation of difference *within* the nation, within its spaces of ascription. They thus never simply involve ascriptions of difference in themselves but mediate in and around the attempt to *inscribe* oneself in the nation.

Nevertheless, in the late twentieth and early twenty-first-centuries, in the political culture of the United States, there is the widespread perception that the nation's pedagogy and therefore its spaces of ascription are confused and threatened with failure. Though highly overdetermined, one variant of this perception places the onus of the specter of failure on the transformations that multiculturalism has wrought. Captured by the language of balkanization and fragmentation, this critique of multiculturalism argues that whatever merits multiculturalism may possess in terms of countering Eurocentrism or an unduly harsh form of assimilation, it is jeopardizing the ability of the nation to cohere as a communal agent by fragmenting that space of ascribing solidarity. For many left/liberal commentators, this threat against the space of communal agency jeopardizes the very ability of the nation to address and ameliorate those sets of problems with which multiculturalism is ostensibly concerned. By including the perspectives of and narratives about minorities through discrete categories of race, they would seem to reify and reconfirm the invidious distinctions that they ostensibly struggle against. By confusing antiracism with self-ascriptions of difference, they would seem to undermine the integrationist vision of the early civil rights era and therefore its mechanisms of redress. Moreover, both dilemmas are heightened by the involvement of the state. In the former, multiculturalism seems to sanction the state's involvement in ascribing difference. In the latter, the confusion of the struggle against racist discrimination with self-ascriptions of difference undermine the legitimate rationale for and public support of affirmative action policies.

It is out of these explicit concerns that cosmopolitan arguments around multiculturalism began to emerge in the mid-1990s. In its liberal variants, multiculturalism's call for the recognition of difference always posed a tension with liberal ideals of moral and political equality and its vision of a maximally unbound individual autonomy. But the turn toward such cosmopolitan reimaginings sought to square these liberal ideals with the recognition of the finitude of autonomy, and this in increasing relation to the crucial mediator of the Nation. Contemporary cosmopolitanism, then, concerned the attempt not to be unduly restricted by that finitude, indeed, to cultivate an openness to the diversity of the world in and through that finitude. Whether through renewed sensitivity to the nation-building imperatives advanced by Will Kymlicka or Rogers Smith or through the attempt to figure a "cosmopolitan patriotism" found in the work of Kwame Anthony Appiah, the nation became the prime mediator of and consolidating force for cosmopolitan forms of communal solidarity and agency. It is thus in what I have called the nation's ascriptive space that cosmopolitan variants mediated history and the present, offering narratives that inculcate certain values and ideals, while attempting to forge a sense of communal agency that will sustain, reproduce, or realize these values. In the American context, David Hollinger best exemplified this attempt to link the liberal cosmopolitan approach within the space of national solidarity as its best guarantor and agent. His *Postethnic America: Beyond Multiculturalism*, published in 1995, unapologetically advanced the space of the nation, in particular, that of the American nation, and how it ought to be of "postethnic" ascriptive significance, a space that in his eyes was jeopardized by multicultural ascriptions, specifically, its ethnoracial particularism.

As an American intellectual historian, Hollinger was well versed in the pathways of the nation's ascriptive spaces. For if the task of the intellectual historian is to connect intellectual ideas with their emergence/influence in history, then the central fulcrum of that task revolves around context, discourse, and the temporal life of ideas. And insofar as the nation is a prime element in those ideas, disclosing the temporal life of ideas hinges on the particular ways in which those ideas are ascribed/inscribed within the nation. As such, Hollinger in his works has always been attentive to the boundaries of ideas, their locatedness within space and time, and the particular tensions that shape their ascription by individuals. In the collection of essays *In the American Province: Studies in the History and Historiography of Ideas*, Hollinger sought to probe the "provincialness" in the life of American ideas even while situating them within the larger world of the "Europe-centered west."[62] For Hollinger, what marks that provincialness of American ideas is paradoxically their "antiprovincialism." Tracking primarily though not exclusively the intellectual milieu of the Progressive era and the subsequent emergence at midcentury of an "American liberal intelligentsia," this "antiprovincialism" generally possessed two forms:

> To be in the American province is good enough for some of us, but for many American intellectuals it has been instead an appalling confinement, a condition to be overcome in the interests of an experience and an identity as great and various as "the West." For yet other Americans, including some intellectuals, this same America has been an expanse so diverse and multitudinous as to render absurd any feeling for it as a "province," a concept better applied to America's regional, ethnic, and religious parts.[63]

What seems to bound Hollinger's depiction of the "antiprovincialism" of American intellectual life lies in its generative ambiguity between viewing the "American province" as an "appalling confinement" and celebrating the "expansive" distinctiveness of that location while figuring its provinciality to its parts. For Hollinger, both elements converged to generate a "cosmopolitan ideal" that "is the desire to transcend the limitations of any and all particularisms in order to achieve a more complete human experience and a more complete understanding of that experience."[64]

Hollinger's efforts to illuminate this cosmopolitan ideal as bridging the antiprovincialism of his intellectual figures led him thus to posit this cosmopolitan ideal as the true province of American intellectual life.[65] Whether through figurations of the escape from the Old World into the New, the historical "art" of a Perry Miller, or the tensions within a modernist mindset opened up by ethnic immigrants between the World Wars, Hollinger situates these strands together as embodying something of a cosmopolitan spirit in American intellectual life and therefore embodying the ascriptive location of the American intellectual imaginary. Hollinger does not explore the peculiar anxieties attendant to such a location,[66] between a predominant concern against the provincialisms in which one finds oneself or in which one has left behind and the move to see this antiprovincialism as the distinctive locus of the American imaginary. Instead, this conception of America's distinctive province provides the genealogy for his defense of the "national culture" of the United States and the need to reinvigorate the solidarity of its "liberal nationalism." Calling the United States "the most successful nationalist project in all of modern history" and a "major point of reference in the extensive new literature developed under the sign of 'liberal nationalism,'" Hollinger holds the liberal nationalism of the United States as an example if not a model at the forefront for the realization of the cosmopolitan ideal in the world at large.[67]

Mindful of charges of American exceptionalism, particularly subsequent to his intervention within multicultural debates, Hollinger has always been quick to emphasize the troubled racial and ethnic history of the United States,[68] though this is usually qualified through "contrasts" that compare favorably and/or position the United States to offer distinctive possibilities for negotiating through the increasingly pressing problems of national culture and political solidarity.[69] For instance:

> . . . the United States has exemplified both democracy and the principle of civic nationality for a longer period of time than have any of the comparably multiethnic societies. It has done so with a population more ethno-racially diverse than that of most of the comparably civic nations of the globe. And, it has maintained a greater measure of cultural particularity of its own—an American culture the depth and character of which are frequently contested, to be sure—than have most of the other, comparable entities. The national community of the United States—the "we" that corresponds to American citizenship—*mediates more directly than most other national communities do* between the species and the ethno-racial varieties of humankind. [original emphasis][70]

Now whether or not Hollinger successfully negotiates charges of exceptionalism is less important than the passage's clear Hegelian undertones. In the context of a chapter devoted to analyzing the prospects for realizing a cosmopolitan postethnic ideal and for reinvigorating a national culture of the United States, Hollinger clearly positions the latter as the instrument for actualizing the former. He states, "when this Chinese ethnic, or a white southerner, or any other American rooted in any one particular enclave within the United States manages to identify with the American people as a whole, that American takes a tiny but ideologically significant step toward fraternal solidarity with the species."[71]

It is hard not to read Hollinger in these passages as identifying American national culture with "bearing the ark of the liberties of the world," even as he expressly forewarns against Herman Melville's famous quote. Indeed, he claims that his points are "more modest."There is surely something right about his claims that the United States possesses some "ideological resources" that are simply "too useful" to pass up with regard to developing a truly civic and cosmopolitan culture. And for Hollinger as for Smith before him, the signifier of the nation and therefore the significance of its ascriptive capacities make the dismissal of attempts to forge a national solidarity a highly dangerous prospect in a world rife with fundamentalisms on the one hand and the deterritorializing flows of global capitalism on the other. Yet, even if we accept in the United States this project of realizing a more cosmopolitan national culture, how exactly are we to move beyond the "ethnic particularisms" so prevalent in America's "predominantly ethnic history"? How are we to ascribe/inscribe ourselves in this liminal space as cosmopolitanism's province? What anxieties attend this move of communal founding and channel this process through which "the 'we' that corresponds to American citizenship *mediates* . . . between the species and the ethno-racial varieties of humankind?" Probing these questions takes us to the specific locus of Hollinger's arguments against multiculturalism and the subtle manner in which he weaves a captivity narrative around the way in which the "ethno-racial pentagon" of contemporary American institutional and cultural life has usurped and threatened a core and "official" civic ideology.

At the start of chapter 2, "Haley's Choice and the Ethno-racial Pentagon," Hollinger articulates the three main points that drive the arguments of his book:

> the United States is endowed with a *non*ethnic ideology of the nation; it is possessed by a predominantly *ethnic* history; and it may now be squandering an opportunity to create for itself a *post*ethnic future in which affiliation on the basis of shared descent would be more voluntary than prescribed. [original emphasis][72]

Alex Haley's choice, in which he chose to identify as black rather than with his Irish ancestry, thus reflects the tragic outcome in which the nation has turned its back on its postethnic future. For Hollinger, the legacies of racism and white supremacy compromised the nation's nonethnic ideology, but, rather than reasserting these Enlightenment universal ideals, contemporary multiculturalism has instead chosen to "close the gap" between the first two points by emphasizing its ethnic dimension.

Originating in affirmative action policies that institutionalized five main ethnic and racial categories for the purpose of statistical measurement, Hollinger argues that multiculturalism has adopted these categories for normative aims far beyond its institutional instrumental rationale.[73] By conflating categories designed to redress discriminatory injustice with normative and descriptive categories of culture, he believes multiculturalism has transformed the ethnoracial pentagon into an ideology of the nation, therefore eclipsing its presumed "nonethnic" ideology and the possibility of a shared national solidarity. The ethnoracial pentagon, he argues, "is an implicit prescription for the principles on which Americans should maintain communities; it is a statement that certain affiliations matter more than others."[74] Prescribing categories in which Americans come to ascribe/inscribe themselves, the ethnoracial pentagon and its multicultural rationale thus "bring to a point of tragic contradiction two valuable impulses in contemporary America: the impulse to protect historically disadvantaged populations from the effects of past and continuing discrimination, and the impulse to affirm the variety of cultures that now flourish within the United States and that flourish even within individual Americans."[75] In addition to distorting the rationale for discriminatory justice, Hollinger believes that this "tragic contradiction" also imperils the very basis for a shared civic solidarity. Indeed, for Hollinger, multiculturalism and its ethnoracial basis "demands for America a future *even more ethnic than its past*" (my emphasis).[76] And its reliance upon the ethnoracial pentagon constitutes a "sweeping movement from species to ethnos."[77]

Since Hollinger's ultimate goal is the reinvigoration of a peculiar liberal American exceptionalism, he makes clear that his critique of multiculturalism is not meant to sanction a return to an unreconstructed "species-centered" discourse of universalism. The "post" in his postethnic perspective is meant thus to signal a recognition of what I have called the finitude of autonomy. Validating the historicist trends embodied in the work of Thomas Kuhn and Richard Rorty, Hollinger differentiates his postethnic ideal by arguing that "a postethnic perspective recognizes that most individuals live in many circles simultaneously and that the actual living of any individual life entails a shifting division of labor between the several 'we's' of which the individual is a part."[78] Indeed, "it is this process of consciously and critically locating oneself amid these layers of 'we's' that most clearly distinguishes the postethnic from the unreconstructed universalist. The latter will be tempted to try to build life-projects outside of, rather than through, particular communities."[79] Yet, given this historicist emphasis, how does Hollinger attempt to establish the postethnic ideal itself? The answer for him lies in the twin polarities of multiculturalism's genealogy and in the increasing trend of what he calls the "diversification of diversity."

Throughout his analysis, Hollinger situates multiculturalism as comprising a tension between two ideals, a cultural pluralist ideal that accepts as given the boundaries of established cultural groupings and therefore the preservation of those boundaries and a cosmopolitan ideal that continually attempts to surpass those boundaries. Both are traceable to debates over cultural pluralism in the early twentieth century, with Horace Kallen and Randolph Bourne as their respective spokesmen.[80] In Hollinger's narration, the cosmopolitan dimension became more prevalent in the '30s and '40s as a "substantial cohort of intellectuals [became] engaged by two major international movements, socialism in politics and modernism in the arts."[81] But as civil rights legislation became institutionalized in the form of affirmative action policies and as identity politics began to affirm and assert various dimensions of particular identities, multiculturalism in his view increasingly foreclosed its cosmopolitan pole and rigidly embraced its culturally plural legacy.

Yet, for Hollinger, the realities of contemporary American life point the way toward reaffirming multiculturalism's unacknowledged cosmopolitan dimensions. Repeatedly citing the rise of mixed-race individuals and their claims to be recognized in the U.S. Census as well as the increasing rates of interracial marriage, Hollinger believes that the discourse of multiculturalism obfuscates the cosmopolitan dynamism of contemporary American life.[82] This "diversification of diversity" thus provides the finitude through which Hollinger believes we can and should uphold a postethnic ideal as the basis for a shared national solidarity. This ideal thus "prefers voluntary to prescribed affiliations, appreciates multiple identities, pushes for communities of wide scope, recognizes the constructed character of ethno-racial groups, and accepts the formation of new groups as a part of the normal life of a democratic society."[83] In relation to ethnoracial affiliations, Hollinger believes that it should be subject to a principle of "revocable consent" that, as a "choice-maximizing principle," is based "on the presumption that people—especially Americans who can invoke the constitutional tradition of the United States—ought to be more free than they now are from social distinctions visited upon them by others."[84] Regarding the struggle against racial discrimination, Hollinger compares the postethnic ideal to that of the religious pluralism of the United States: "both partake more of the private than the public sphere, and neither is to be the beneficiary of outright public subsidies. In the meantime, programs for affirmative action can continue to occupy the political space that was theirs alone before culture began to take over the ethno-racial pentagon."[85]Ultimately, Hollinger believes that a host of problems demands a "species-centered discourse" such as the "physical health of the planet" and that, therefore, national solidarity remains the best agent for addressing these dilemmas. A postethnic perspective, in moving beyond multiculturalism, thus offers for Hollinger the best way of negotiating the terms within which a cosmopolitan community can be imagined and ascribed as an agent for social change.

Hollinger's attempt to forge a basis for cosmopolitanism's province through the language of a postethnic ideal is an eminently laudable effort, and his treatment within *Postethnic America* always seeks to strike a measured and balanced tone. Yet the contingent historicist basis in which he couches his appeals to a postethnic American national solidarity is demarcated and delimited in subtle but problematic ways within that text. And the forces that stand in the way of the realization of a postethnic community trade upon a captivity narrative very prominent in contemporary American political culture, one in which the anxieties attendant to the continuing legacies of racial discrimination are projected and displaced not onto the intractability of racism but onto the very act of racial identification itself. It is the racial embodiment of individuals, both in the sense of seeing their economic finitude as a result of race and in their attempts to inscribe their appeals within the nation as racial subjects, that is ultimately figured as the threat whose exclusion becomes the necessary supplement for the nation's cosmopolitan becoming. In elaborating this constitutive slippage, I explore three ambivalences in Hollinger's work: the relationship between history and tradition within the American nation, the post-1965 immigrants and consequently the reproduction of the nation, and, finally, the anxious disavowal of racial identification as threatening the bonds of the nation.

As elaborated previously, Hollinger frames the play of multiculturalism in the contemporary United States as a tragic drama between two poles of the American nation, on the one hand its "strictly nonethnic ideology" and its corruption within its "predominantly ethnic history" on the other. Indeed, for Hollinger "the United States has never been without a battle of a kind between the illegitimate ethnic nation and the official civic nation."[86] But multiculturalism encompasses a tragic drama because the victims of America's "ethnic history" have to come to ostensibly reject the official civic nation in favor of a fully ethnicized nation. One of the hallmarks of his postethnic ideal is an imagined space in which individuals of whatever ethnoracial affiliation can come together in their finitude to plan a contingent civic future together. Such a coming together "is built and sustained by people who honor a common future more than a common past."[87] But this vision of a contingent future is constrained and delimited in Hollinger's formulation by the dichotomies of the nation's core ideology and of its corruption in history, of an official constitutive center that is both origin and future yet outside history, in perpetual tension with the nation's temporal life.

To "write the story of the nation," according to Homi Bhabha, is to be involved in an "archaic ambivalence" precisely because the "writing" of the nation, its temporal ascription/inscription, always sits in an ambivalent relation to its imputed core identity, an identity that constrains its play in history. Like Smith, as discussed before, the nation-building imperatives of the United States' temporal life involve inescapable anxieties around the space of its liberal ascription. Even as Smith documented that space, it became ultimately elided through his split between a liberal tradition and an ascriptive tradition. Indeed, the notion of an uncorrupted liberal tradition became the possibility for assuaging the anxieties of its own ascriptive future.

If Hartz bemoaned a persistent liberal American ascriptivism and Smith feared the corruption of that ascriptivism, Hollinger seems to fully embrace the possibilities of that ascriptive moment, when the nation's inhabitants fully mediate their finitude qua the nation. At one point Hollinger asserts that an "ideal nation" would possess "a national ethnos of its own"[88]—a paradoxical claim that seems to undermine the very distinction between a civic and an ethnic nation. By national ethnos he meant a national culture, a civic religion, yet the signifier of ethnos suggests a basis of identity that is noncontingent, a center that constrains its possible play. Ultimately then, it is not the pragmatic problems of multiculturalism and its tensions with racial justice that undergirds the "beyond" of his "postethnic" ideal. Those problems, real enough, do not foreclose by themselves the contingent rewriting of the nation's ascriptive space. Rather, it is the anxieties generated by that contingent future, one in which multiculturalism seeks to rewrite the nation through "ethnoracial particularism," that propels him to situate it within a narrative of an illegitimate and corruptive play of an official civic core. And in this narrative, a cosmopolitan postethnic ideal operates less as a contingent possibility than as the reassertion and reconfirmation of a constitutive center of the American nation, one that reimagines/remembers its liberal dream of a community of freedom through the specter of its racial rewriting.

If I have characterized Hollinger's depiction of multiculturalism as employing a captivity narrative it is because the convergence between the indictment of the nation by the civil rights era and the question of national reproduction raised by post-1965 immigration represents such a highly cathected site of ambivalence for his project of national reinvigoration. *Postethnic America* tells primarily a story of tragedy. In the aftermath of the civil rights struggles, part of which involved the liberalization of immigration policy, these immigrants came to increasingly identify with the categorical map instituted through affirmative action entitlements. They thereby infused "culture" into categories meant to eliminate discrimination, reified those same categories, and substituted them for a common national culture. Hence, rather than embracing and enacting the promise of the nation, these immigrants perpetuate an endless cycle of victimization by the nation and foreclose the very possibility of national solidarity able to transform the economic inequalities of American life. But this tragedy in *Postethnic America* is depicted far more menacingly in other works.

In his salutary review of Hugh Davis Graham's *Collision Course: The Strange Convergence of Affirmative Action and Immigration Policy in America*, Hollinger places great emphasis on the "unintended consequences" of their "strange" convergence.[89] Noting how the "sponsors and backers" of the Immigration and Nationality Act of 1965 did not believe that it would "significantly change the number of immigrants or their predominantly European points of origin," he depicts the subsequent shape and scope of immigration as a "radical departure from the Great Society's clearly expressed intentions" where "without congressional approval and without even a national debate on the issue, 26 million late twentieth century immigrants—*the number, as it happens, of African Americans in the United States in 1980*—found themselves eligible for at least some affirmative action programs" (my emphasis).[90] The resentment contained within these statements goes far beyond the challenge of rendering affirmative action policies fair and is magnified by two sleights of hand. By depicting post-1965 immigration as a "radical departure," Hollinger severs any connection the liberalization of immigration policy has with the egalitarian spirit of the civil rights era.[91] Through the shibboleth of a comparison with the numbers of African Americans, Hollinger raises the specter that these immigrants have illegitimately captured a program meant solely for its true and proper targets.

A source of special ire for Hollinger are family reunification provisions that "allowed a naturalized immigrant to bring to the United States not only a spouse and children, but also any number of siblings, that turned out to be very numerous indeed. These siblings, upon becoming citizens, could do the same, creating chain migrations. The framers of the act did not calculate how rapidly the extensive kinship networks of a single immigrant from countries with high birth rates could produce huge numbers of legal immigrants."[92] Of course, there is nothing factually wrong with what Hollinger articulates, yet one has to ask what these statements serve if it is not to conjure an image (a well-worn image) of an illegitimate and menacing immigrant other, whose "high birth rates" and "vast chain migrations" take advantage of and overwhelm a national community attempting to rectify its failure with respect to African Americans.

The final lynchpin of this captivity narrative is sealed in what he formulates as a "will to descend." A play on Nietzsche's will to power, Hollinger defines the will to descend as "the claiming, on behalf of a particular community of descent, of contributions to civilization the value of which is already recognized in a social arena well beyond the specific community of descent seeking empowerment through genealogy."[93] Presumably, the prime participants in these "power-intensive genealogies" are multicultural adherents who mask their claims on the nation through a language of victimization when in reality they are making a play for power. Does this mean that the postethnic perspective involves a corresponding "will to ascend"? Hollinger does not formulate it as such, but the innocent imagery of mixed-race individuals and of interracial marriages clearly signals the valenced dichotimization in which the nation becomes the source of salvation.

Ultimately, it is not even a concern with the continuing struggle against racism that forms the primary "victim" of this captivity narrative but a certain formulation of the nation itself. The one example he gives of this "will to descend" is one involving African Americans, specifically Martin Bernal's *Black Athena: The Afro-Asiatic Roots of Classical Civilization*.[94] The captivity narrative he weaves, of immigrants illegitimately seizing the nation, of individuals masking their "will to descend," turns not upon the challenge of rectifying racial injustice but upon a slippage between racism and racial identification. Indeed, it is the anxieties of that unsettled "quarrel" of the civil rights era's attempt to rectify the nation's racist legacies that threatened the liberal "dream" of the nation. Out of that liminal space, Hollinger attempts to remember a cosmopolitan vision of the nation by projecting that anxiety not upon the continuing intractability of racism but upon the bodily inscription of racial identification within the nation. One gets the sense that affirmative action would be fully successful in ameliorating racial injustice if only the civil rights struggle had not evolved into affirmations of racial identification. As evidence of this, Hollinger devotes no attention to strengthening affirmative action programs beyond severing its cultural consequences, beyond severing the ability of individuals to inscribe themselves within the nation from the finitude of that historical location. And the imaginary of the liberal American nation is reinscribed against the shadows of racial identification rather than from the ground of racial inequality.

There is much of value and insight in Hollinger's treatment of multiculturalism, in the tensions within its struggle to imagine a community free from the cultural bases of economic and political racism. But Hollinger consistently attempts to separate culture from racism, seeing their link to each other as the result of a confused and tragic confluence of racial identification. Yet the space between culture and race speaks to the liminal anxieties of the nation's becoming, both in the past and in the present. One senses in him the desire for a sovereign agent able to sort through and sever their Gordian knots. If there are echoes of Woodrow Wilson in the way in which I have situated both of them, it is not to question Hollinger's concern over ameliorating racial injustice but to draw attention to what is a common set of dynamics and a common source of anxiety. In the liminal spaces in which the American nation attempts to found its community and assert its solidarity, in the move to ascribe a dream of a unique community for all within its finitude, that dream, I have tried to show, has always existed in an ambiguous constitutive relationship to racialized members within its confines. The anxieties that occur as they resolve their proper place have often been manifested in a metonymic slippage in which difficulties confronting the nation's becoming, anxieties constituting its ascriptive space, are tacitly identified with and displaced onto those racialized others, thereby securing the boundary through which that nation's being can be imagined and assured of its presence. The quarrel is not forgotten but displaced onto the remains of race endlessly repeated. To be a racialized subject has thus always meant being a split subject and thus always the occasion for establishing the imaginary of freedom.[95] And in that metonymic displacement, a whole host of temporal anxieties are resolved: between the contingency of history and an identity secured elsewhere (tradition, blood), between the freedom of autonomy and the finitude of its location, between the nation's proper ascriptive space and the disavowed ascriptions of others. Insofar as cosmopolitanism needs its other for its eschatological ascription, we will not have moved beyond the multicultural moment of our contemporary impasse.

***

> . . . as always, coherence in contradiction expresses the force of a desire.
>
> —Jacques Derrida[96]

The paradox of Wilson's speech at Gettysburg remains one only if we adhere to the strict split between liberal ideas and the imaginative spaces through which they are made flesh and given meaning and direction. To insist on the logical incoherence of ideas of freedom and autonomy, equality and democracy, with particular ascriptive markers obscures rather than reveals the imaginative spaces of the contested past just as it forecloses the possibilities of the present and future. But if there is no necessary split between them, indeed, if they cannot be split, this also means that there is no necessary logic connecting such ideals with the pernicious exclusions that have been so strongly grooved into the American imaginary. Exploring and unraveling these connections then requires that we expand our understandings of the roots of racial marginalization and exclusion beyond their locations in what we typically comprehend as acts of explicit demonology. Exclusion lies not in the name—the names we give others or the names we give ourselves—but in the ascriptive anxieties of desire and the world made through it.

The rhetorical structure of the quarrel forgotten exposes a deeper connection between American exceptionalist dreams of freedom, autonomy, and racial exclusion. That connection coalesces around the anxieties of ascription itself, around the desire for coherence inoculated against its temporality, around the disruptive presences that both enable and threaten those illusions—from Puritans in the wilderness, to the uniquely American in the frontier, to a color-blind American empire in a world where "they hate us. They hate what America stands for."[97] The absent presence of race has been the paradigmatic though not sole variable in the American exceptionalist equation. Its constitutive role generates the possibility of imagining an exceptionalist presence but only upon control of and mastery over the ascriptive desires of those excluded. The one strand embraced from the ferment of the civil rights era comes with a built-in self-destruct timer. Black social desire, the diverse claims of racial subjects, become the quarantined containers for the anxieties of the nation's rewriting. Can we risk not setting it free?

NOTES

1. Quoted from Sacvan Bercovitch, *Puritan Origins of the American Self* (New Haven: Yale University Press, 1975), 19. An earlier version of this chapter appeared as "Reconstructing the 'Problem' of Race," *Political Research Quarterly* 61, no. 4 (Dec. 2008): 660–670.
2. David W. Blight, *Race and Reunion* (Cambridge: Belknap Press, 2001).
3. Ibid., 8.
4. Nor was this the first instance in which a declaration of fraternal solidarity depended in some fashion upon the excision of slavery. The pattern was demonstrated when the slavery clause of the Declaration of Independence, charging that the king had "waged a cruel war against human nature" by assaulting a "distant people" and "captivating and carrying them into slavery in another hemisphere," was stricken by southern delegates. Adrienne Koch and William Peden, eds., *The Life and Selected Writings of Thomas Jefferson* (New York: Modern Library, 1944), 25.
5. Blight, *Race and Reunion*, 9.
6. "Address at the Gettysburg Battlefield, July 4, 1913," in *The Papers of Woodrow Wilson*, vol. 28, ed. Arthur S. Link (Princeton: Princeton University Press, 1978), 23.

7. Ibid., 24. For the special place of the jeremiadic tradition in American discourse see Sacvan Bercovitch, *The American Jeremiad* (Madison: University of Wisconsin Press, 1978). For an analysis of its differential uses and consequences for American politics, see George Shulman, "American Political Culture, Prophetic Narration, and Toni Morrison's *Beloved*," *Political Theory* 24, no. 2 (May 1996): 295–314.
8. Bercovitch, *American Jeremiad*, 25.
9. Ibid., 23.
10. Ibid.
11. By citational performance, I am drawing upon the work of Judith Butler. See her *Excitable Speech: A Politics of the Performative* (New York: Routledge, 1997).
12. Indeed, almost all the presidential speeches discussed in this book seem to employ some version of this "amnesiac redemption." Perhaps that is the very basis of its jeremiad: forget lest we be doomed. Only one speech truly stands in contrast: Lincoln's Second Inaugural.
13. See David Hollinger, *Postethnic America: Beyond Multiculturalism* (New York: Basic Books, 1995), 131–132. Hollinger will be the focus of attention later on in the analysis. For now, I simply wish to pose his question whether we should see Wilsonianism as outside the nation's ideology because it is rooted in an ethnic philosophical anthropology.
14. Rogers M. Smith, "Beyond Tocqueville, Myrdal, and Hartz: The Multiple Traditions in America," *American Political Science Revew* 87, no. 3 (Sept. 1993): 549–566, and *Civic Ideals: Conflicting Visions of Citizenship in U.S. History* (New Haven: Yale University Press, 1997).
15. Jacques Derrida, "Structure, Sign and Play in the Discourse of the Human Sciences," in Derrida, *Writing and Difference* (Chicago: University of Chicago Press, 1978), 278–279.
16. Ibid., 279.
17. Ibid., 279. As he states, ". . . the movement of any archeology, like that of any eschatology, is an accomplice of this reduction of the structurality of structure and always attempts to conceive of structure on the basis of a full presence which is beyond play."
18. Ibid., 292.
19. Of course, one could point to the Constitution itself, and indeed this is undoubtedly true. Yet the Constitution is a far more complex text in terms of literally governing the American polity. Most of all, it is a malleable text. Those who attempt to appeal to the Constitution in its symbolic role as center of political culture eitehr must be committed to a very thin procedural notion of American political culture or else are implicitly referring to other texts from which to import symbolism into the Constitution. For an account that explores the symbolic challenges raised by the Constitution, see Daniel Lessard Levin, *Representing Popular Sovereignty: The Constitution in American Political Culture* (Albany: SUNY Press, 1999).
20. Martin Luther King Jr., "I have a Dream," in *A Testament of Hope: The Essential Writings of Martin Luther King*, ed. James M. Washington (New York: HarperCollins, 1986), 217–220.
21. In exploring King's speech as occupying the center of American political discourse around race and nation today, I am not making any definitive claims as to King's own intentions. He concludes the speech: "When we let freedom ring, when we let it ring from every village and every hamlet, from every state and every city, we will be able to speed up that day when all of God's children, black men and white men, Jews and gentiles, Protestants and Catholics, will be able to join hands and sing in the words of the old Negro spiritual, 'Free at last! Free

at last! Thank God Almighty, we are free at last!'" To sing the American dream through the "words of the old Negro spiritual" signals King's attempt in the speech to rewrite and claim the patriotic idioms of the nation through his own marked location. Hence a full exploration of the dynamics of racial absence and presence within the text is more complex than can adequately be dealt with here.

22. For an analysis of this "bracketing" and its consequences for civil-rights-era mythology, see Nikhil Pal Singh, *Black Is a Country* (Cambridge: Harvard University Press, 2004).
23. For an analysis that raises the specter of their intersection, see Hugh Davis Graham, *Collision Course: The Strange Convergence of Affirmative Action and Immigration Policy in America* (New York: Oxford University Press, 2002).
24. Hollinger, *Postethnic America.*
25. Ibid., 19, 136.
26. Louis Hartz, *The Liberal Tradition in America* (New York: Harcourt, Brace, 1955).
27. For an account of the exclusionary consequences of liberalism's "theoretical core," see Uday S. Mehta, "Liberal Strategies of Exclusion," *Politics and Society* 18, no. 4 (1990): 427–454.
28. Hartz, *The Liberal Tradition*, 31.
29. Respectively, Philip Abbott, "Still Louis Hartz after All These Years: A Defense of the Liberal Society Thesis"; Richard Iton, "The Sound of Silence"; Sean Wilentz, "Uses of *The Liberal Tradition*," all in *Perspectives on Politics* 3, no. 1 (March 2005): 93–109, 111–115, 117–120.
30. For a similar "structuralist" reading of Hartz, see Anne Norton, "Engendering Another American Identity," in *Rhetorical Republic: Governing Representations in American Politics*, ed. Frederick M. Dolan and Thomas L. Dumm (Amherst: University of Massachusetts Press, 1993), 125–142.
31. Michel Foucault, *Discipline and Punish* (New York: Vintage, 1977), 31. He states: "I would like to write the history of this prison, with all the political investments of the body that it gathers together in its closed architecture. Why? Simply because I am interested in the past? No, if one means by that writing a history of the past in terms of the present. Yes, if one means writing the history of the present."
32. Hartz, *The Liberal Tradition*, 71.
33. I purposely leave vague what that "fragment" consists in. Typically, Hartz is interpreted as viewing the contents of that fragment as containing an unburdened Lockian set of political ideals. This is for the most part true of Hartz, but he also sees that fragment as a *movement* of fragmentation. It is a relational separation that preserves, in a Freudian sense, the ghostly remnants of what is left behind; it is, as well, a fragment of the *wound* of separation. For example, he calls the liberal society a "fatherless tribe," while the European experience of revolution engenders an inner and outer struggle that "like the slaying of a Freudian father . . . goes on in a sense forever" (71, 65). How to reconcile these formations? One could read him as claiming that the liberal society therefore is freed from this burdened struggle. Alternatively, the groundlessness of a condition of "fatherlessness" imperils all the more the search for paternal authority, that is to say, drives all the more the desire to contain and restrict political contingency. For a related exploration of the problem of founding authority, see Bonnie Honig, "Declarations of Independence: Arendt and Derrida on the Problem of Founding a Republic," in *Rhetorical Republic; Governing Representations in American Politics*, ed. Frederick M. Dolan and Thomas L. Dumm (Amherst: University of Massachusetts Press, 1993), 201–225.
34. Hartz, *The Liberal Tradition*, 16.

35. Ibid., 3.
36. Ibid., 62.
37. Ibid., 3.
38. Ibid., 62, 63.
39. Ibid., 14, 17.
40. Ibid., 115–117, 184–197, respectively.
41. Or perhaps we must return to Locke's statement "In the beginning all the world was America . . . " and rethink the absences contained in the liberal tradition.
42. Hartz, *The Liberal Tradition*, 6.
43. Ibid., 11.
44. This is not quite true. The ideological energies prior to the Civil War represent for him "the great imaginative moment in American political thought" (176) even as he depicts the "feudal dreams of the South" as ultimately demonstrating the gravitational power of the American liberal formula.
45. For Hartz, the paradigmatic figure emblematic of this liberal Burkean Americanism was Woodrow Wilson, who displayed both the isolationist and the messianic poles characteristic of it, on the one hand viewing the outside world as filled with threatening others and on the other hand having the propensity to view and construct the outside world in our own image.
46. Hartz, *The Liberal Tradition*, 309.
47. Ibid., 14.
48. Ibid., 12.
49. Ibid., 13. Instead of directing their energies toward the dogmatism at the center of American liberalism, they "contributed" to its strength. For Hartz, "in their demonology the nation never really sinned: only its inferior self did, its particular will, to use the language of Rousseau" (31).
50. Ibid., 14, 308.
51. Hartz seems to have carried on a lifelong preoccupation and struggle with the contexts and dilemmas of transformative political agency, all the way to his analysis of "inventive power" and the anxiety of "active and passive impulses" in his little-known work, *A Synthesis of World History* (Zurich: Humanity Press, 1984). See also Patrick Riley, "Louis Hartz: The Final Years, the Unknown Work," *Political Theory* 16, no. 3 (August 1988): 377–399.
52. Hartz, *The Liberal Tradition*, 309.
53. Smith, "Beyond Tocqueville," 550.
54. For comments and critiques of Smith's work as well as Smith's responses, see Jacqueline Stevens, "Beyond Tocqueville, Please!," *American Political Science Review* 89, no. 4 (Dec. 1995): 987–995; Karen Orren and Stephen Skowronek, "Structure, Sequence, and Subordination in American Political Culture: What's Traditions Got to Do with It?," *Journal of Policy History* 8, no. 4 (1996): 470–494; James A. Morone, Eldon Eisenach, Wilson Carey McWilliams, and Rogers M. Smith, "Symposium on *Civic Ideals*," *Studies in American Political Development* 13 (Spring 1999): 184–244; and Ira Katznelson, "Civic Ideals: Conflicting Visions of Citizenship in U.S. History," *Political Theory* 27, no. 4 (August 1994): 565–570.
55. Smith, *Civic Ideals*, 6.
56. Ibid., 481–484.
57. Ibid., 492–493.
58. Ibid., 500.
59. Smith's *Stories of Peoplehood: The Politics and Morals of Political Membership* (Cambridge: Cambridge University Press, 2003) seems to acknowledge this dilemma in grappling with the more ethical and democratic challenges facing political authority and cohesion, rather than through any appeal to logical or philosophical determinations.

60. By "postcolonial" I mean the demographic migration of immigrants from non-Western societies and the increasing prominence of racialized groups in the civic and cultural life of the nation.
61. Homi Bhabha, "DissemiNation; Time, Narrative, and the Margins of the Modern Nation," in Bhabha, *The Location of Culture* (New York: Routledge, 1994), 204.
62. David Hollinger, *In the American Province* (Baltimore: Johns Hopkins University Press, 1985).
63. Ibid., vii.
64. Ibid., 59.
65. In his *Science, Jews, and Secular Culture; Studies in Mid-Twentieth Century American Intellectual History* (Princeton: Princeton University Press, 1996), Hollinger attempted to document the efforts of Jewish liberal scientists and intellectuals to secularize American public culture against the religious provincialism extant in the American academic setting and in the public at large.
66. Of course, this is a theme woven across American history: from anxieties over consumer virtue during the founding, Carroll Smith-Rosenberg, "Dis-covering the Subject of the 'Great Constitutional Discussion,' 1786–1789," *Journal of American History* 79, no. 3 (Dec. 1992): 841–873; to anxieties over the market revolution, Michael Rogin, *Fathers and Children: Andrew Jackson and the Subjugation of the American Indian* (New York: Knopf, 1975); from anxieties over industrial expansion, Susan L. Mizruchi, *The Rise of Multicultural America: Economy and Print Culture, 1865–1915* (Chapel Hill: University of North Carolina Press, 2008); to multiple anxieties over gender, marriage, and the family, Robert O. Self, *All in the Family: The Realignment of American DemocracySince the 1960's* (New York: Hill and Wang, 2012), and Priscilla Yamin, *American Marriage: A Political Institution* (Philadelphia: University of Pennsylvania Press, 2012).
67. David Hollinger, "Authority, Solidarity, and the Political Economy of Identity: The Case of the United States," *Diacritics* 29, no. 4 (Winter 1999): 117, and "National Solidarity at the End of the Twentieth Century: Reflections on the United States and Liberal Nationalism," *Journal of American History* 84 (Sept. 1997): 565.
68. Although paradoxically, he will also offer American history as an example of the successful "incorporation" of ethnoracial groups in providing a continuing basis for political solidarity, through "immigration, conquest, and enslavement-and-emancipation." "Authority, Solidarity, and the Political Economy of Identity," 117.
69. David Hollinger, "National Culture and Communities of Descent," *Reviews in American History* 26, no. 1 (1998): 312–313.
70. Hollinger, *Postethnic America*, 140–141.
71. Ibid., 142. The chapter title "The Ethnos, the Nation, the World" itself illustrates the Hegelian dialectic through which Hollinger situates the realization of the idea of cosmopolitanism through its negative sublation to the finitude of ethnos.
72. Ibid., 19.
73. For analysis of the changing racial categories in the history of the census, see Melissa Nobles, *Shades of Citizenship; Race and the Census in Modern Politics* (Stanford: Stanford University Press, 2000), and Sharon M. Lee, "Racial Classification in the U.S. Census, 1890–1990," *Ethnic and Racial Studies* 16, no. 1 (1993): 75–94. For analysis of affirmative action racial and ethnic categories, see John Skrentny, *The Minority Rights Revolution* (Cambridge: Belknap Press, 2002), and Victoria Hattam, "The 1964 Civil Rights Act: Narrating the Past, Authorizing the Future," *Studies in American Political Development* 18 (Spring 2004): 60–69. For different approaches to the future of racial and ethnic categories in the Census see the collected articles in *Daedalus* 134, no. 1 (Winter 2005).

74. Hollinger, *Postethnic America*, 24.
75. Ibid., 49.
76. Ibid., 23.
77. Ibid., 50.
78. Ibid., 106.
79. Ibid.
80. For a different approach to these debates over cultural pluralism and the rise of a terminology of ethnicity see Victoria Hattam, *In the Shadow of Race: Jews, Latinos, and Immigrant Politics in the United States* (Chicago: University of Chicago Press, 2007).
81. Hollinger, *Postethnic America*, 97. In *Postethnic America*, Hollinger downplays this tension among the intellectuals of *Partisan Review*, portraying them instead as exemplars of a postethnic ideal. However, the tensions are much more pronounced in his analysis of the Jewish intellectuals during this period found in "Ethnic Diversity, Cosmopolitanism, and the Emergence of the American Liberal Intelligentsia," in *In the American Province*, previously published in *American Quarterly* 27 (1975): 133–151. In that analysis, disagreements over the cosmopolitan ideal became full blown in the mid-1960s with the "expulsion of whites from civil rights organizations by black separatists" and the emergence of the journal *Commentary*. Hollinger, *In the American Province*, 71–72.
82. He might also have included the rise of transnational adoption, primarily from "second-" and "third"-world countries.
83. Hollinger, *Postethnic America*, 116.
84. Ibid., 118.
85. Ibid., 124.
86. Ibid., 136.
87. Ibid., 134.
88. Ibid., 132.
89. Hollinger, "Not What We Had in Mind, But . . . ," *Reviews in American History* 30 (2002): 346–354.
90. Ibid., 346–347.
91. It is only by confining that egalitarian spirit toward African Americans and concomitantly erasing the fact that the 1965 immigration reforms finally removed the racially discriminatory limits on the immigration of Asians and others that Hollinger can radically split these fundamental transformations.
92. Hollinger, "Not What We Had in Mind," 347. In another context, he states, "Within legal immigration, the priority of family reunification may not be as defensible as other bases for selecting immigrants." "National Solidarity at the End of the Twentieth Century: Reflections on the United States and Liberal Nationalism," *Journal of American History* 84 (Sept. 1997): 562.
93. Hollinger, *Postethnic America*, 126. See also Hollinger, "National Culture and Communities of Descent."
94. Martin Bernal, *Black Athena: The Afro-Asiatic Roots of Classical Civilization* (New Brunswick: Rutgers University Press, 1987).
95. Or, as James Baldwin says, "the Negro tells us where the bottom is: *because he is there*, and *where* he is, beneath us, we know where the limits are and how far we must not fall." Baldwin, *Nobody Knows My Name* (New York: Dell, 1961), 133. See also Toni Morrison, *Playing in the Dark: Whiteness and the Literary Imagination* (New York: Vintage, 1993), and George Shulman, *American Prophecy: Race and Redemption in American Political Culture* (Minneapolis: University of Minnesota Press, 2008).
96. Derrida, "Structure, Sign, and Play in the Discourses of the Human Sciences," 279.
97. George Bush, Press Conference, September 13, 2001, accessed February 1, 2014, www.washingtonpost.com/wp-srv/nation/transcripts/bushtext2_091301.html.

4 In Defense of Women

The Cultural Defense and "Dementia Americana"

> Who fails to recognize there the peculiar needs of that remarkable community shaped to conquer the world? . . . every time men come together to form a particular society, a conception of honor is immediately established among them, that is to say, a collection of opinions peculiar to themselves about what should be praised or blamed.
>
> —Alexis de Tocqueville[1]

> The admiring fascination exerted on the people by "the figure of the 'great' criminal' . . . can be explained as follows: it is not someone who has committed this or that crime for which one feels a secret admiration; it is someone who, in defying the law, lays bare the violence of the legal system, the juridical order itself.
>
> —Jacques Derrida[2]

In his article " 'Make My Day!': Spectacle as Amnesia in Imperial Politics," Michael Rogin argued that the appeal of the Reaganite politics of the 1980s lay in its replication of a persistent pattern in the nation's political history. Sutured together through the centrality of spectacles, the 1980s had witnessed the resurgence of an imperialist politics alongside a perplexing critical amnesia a mere decade after the mass indictments over the Vietnam War and the civil rights era.[3] Reagan was a master of the spectacle form, Rogin claimed, by which he meant Reagan's fluid ability to establish affectations of intimacy and action with a mass public through pop cultural references that continually displaced the lines between fiction and reality. For example, by invoking Clint Eastwood's famous line in the movie *Sudden Impact*, in which a white policeman dares a black hoodlum to shoot his white female hostage, Reagan established with the public an intimate appeal to a restorative violence. The eager threat of the line was not restrained by the technicalities, anxieties, or corruptions of the juridical order; indeed it derived from an illicit fantasy of individual autonomy premised on the "need to forget the web of social ties that enmesh us all and the wish for an individual power so disjunctive with everyday existence."[4] Through the spectacle of these populist substitutions, Reagan thus tapped into a form of political rhetoric that had a long history in rendering the nation's political culture usefully blind to its own imperialist excess and racial violence.

Yet, far from simply being a device for forging intimate connections between president and mass public, Reagan's use of spectacle enabled the expansion and passive enjoyment of more covert, disavowed, and indirect aims. By displacing the deeper implications of its movements, Reagan's use of spectacle instead attracted identifications with its surface play. As exemplified in the Iran-Contra scandal, "covert spectacles . . . display state-supported American heroes in violent, racial combat."[5] Yet the exposure of Reagan's unaccountable aims seemed all the more to enhance their specular attraction. The fascinating public testimonies of secret extrajuridical agents acting to defend and preserve the state from hidden threats not only offered entertaining political theater but also served to incite support for their juridical expansion. Such spectacles, Rogin argued, displayed three key elements. First, such spectacles routinized a voyeuristic, passive political relation with the content of the spectacle. While one was drawn into the economy of imaginative identification with the spectacle, one's direct connection with it was one of powerlessness and "vicarious participation." Second, the play of such identifications traded upon the tacit acceptance of distinctions between an inclusive intimacy and demonized threats. For Rogin, "political spectacles display centrifugal threats—threats to the subject and threats to the state—to contain as well as to enjoy them."[6] Rogin argued that the aims driven by political spectacles required the active maintenance of such configured threats. They must be readily "repeatable," standing in indistinguishably and masking a variety of context specific political aims.[7] Reagan could achieve the expansion of the military *and* dismantle the welfare state through specular identifications with heroic Rambo-like freedom fighters in Afghanistan and Nicaragua against the machinations of the "evil empire" of the Soviet Union. Finally and perhaps most important for Rogin, this specular form of American politics was tightly bound to its traditions of political demonology, most notably those grooved in the conquest of Native Americans and in its history of slavery and racial abjection.

By blurring the line between fantasy and reality, passive voyeurism and active endorsement while tapping into enduring traditions of political demonology, such identifications could be disarmed of their more alarming implications even while tacitly building intimate support for more specific policy goals. If the civil rights, feminist, and antiwar/anti-imperial struggles challenged America's racial, patriarchal, and imperial history, bringing about a crisis in its global self-representation as the land of freedom and equality, Reagan's use of specular forms of identification allowed the "Reagan regime [to] put America back together again by exploiting and disavowing the 1960's."[8] Severing American ideologies of racial demonology from their embodied histories into the realm of specular cultural forms of identification fostered the productive reworking of those "traditions" and thus allowed Americans to "both have the experience and not to retain it in memory,"[9] indeed, to forestall the examination of their roots in historical memory. Ultimately, such "historical amnesia allows race and countersubversion to continue to configure American politics by disconnecting current practices from their historical roots."[10] And, through their "colonization of everyday life," the specular form "turn[s] domestic citizens into imperial subjects."[11]

Rogin's articulation of specular politics as a key factor in revitalizing racial demonology in the post–civil rights era is especially rich in considering the discourse of multiculturalism. For surely multicultural discourses have been engaged in the reworking of racial demonology, at the very least in normatively expanding political and cultural accommodation across racial and ethnic lines. But insofar as the fault lines of its battles continue to slip into struggles between abstract conceptions of universalism or between a neutral, unifying culture and the novel recognition of difference, it seems fair to suspect that the workings of political amnesia are afoot. If so, what spectacles have shaped and contoured our apprehension of multiculturalism? Have such spectacles allowed the reworking of traditions of racial demonology—to have the vicarious experience of them but to forestall their critical apprehension in historical memory? Have they transfigured issues of cultural difference through what Rogin termed "amnesiac representation"?

Certainly in the American context, one of the most readily identifiable spectacles in multicultural debates have been controversies surrounding the "cultural defense" during the late 1980s and 1990s. Primarily involving homicide, Asian defendants, and supposed culture differences around gender and sexual propriety, these cases gained prominence through attempts to introduce culturally based defenses as either mitigating of guilt or exculpatory altogether.[12] Yet, despite the fact that there exists no formal "cultural defense"[13] and that it emerged in only a small handful of cases, the uniquely compelling dramas within them became especially productive grist for tapping into larger anxieties and hopes and therefore became lightning rods within multicultural debates. In fact, the same few cases began to appear repetitively in the mainstream press as well as academic and legal journals—so much so that a prominent academic text would pose these same trials as synonymous with the analysis of multiculturalism itself, thereby expressing in its title, *Is Multiculturalism Bad for Women?*, the generalized threat multiculturalism allegedly posed for women in Western liberal democracies.[14]

This chapter thus reexamines two of the most prominent cases discussed in relation to the cultural defense, *People v. Dong Lu Chen* and *People v. Fumiko Kimura*, but examines them as exemplary texts of specular imperial politics.[15] Both trials elicited rich political imaginaries over private violence and public honor, cultural irrationalism and legal technicality, and they mobilized as well specters of foreign cultures and the threats they posed to the body politic. The attention drawn to them encouraged a voyeuristic identification with the state as under assault while reworking not just older forms of racial demonology but also older gender constructions as well. Perhaps most important, these specular investments fostered an amnesiac representation of cultural difference that obscured its own home-grown origins. Far from being the occasion of empowering recognition for a politics of difference, the *spectacle* of the cultural defense ultimately served to revitalize a liberal sovereign imaginary by recycling older alterities of race and gender into newly formulated threats from without.

Lost amid the spectacle of the cultural defense have thus been legitimate efforts to formulate ways for pluralizing American jurisprudence.[16] Yet, precisely because these trials quickly became sensationalized, these efforts have faced a vexed, compromised, and ambivalent struggle. Part of the concern in this chapter is that we not subsume spectacle for the more complex questions they raise—that we move beyond the surface attractions of the trials themselves and consider more deeply how the cultural defense emerges in American jurisprudence out of a more complex lineage of sedimented constructions of race, gender, and political sovereignty. While I critique the specular uses of the cultural defense in liberal multicultural discourse, refusing the amnesiac colonization of its elements must involve tracing the threads backwards for the lines of fragility, the fissures of difference and alterity, that may allow us to consider them differently in the present context. The ambivalent encounter in attempting to retrieve critical political possibilities in legal, juridical formations has long been signaled by the best work in Critical Race Theory.[17] Such envisionings must puncture law's sublation of politics, retrieve historically shaping contexts, and balance openings of political possibility with their consolidating juridical effects. It is a risky venture, for such counter identifications and sympathies can also sanction alternatively dangerous and reactionary politics.

Rogin argued that "political amnesia works . . . not simply through burying history but also through representing the return of the repressed."[18] Legal trials in their efforts to sublate politics often bear the traces of what cannot be definitively or legibly represented.[19] The two trials most discussed in relation to the cultural defense offer differing sympathetic pathways in their constructions of cultural difference. In the differing controversies they generate and the texts of the trials themselves, one therefore witnesses two different kinds of the specular repressed: one that recalls the specter of racial miscegenation transposed onto the defense of the state, the other the feminization of culture as nonautonomous and politically unintelligible and illegible. The two racial and gendered sets of meanings, however, are bound together on a deeper level through masked identifications with a tacit discourse of sedimented normativity that bases its conception of political sovereignty on the extrajuridical defense of honor premised on the confinement and subjection of a domestic sphere.[20]

It is this discourse of sedimented normativity that, I argue, shadows the development of the cultural defense, providing the surface enjoyments the spectacles repress and contain. To elucidate this sedimented normative construct I begin by examining that nineteenth- and early-twentieth-century legal "artifact" known variously as the Unwritten Law or Dementia Americana.[21] Only then can we come to understand how the cultural defense emerges in late-twentieth-century American jurisprudence, and only then can we arrive at a deeper understanding of their specular appeal in liberal multicultural discourse. But to properly situate the Unwritten Law's fecund connections to criminal/juridical elaborations as well as its enduring power governing racial spectacles, I first turn to a different racial spectacle and sensationalized crime trial, one that has been largely forgotten or repressed in post-'60s juridical transformations.

DEMENTIA AMERICANA AND DEMOCRATIC EXCESS

> . . . If you desire to give it a name, I will ask you to label it *dementia Americana.* It is that species of insanity which makes every home sacred . . . which makes a man believe that the honour of his wife is sacred . . . which makes him believe that whoever invades the sanctity of that home, whoever brings pollution upon that daughter, whoever stains the virtue of that wife, has forfeited the protection of human laws and must look to the eternal justice and mercy of God.
>
> —Delphin M. Delmas, defense attorney for Harry Thaw[22]

In a *Time* magazine article of February 18, 1952, Hawaii was showcased as a society in profound and promising transition. Titled "The Brown and White Mosaic," the occasion of the article was the impending congressional petition the following week for Hawaii to be admitted into statehood, something that had been repeatedly denied for almost a century.[23] What was different this time, the author argued, was that changes over the past decade since the "Jap attack on Pearl Harbor" had raised Hawaii as a model of "racial relations in the world." Among the changes listed was the boom in postwar prosperity, the breakdown of old colonial and economic monopolies in favor of a balance of corporate professionalism and restrained labor unionism, and the growing political incorporation of some of its racial and linguistic "minorities." What could threaten that transition were the communist sympathies of some of its labor leaders,[24] but the author believed these to be relatively insignificant since most of Hawaii's minorities and, therefore, overwhelmingly, its union members had long practiced a form of ethnic group advancement. Still, if there was a problem threatening the future of Hawaiian economic prosperity, it was that its agricultural economy could not be sustained at its profitable level and that Hawaii would be increasingly forced to remake itself as a tourist destination. Framing a kind of early multicultural argument as a resolution of some of Hawaii's longstanding problems, this article provides a snapshot of a Hawaii that was indeed undergoing seismic transformations not only after the war but also in the decade proceeding it.[25]

What the article did not mention, however, was that twenty years prior to its publication, in the early months of 1932, a quite different image of Hawaii was occupying the minds of not just its population but also the newspapers, editorials, and radio commentaries of the nation at large. That spectacle dealt with the question of alleged interracial gang rape and the subsequent "honorable" murder of one of the defendants in the case by a group consisting of the "rape victim's" mother, husband, and a few of the husband's fellow naval servicemen after a jury failed to convict the defendants. The ensuing Massie trial captured the nation's attention during those months from December 1931 to well into the fall of 1932 with its images of a distant dark colony where white women were being raped with impunity, of an ineffective juridical establishment that failed to convict the alleged rapists, of the rising ambition and power of the U.S. military in the Pacific arena, and of the outrage of a racially mixed jury's ability to pass judgment on a high society mother's and military husband's righteous violence to restore a daughter and wife's honor.[26] Of the "trials of the century" we no longer remember the Massie case well, yet at the time the *New York Times* published "almost two hundred stories on the tumultuous happenings in Hawai'i" and the Associated Press editors voted the Massie affair "one of the top world news events of the year—and single most important criminal trial in the country."[27] In addition, Congress held emergency hearings on law enforcement conditions in Hawaii, the case spurred a "remarkable" and extensive Justice Department fact-finding mission on such conditions, and Senate bills were proposed to alter Hawaii's juridical structure and restrict its popular sovereignty. No less than Clarence Darrow himself, the famed lawyer of the Scopes Monkey Trial and the Leopold and Loeb murder case, was on hand to stamp the defense of the Massie trial with his own brand of rhetorical flourish.

David Stannard's narrative of the case develops rich personal characterizations of the individuals involved as a window into the larger social and political forces that shaped its spectacle. Thalia and Thomas Massie, a young but troubled couple, arrived in Hawaii in 1930 when he was assigned to a submarine squadron after completing his training in New London, Connecticut. In the early morning hours of September 13, 1931, after Thalia and Thomas had attended a cocktail party and had become separated, Thalia was found wandering on the side of the road with a swollen and bruised face. She claimed to have been raped by "five or six Hawaiians." Though her story would change numerous times in the months ahead, a racially mixed group of five youths was rounded up and tried on November 16 for her alleged rape. A verdict of a hung jury was delivered on December 7.[28] Since the local white establishment feared the negative publicity that the case might generate, news of this initial trial was largely subdued, and the case would have probably faded into obscurity. However, the nation's attention was focused on Hawaii in December 1931 because massive war games were to take place over the next two months, and the build-up of military forces was a daily news item in the continental and local newspapers.

Lurid stories and rumors of sexual rapaciousness began to be the focus of media attention in Hawaii. Admiral Yates Stirling, the top military official in the islands, seized upon the opportunity to demand that the military take over the administration of the islands. In a cable he sent to the secretary of the navy and to the chief of naval operations, Stirling confirmed the fears about the safety of naval wives coming to Hawaii and whipped them up further by including a local article claiming "forty rapes" in the islands over the past year while lamenting the likelihood of "mixed blood juries rendering justice in cases involving rape because of apparent apathy toward the crime of rape."[29] Admiral William Pratt, the chief of naval operations, replied the next day with outrage over the situation in Hawaii, declaring that he was unwilling to send the fleet to Honolulu unless the situation was fixed. "American men," he stated "will not stand for the violation of their women under any circumstances. For this crime they have taken the matter into their own hands repeatedly when they have felt that the law has failed to do justice."[30]

If Pratt's words signaled the atmosphere of a lynching to come, the murder of Joe Kahahawai , one of the defendants in the original trial, on January 8 seemed to confirm it. His body was found wrapped in a bundle in the back of a car driven by Thalia's mother, Grace Fortescue, along with Thomas Massie and Edward Lord, a fellow naval servicemen. The question of their guilt (along with that of Deacon Jones, another naval friend, who stayed behind to clean up the crime scene) in the murder of Kahahawai seemed clear. The remaining question, which occupied the editorials of the nation's papers and Congress over the next few months, was whether justice would be served, that is, whether justice would be travestied in convicting the mother and husband for defending the honor of Thalia Massie. The democratic right of Hawaii's multiracial population to decide that issue placed the question in doubt. Calls for martial law were voiced repeatedly in the press. Indeed, just a week later, emergency weekend hearings were called before the Senate committee on Territories and Insular Affairs over the "racial chaos" taking place in Honolulu. A prime concern was whether the impending trial could be moved to a different venue, ostensibly to a more "objective" locale.[31] Out of those hearings and over the course of the next year, the Senate would consider and pass a number of bills to restrict the democratic sovereignty of Hawaii. These included provisions for the presidential appointment of an attorney general, a "high sheriff," and a chief justice for the territory of Hawaii, the authorization of circuit court judges in Hawaii to comment upon trial testimony, the altering of electoral district apportionment, and the removal of residence and citizenship qualifications for appointment to office.[32]

The fears and anxieties of racial popular sovereignty in Hawaii to which these bills responded placed all the more emphasis on the course and conduct of the coming trial. In this regard, there was perhaps no one better than Clarence Darrow to evoke the consciences and sympathies toward the defendants that "justice" would require. At first glance, it might appear that

Darrow's decision to represent the defendants was questionable or hypocritical. Darrow had long made a reputation for himself by representing racial minorities or striking union members—he had just withdrawn a year earlier from the defense of the Scottsboro Nine case (in which nine black teenagers were arrested for the alleged rape of two white women) over disagreements with the legal defense sponsors, the NAACP (which had sponsored him) and the International Labor Defense. Here he would essentially be defending lynch law. But cast in the mold of a populist muse, Darrow had always employed defenses that appealed to and relied upon jurors' sympathies in their role as consciences of their communities.[33] He frequently advocated the technique of jury nullification in appealing to a higher law that would sanction or at least forgive violations of the particular laws in question.[34] In his seven-hour summation of the 1926 Sweet case, involving eleven Detroit blacks charged with murder after firing into a white mob that had surrounded their house, Darrow pleaded the all-white jury to "look into your own heart." "Put yourselves in their place," he implored. "Make yourselves colored for a little while. . . . It won't hurt. You can wash it off."[35] The Massie case, no doubt, would present a unique challenge of cultivating jury sympathy. Besides, he would be playing to a national audience in what was to be his last trial.

Technically, Darrow's defense in the Massie-Fortescue trial hinged on temporary insanity. He sought in the course of the trial to place the murder weapon in the hands of Thomas Massie while emphasizing his distraught mental condition over the alleged rape of his wife and the subsequent acquittal of the five defendants. But one should not conflate technical strategy with the larger narrative defense Darrow sought to evoke, especially in stoking more subtle forms of jury nullification. For Darrow's defense also appealed to the sense that what Massie and the others had done was right and honorable, reasonable and tragic. In his closing argument, he invoked the classic resonances of the Unwritten Law, arguing that true justice was lodged "somewhere deep in the feelings and instincts . . . a yearning for justice, an idea of right and wrong, of what is fair between man and man, that came before the first law was written and will abide after the last one is dead."[36] True justice "existed independent of laws, independent of rules that often destroy it." Rather, it was founded in and nourished by the "devotion of mothers, of husbands—and when that dies in the human heart, then this world will be desolate and cold and will take its lonely course around the sun alone."[37] Despite the outright racism in the popular and media perceptions of the case and in debates of the Unwritten Law, Darrow ironically appealed to the imaginative reverse of what he had implored in the Sweet case, asking the racially mixed jury "to *forget* race and look upon this as a *human* case" (emphasis added).[38]

Such ambivalences between insanity and honor, between the letter of the law and its imagined foundations, and between the irrational threat of race and appeals to the human should not be glossed over. Indeed, they are the keys to grasping how the Unwritten Law has helped constitute the meanings of criminal responsibility in its recognized defense of homicide. They are also imperative for apprehending the Unwritten Law's ghostly presence as a form of sedimented normativity shaping the interpretive course of the two "cultural defense" trials discussed later. But, to elucidate this, we will need to examine more closely the ghostly history of the Unwritten Law in its encounter with the evolving legal system of nineteenth-century America.

In its most paradigmatic form, the Unwritten Law concerns the right of a husband to commit violence and even kill another man who has seduced and corrupted the husband's wife. Such violence is perceived as a restoration of the husband's honor and as necessary for the dignity he shares with other men. It therefore houses a conception of sovereignty and autonomy based historically on the recognition that the husband is the sovereign representative of his domicile. British common law long recognized a narrow and restricted form of this sanctioned violence if the husband acted in the immediacy of witnessing or catching the seducer in the act. This was known as *in flagrante delicto*. Along with its other familial sanctions of violence, self-defense or the protection of property against a robber, this principle became the basis of provocation defenses that usually mitigated what might be murder charges to manslaughter. Yet right away one notices a tension here between the righteousness of the extrajuridical violence to restore honor and the juridical necessity to restrict, tame, and subjugate it. This tension seems key if we are to understand what is gained by its designation as the Unwritten Law, for the sources of its restorative power lies precisely in its being unwritten, as prior to and beyond its juridical writing. The law may come to recognize it or versions of it, but such recognition will never fully sublate it.[39] It is thus by its nature always codifiably uncertain and contested precisely because the power it invokes lies not in law but beyond it.

This juridical uncertainty and contestation that the Unwritten Law embodies explains its emergence and proliferating expansion in a series of sensational trials in mid-nineteenth-century America. Both Robert Ireland and Hendrik Hartog situate its emergence in the milieu of transformations in the public legal rights of wives. At the same time, discourses of mothers and wives as the bearers of republican virtue could in the "zero-sum game of marital struggles" lead husbands to perceive a loss of prestige, honor, and control.[40] Likewise, Ireland speaks of a growing fear of libertinage that was magnified and intensified by republican discourses that stressed the public political significance housed in the virtue of the women in their lives. In all of these analyses, the emergence of Unwritten Law claims in court became symptomatic patriarchal expressions over the anxieties induced by changing political discourses and formations.[41] Invocations of the Unwritten Law attempted to tap into an assuaging originary sovereignty that in the imaginary could restore proper order in the face of fears of sexual excess and the growing political agency of women.

As a discursive normative appeal to a "higher law" that by its nature had no legal standing,[42] the Unwritten Law depended upon the imaginative sympathies of the community of actual and prospective jurors.[43] But, rather than a purified and static doctrine, the construct of the Unwritten Law emerged at the site of contesting the law in specific trials; therefore, one notices its semantic drift. Ireland includes cases involving brothers who avenged the sexual dishonor of their sisters[44] and even the case of a "vengeful female" who killed her fiancé after he broke off the engagement and subsequently sought to "entice her to an assignation house."[45] None of the most celebrated cases fits the standard of catching the seducer in the act. Indeed, the Harry Thaw case involved a relationship of "sexual dishonor" involving his wife that had begun before Thaw met his wife and ended prior to their marriage. Likewise in the Massie trial, even if Darrow sought to place the murder weapon in the hands of the husband, it was clear that the kidnapping of Joe Kahahawai and the attempt to restore Thalia Massie's honor was orchestrated by the mother, Grace Fortescue, an act that Darrow did not disavow but explicitly included in his sympathetic evocations of the Unwritten Law. What this semantic drift suggests is that the Unwritten Law became the imaginative symbol of originary communal norms (patriarchically inflected) that, freed from its literal confines within archaic notions of a husband's honor, could be transposed upon the community at large and symptomatically actuated by perceived anxieties of sexual excess and fears of sexual subversives in a community's midst. Such Unwritten Law trials became spectacles precisely because they articulated anxieties over sexual control writ large upon the juridical order and provided a discourse of original sovereignty housed in notions of honor that could supplement the anxieties of that juridical order. And in the personal dramas articulated in these trials, they could provide exemplary even if extreme instances of imaginative action and identification.

What brings about semantic drift? Besides situating the Unwritten Law in larger currents of social fears and juridical transformations, one also must attend to its workings within the arena of the criminal trial specifically, what Martha Merrill Umphrey calls the "dialogic production of law."[46] Umphrey argues (using Bakhtin) that the spectacles of Unwritten Law cases represents the discursive instability of meanings of criminal responsibility in mid- to late-nineteenth-century American criminal jurisprudence and that, through the course of these trials, new legal meanings of honor and insanity and therefore the categories of provocation and insanity itself were juridically developed and elaborated. As stated previously, the Unwritten Law gained purchase in British and American jurisprudence through its more narrow sanctioning as part of specific provocation defenses. But the standard of *in flagrante delicto* was not met in virtually all of these high-profile cases. This, in addition to the fact that provocation defenses usually mitigate rather than exculpate the offense, led defense attorneys to progressively elaborate different hybrid arguments of temporary insanity, since insanity represented an exculpatory defense. But, in addition to the outcome sought, such arguments also depended upon the dynamics of legal contest. For defense attorneys could not introduce evidence of provocation and, therefore, counternarratives of criminal responsibility and social subversion[47] without relying on a claim of some form of insanity. Hence, we find the progressive elaboration of different articulations of temporary insanity such as mania transitoria, irresistible impulse, monomania, moral insanity, the heritability of insanity, and, perhaps its crowning appellation, dementia Americana. And, in support of these articulations, defense attorneys would introduce batteries of medical experts and alienists.

If such articulations of the Unwritten Law in its encounter with juridical law seemed to pull provocation and insanity toward each other, these tensions could be productive of juridical and more diffuse normative effects. Writers of the law could respond to the instabilities generated by such defenses by attempting to restabilize the law through new notions of provocation and insanity. The 1861 Texas statutes expanded the *in flagrante delicto* rule to include any "opprobrious words or conduct directed at a female relative" and made such a provocation defense exculpatory rather than merely mitigating.[48] Umphrey also cites changes in successive editions of Francis Wharton's nineteenth-century definitive tract *A Treatise on the Law of Homicide*. Umphrey argues that Wharton's discussions of provocation become successively more expansive to include communal norms of honor and a notion of "injury [that] seems to be a violation of the defendant's sovereignty by harm done to a dependent."[49] Collectively, these changes wrought two juridical consequences. First, this spurred a burgeoning cottage industry in the late nineteenth century around the dialogic refinement and elaboration of notions of insanity through testimony by the proliferation of medical "experts" who frequently built upon each other's performances. Second, understandings of provocation expanded from more narrowly prescribed situations toward sympathetic understandings of "reasonable" distress over egregious injuries.[50]

But beyond attempts at restabilizing legal categories and meanings, the complex, contradictory efforts of defense attorneys to engender sympathetic identifications with their defendants along with the alienating difference of insanity could likewise spawn complex affectations in the jury and the public at large. Ireland notes how newspaper editorials around many of the most celebrated cases were derisive of the attempt to use insanity as an excuse for their actions,[51] viewing it, as we do now, as a kind of *dishonorable* legal trick and technicality. But such cynical derision, far from being a rejection of the Unwritten Law, attests to its power in shaping the underlying terms of interpretation. Ostensibly, it would have been more honorable for such defendants to challenge the law, to claim the righteousness of their actions, even to accept their juridical punishment and fate rather than escaping into juridical subjection.[52] The discourses of the Unwritten Law, introduced through the spectacles of these trials, are thus not ultimately determined by the particular fates of these trials, even as they are shaped and contoured by them, even as they exert a ghostly force on the evolution of criminal codes of responsibility.

By the time of Harry K. Thaw's trial in 1907 and its figuration as a kind of dementia Americana, the Unwritten Law had become a ghostly, tacit, and *illegible* symbol of an extrajuridical source of moral propriety—a form of sedimented normativity, an inherent hegemonic cultural defense, an incipient identity politics—that was generative of the juridical order even if it could not be affirmatively translated into its terms, even if it resisted and violated the law. If it was intelligible as a kind of insanity, it was an insanity that appealed to something "we" all irresistibly shared, an attachment to notions of personal honor and sovereign autonomy that lay prior to and beyond whatever rights the law recognized and granted, an insanity that could propel acts of extrajuridical violence that nonetheless fostered imaginative sympathy and identification. Dementia Americana thus captured something of the economy of ironic identification and "motivated disavowal" that the spectacles of the Unwritten Law both repressed and enjoyed. If such extrajuridical violence could not be legally sanctioned, it could still be imaginatively excused through other sympathetic means.

Such "sympathetic means" can clearly come to shape not just explicit trial evocations of the Unwritten Law but also its workings on an implicit generalized level. For the late nineteenth and early twentieth centuries were also the age of racial lynching. Though none of the articles mentioned explicitly analyzes the relationship between the Unwritten Law and racial lynching, it seems clear that the underlying discourses of sexual honor and racial sexual subversion had come to legitimate, if extrajuridically, the widespread murder of blacks and other racialized individuals over perceived affronts of sexual dishonor. If so, so pervasive had the Unwritten Law become as a symbol of sedimented sovereign normativity that sympathetic identifications with it did not even need the pretext of a trial challenge for its evocation, since the vast majority of these lynchings had never even made it to trial. Undoubtedly, the epidemic of racial lynchings in these decades signified the attempt to restabilize white supremacist notions of political sovereignty over and against the expansions of rights and freedoms for the nation's racial subjects as well as expansions of rights for women. That Jim Crow legislation operated apace through attempts to restrict such rights and freedoms could thus *perversely* come to signify juridical attempts at restabilization by removing and restricting such potential sources of provocation and extrajuridical violence.

The spectacle of the Massie trial thus brought into conflict in the nation's imaginary on one hand Unwritten Law discourses of implicit racialized and gendered norms of sovereignty and on the other a juridical order that was identified in the press as racially other and in democratic excess. The racial make-up of the jury became a consuming, even fetishistic item in the press[53] precisely because, as jury members, individuals were not simply subjects of the law but also empowered as its authorizers and adjudicators. It was their sympathies and identifications that would pronounce legitimacy or disavow the tacit claims of normativity housed in the Unwritten Law. In the prosecution's closing arguments, associate prosecutor Barry Ulrich reminded them of this fact, stating, "Far more hangs on this trial than the fate of these four defendants. Our power of self-government is being questioned. You jurors, the judge, the people of this Territory are on trial, charged with not being able to govern ourselves."[54] After forty-eight hours of deliberation, the verdict was announced on April 29—all four defendants guilty of manslaughter with leniency recommended. For the next five days, while the nation waited for sentencing, expressions of outrage filled the nation's editorials and radio programs. Many had expected the seven whites on the jury to acquit the four defendants, believing that at least they would recognize the honor in the defendants actions and that therefore there could be no worse outcome than a hung jury. In addition, more than a hundred congressmen from both parties had signed a petition demanding that President Hoover or Governor Lawrence M. Judd pardon the convicted killers, expressing "deep concern for the welfare of Hawaii."[55] In the end, the four defendants were sentenced to ten years in prison, but this was simultaneously announced with Governor Judd's commutation of their sentence to the time they had spent in his office, exactly one hour.

Ultimately, Stannard situates the outcome of the Massie affair as an inspiring narrative of individuals and a racialized community that challenged the importation of lynch law into Hawaii and the racist, imperialistic pressures brought to bear on their limited and meager democratic sovereignty. And in the context of the challenge that was involved in even bringing the trial to surface, Stannard's narrative is persuasive especially in factoring the changes in Hawaiian politics that followed the catalyst of the trial.[56] Yet this ought not to be confused with disrupting the Unwritten Law or its ghostly presence within the categories of criminal responsibility. The compromise reached in the verdict itself—a conviction of juridical manslaughter alongside a political commutation—reflects already the ambivalent structure of the Unwritten Law in its influence on the evolution of legal meanings and categories of criminal responsibility. The spectacle of the Massie affair left intact the discourses surrounding the Unwritten Law; indeed, as spectacle it all the more confirmed its status as an implicit normativity providing the imaginative and sympathetic identifications through which the fantasy of asserting martial law in Hawaii could be entertained as appropriately restoring order and protecting white womanhood in a subversive racialized territorial holding that straddled the liminal border of the juridical political order. And through such spectacles of lurid criminality and miscegenating subversion, discourses of the Unwritten Law could provide the means for parsing the ultimate authorizers and sovereign agents of the political order as well as its proper subjects, could provide the means for parsing the categories of provocation and insanity.

SPECTACLES OF ACTION AND SUBJECTION IN THE CULTURAL DEFENSE

> The prestige of patriarchy is revived around madness in the bourgeois family . . . Thus in the modern world, what had been the great, irreparable confrontation of reason and unreason became the secret thrust of instincts against the solidity of the family institution and against its most archaic symbols.
>
> —Michel Foucault[57]

In American criminal jurisprudence there is no criminal act without a guilty mind. Encapsulated in the concept of mens rea, itself derived from the Latin formulation *actus not facit reum nisi mens sit rea* (an act does not make one guilty unless his mind is guilty), the necessity of a guilty mind seems to imply the recognition of distinctions between legal guilt and moral guilt. Moral guilt thus bases itself on the violation of moral norms. Theoretically, arguments of cultural pluralism that assert the primacy of normative difference could base a cultural defense through shades of difference regarding moral norms, arguing that defendants do not possess the established and dominant moral and social norms with respect to a certain criminal act and therefore ought to be less culpable.[58] A related though weaker version of the cultural defense rests on the notion of individualized justice, that justice and therefore the treatment individuals receive before the law should take into account the specific nature of not just the act but also the actor. Defenders of this view make such an argument more palatable by folding it within the principle of equal treatment before the law, with the corollary that different individuals should be treated equally through their difference.[59] Yet a third view adopts a more critical stance, seeking to contest and politicize the inherent moral and political assumptions bound within Western masculinist jurisprudential standards of mens rea. The cultural defense can thus seem to offer a mitigating recourse for the harm done in judging cultural minorities according to such standards as well as to expose their hegemonic bias.[60] All three forms of argument should not be seen as mutually exclusive since all of them base themselves in accounts of mens rea. Rather, they differ in their emphasis and in the aims for which the cultural defense is placed.

The development of American criminal jurisprudence has tended to collapse questions of moral guilt into questions of rational capacity and reasonable intention. Hence, mens rea is taken to mean the state of mind of the defendant and is determined by distinctions between rational ability and insanity, volition and nonvolition.[61] The two are not synonymously treated in criminal trials. For example, one can be judged rationally sane while committing a nonvolitional act or insane while demonstrating volitional intention. Paradigmatically, insanity represents the lack of mens rea and therefore is an exculpatory defense. Provocation-type defenses such as the Battered Women's Syndrome defense or heat-of-passion defenses do not generally assert mental insanity but claim variations of rational nonvolition.[62] The idea is that a defendant, though rationally sane at the time of trial, may nevertheless have acted under compulsion from either external or internal factors and therefore ought to be judged less culpable. But the space between provocation and insanity is subject to great variation, depending as it does upon not only the statutes of particular states but also, significantly, the sympathies of trial judges and juries.

Since there exists no formalized cultural defense, these constraints impact heavily on the legibility of cultural factors. As we saw with cases of the Unwritten Law, the ability to introduce counternarratives of criminal responsibility devolved into trial formulations that were parasitic on insanity. Only through developing novel notions of temporary insanity could evidence of such narratives enter into the court's consideration. Even more so in cases of the cultural defense, such constraints have shaped the manner in which cultural factors are perceived. What we find in case after case is that cultural differences, when successfully introduced in the courtroom, become elided as either sources of insanity or forms of alien automaton-like action.[63] But, beyond this, it is differences in the outcomes of these cases and the manner in which they have evoked sympathy or disavowal, particularly for those that have been high profile, that have generated much of the controversy and spectacle surrounding them. They are also differences, I argue, that demonstrate the specular "motivated disavowal" enabled by them, providing amnesiac representations of sedimented norms of racial and sexual subversion, while legitimating imperial subjection more broadly.

The most controversial case and for many the case that raises the specter of the cultural defense is that of *People v. Dong Lu Chen*.[64] In 1988, Dong Lu Chen, a Chinese immigrant employed as a dishwasher and garment worker, killed his allegedly adulterous wife, Jian Wan Chen, with eight hammer blows to the head and therefore faced a charge of murder. In a nonjury trial, the Brooklyn Supreme Court judge presiding over the case was widely viewed by prosecuting attorneys as a tough-minded law-and-order judge. And yet Judge Edward Pincus surprised many by reducing the murder charge to second-degree manslaughter and giving Dong Lu Chen the lightest possible sentence—five years' probation. Instrumental to the reduced charge was the introduction of a "cultural defense" in which it was argued that Chen's "traditional" Chinese culture drove him to an uncontrollably violent state because of the intense shame that infidelity had brought on him and his family. Judge Pincus found persuasive the "expert" testimony provided by Burton Pasternak, a white anthropology professor, who testified that adultery in China constituted an "enormous stain," a "damaging reflection on his ancestors and his progeny."[65] Where divorce might be an option here, divorce in China would represent virtually "the end of a person's real life" since divorce as a result of a wife's adultery would indicate that the husband had lost "the most minimal standard of control over his family."[66] Further, Pasternak argued that had Chen been in China, social kin would have served as a safety valve, intervening to prevent any violence. Hence, in America, Chen effectively had nowhere to turn, and the pressure of his cultural precepts drove him to act violently. Calling Pasternak "perhaps, the greatest expert in America on China and interfamilial relationships," Judge Pincus was persuaded by Pasternak's testimony that Chen's culture was a contributing factor in the defendant's mental state at the time of the act. Indeed, he had this to say:

> I was convinced that what had happened at that time was because he had become temporarily, totally deranged. I didn't feel that he had formed an intent to murder. He was the product of his culture. The culture was never an excuse but it is something that made him crack more easily. That was the factor, the cracking factor.[67]

Under the interpretation of Bruce Pasternak and Judge Pincus, cultural difference thus served as the mechanism to explain Chen's murderous act. He could not fully appreciate the wrongfulness of his act because of the irrational pressure that Chinese culture was brewing within him. Hence, he lacked the requisite mens rea for a murder conviction and faced a much lesser charge of second-degree manslaughter.

During the sentencing phase, Judge Pincus evoked the tragedy of the case, speaking of the defendant as also a "victim, a victim that fell through the cracks because society didn't know where or how to respond in time."[68] Moreover, he placed the future fate of that tragedy upon his daughters, telling a reporter, "Now there's a stigma of shame on the whole family. They have young, unmarried daughters. To make them marriageable prospects, they must make sure he succeeds so they succeed."[69] Identifying with the language of honor evoked by Pasternak, Pincus sought to extract a "promise" from Chen:

> I must have a promise from the defendant on his honor and the honor of his family he will abide by all the rules and conditions that I impose. . . . And if he does not obey and he violates any of these conditions, not only does he face jail, but this will be a total loss of *face*. [emphasis added][70]

Pincus's outrageous masculinist identification with what was presented as cultural difference became the spark for media and academic outrage as well as generating political protests far removed from the procedures of the court.[71] Because of cases like this one, many have found the results of the "cultural defense" less than salutary, claiming that the "cultural defense" has led to the sanction of domestic violence within immigrant communities or else the subordination of women more generally. In the immediate aftermath, a coalition of Asian American community activists and white feminists protested the decision, arguing against both the cultural testimony and the light sentence. But they differed in how they critiqued their combination. District Attorney Elizabeth Holtzman's statement was emblematic of the position of the National Organization for Women (NOW):

> There should be one standard of justice—not one that depends on the cultural background of a defendant. There may be *barbaric customs* in various parts of the world—that cannot excuse criminal conduct here. Anyone who comes to this country must be prepared to live by and obey our laws. And people like Mrs. Chen are entitled to the protection of our laws. This sentence suggests that women's lives, and particularly minority women's lives, are not valued. [emphasis added][72]

The response from the Asian American groups was more ambivalent. Though they too protested the light sentence and the troubling message the verdict would send to already battered Asian American women, their concerns were also directed at the use or misuse of Chinese culture instrumental in the decision. They believed that culture should in certain circumstances be taken into account. But who would get to define "Chinese culture"? What forms of accountability or input could Asian American groups have on testimony advanced in their name? Hence, Monoma Yin of the Committee Against Anti-Asian Violence stated, "We have always wanted a more culturally informed judicial system but this case completely crosses the line to the point of excusing a murder. The judge is using a very archaic academic interpretation."[73] As Leti Volpp discusses, these lines of ambivalence and difference ultimately fractured the coalition between Asian American activist groups and white feminists. Holtzman's position seemed to repeat the great void that existed between white feminist concerns and issues of cultural difference. In citing her concerns over the protection of women's lives, she implicitly accepted the figuration of Chinese culture within the "expert" testimony of Pasternak as irreducibly different, as a menace to women. Despite her objection to Pincus's sentence, she placed the blame, ultimately, not on Pincus or even on Chen for that matter but on the barbarism of cultural difference and its miscegenating threat to women and the laws of the state. When this specular image exploded again during the O.J. Simpson trial,[74] reenacting the scene of racial miscegenation, some women's advocacy groups would recall the Chen case.[75] By the time of Susan Moller Okin's intervention in the multiculturalism debates, that image—contemporary, yet not so contemporary—had been well grooved in the imaginary. On its surface, it was a drama of cultural menace and subversion, a call to preserve the state and its laws from cultural miscegenation, a call to protect women through the subjection of cultural difference.

To be sure, Okin's essay, despite its provocative title, is more nuanced than I give credit for. I single out her text not because it is the most egregious example—far from it—but because it shows the extent to which the spectacles of the cultural defense had taken hold. As she claims, she simply wants to note tensions between multiculturalism and feminism and to "caution" against their easy association—a point that is unquestionably correct and important, going both ways. Still, perhaps despite herself, she cannot refrain from identifying the latter with the Western liberal state, thereby flattening whatever tensions exist within her own "associative chains."[76] In her reply to the various commentaries on her original essay, she makes a point of declaring that "this debate is taking place only because its participants live in liberal societies. . . . In many countries, some of us would be in danger of being silenced, if not placed in physical peril, for expressing views such as we express here."[77] Rather than countering the spectacle of the cultural defense, her conflation of the protection of minority women with the liberal subjection of cultural difference moves within its terms and thus ultimately silences the very women she would protect—those immigrant women or women of color who would critique not only the patriarchal and subordinating aspects of their own hybrid cultural inheritances but also their invisibility within the Western liberal state.[78] To see how the specular politics of the cultural defense forecloses the identifications of immigrant women and women of color through the aegis of the Western liberal state—thereby producing for them only a spectacle of subjection—we must turn to that other sensationalized case, *People v. Fumiko Kimura.* Okin aligns the two cases as being fundamentally equivalent in producing "gender-biased" cultural messages. But this is quite misleading, for the dramas enacted in each case are very different—indeed, they are almost polar opposites in a number of significant dimensions. If there is a unifying "message" to be gleaned from their outcomes, it is one that, as I will show later, points to a sedimented normativity, points to Unwritten Law discourses of racial miscegenation, honorable violence, women's irrationality and confinement and, collectively, their amnesiac *re*-presentation.

The most notable difference in the two cases is that in Kimura's trial, cultural factors did not enter into the official legal proceedings but rather surrounded the case from outside or cropped up in unacknowledged, unexplored ways. There was no "expert" allowed to define Kimura's culture. Indeed, both prosecution and defense asserted the need to see her as insane. Hence, the course of Kimura's trial devolved upon the need to *elide* her reasons for action, troubled though they may have been. On January 29, 1985, along a stretch of Santa Monica beach, the thirty-two-year-old Kimura waded into the Pacific Ocean with her two children, one age four, the other six months of age.[79] The two children drowned while Kimura, close to death, was successfully revived by those on the scene. She was thus charged with two counts of first-degree murder. During the police interrogation, she mentioned a mistress her husband had been seeing, a previously failed marriage, and the sense that she "had failed as a wife."[80] Kimura, apparently, had lived a very isolated life. Though she had lived in the United States for sixteen years, she spoke little English, did not drive, had few friends outside her family, and worked selling hot dogs at Dodger Stadium. Only nine days previous to her actions, she had learned of her husband's infidelity, when his mistress (with whom he worked) called her, distraught over the husband's deceitfulness.

An important dimension of Kimura's case thus concerns the opportunities to identify with and render legible her reasons for action. It seems clear that all parties to her trial, including the prosecution, felt some sympathy for Kimura, and yet the constraints of the law continually placed limitations on the ability to offer those reasons without distorting them in one form or another. For Kimura, those forms consisted of either insanity or an intent to kill. When news of her case spread through the Japanese American community, a petition was circulated and amassed more than twenty-five thousand signatures before it was delivered to the district attorney. The petitioners sought to provide reasons for Kimura's actions and argued for leniency. According to the petition, Kimura's actions were consistent with the practice of *oyako-shinju*, a practice of parent-child suicide in which emotionally distressed parents, contemplating suicide, believe that it is their obligation to take their children with them since it would be more heinous to leave them alone in the world.[81] In cases such as Kimura's, where the parent survives yet the children do not, modern Japanese law, the petition asserted, treated the action as "involuntary manslaughter resulting in a light suspended sentence with probation and supervised rehabilitation." Thus, though Japanese law did not sanction the practice, it treated such cases as a tragedy, and the petition implicitly argued that it should be viewed as the American equivalent of a provocation defense, with a mitigated sentence. Unlike the Chen case, in which a single white anthropologist defined "Chinese culture" *tout court*, Kimura's case sparked a community's push to introduce cultural factors into the court.

Two things need to be asserted with respect to this communal intervention. First, it was not unified. Kimura's case sparked a debate within the Japanese American community.[82] Those who were most sympathetic to her were primarily the older *Issei* or first-generation Japanese Americans. Younger generations, mindful of being perceived as inassimilable foreigners or different, felt that she should be "treated harshly according to American standards." Others resented the attention the case received "when there were other social problems in the community that also deserved attention." Second, it was not uncritical. In addition to the resentment some felt over the exposure of the case, even those sympathetic to Kimura reacted as they did, as Okin claims, not because "women are ancillary to men and should bear the blame and shame for any departure from monogamy"[83] but because "the sympathy which Fumiko Kimura received . . . [was] toward a victim of the social structure that denies the female the opportunity for becoming a self-supporting and self-confident human."[84] Far from being viewed uncritically, Kimura's case evoked reflections and identifications precisely over the *lack* of autonomy of Japanese and Japanese American women while also spurring criticisms of how the media spectacle over the case was *colonizing* the issues that the community faced.

Yet such complex, heterodox, and ambivalent reasons and identifications could not find expression in the court. The two prosecuting attorneys had this to say:

> But what can I do? Two children were killed—and it *doesn't matter* what her reasons were, it's against the law. . . . [emphasis added][85]
>
> If, in fact, she was doing everything according to her cultural precepts, it would have supplied elements of the prosecution case, because then it would have shown she *intended* to kill her kids—intent to kill. I could have probably gotten a first-degree murder conviction. If she was *totally* sane, knew what she was doing, it was a rational decision. I could have shown premeditation, deliberation, and intent to kill—all of those things which are necessary for first-degree murder. [original emphasis][86]

Because of existing constraints in the law and the distinction between provocation and insanity, between *reasonable* causes of violence and insanity, Kimura's attorney had no choice but to elide the cultural dimensions of her case and present her as insane. Though her reasons and agency were hardly something to laud or celebrate, the important point is that they could not find expression within the law as other than guilty intent with malice or completely illegible as insane. Instead of the testimonies of the community surrounding the case,[87] the defense thus rested upon the "expert" testimonies of six psychiatrists who diagnosed her as exhibiting "brief reactive psychosis" with a "high degree of certainty" that she was legally insane at the time of the offense and that "her illness so consumed her that her actions were a direct result of her condition."[88] In the end, Kimura plea-bargained from double murder charges to voluntary manslaughter by reason of insanity. She was given a relatively light sentence of one year in jail with five years' probation, with psychiatric counseling advised. It appears that the light sentence reflects the sympathy she received on the part of both the judge and the prosecution. But such sympathy did not rest upon cultural factors; it rested on eliding her agency as insane and wholly other—despite the efforts of a sizeable contingent of Japanese Americans to render legible her agency, even as such identifications spurred their own complex and contrary affects.

These two cases and similar high-profile cultural defense cases were viewed collectively as raising two images about the late-twentieth-century American juridical order. On the one hand, the rise of cultural defense cases might signal the tolerance of the American liberal democratic state and the multicultural equanimity of its terms of justice. On the other hand, the rise of cultural defenses became the occasion for fears of cultural miscegenation upon the American nation, fears about the contagion of foreign and barbaric cultures, and fears about protecting women and those situated within the domestic sphere. Yet both, though they appear in mutual contradiction, are united in a common anxiety and aim, namely the legitimation of the juridical order as it increasingly incorporates and exerts its influence upon other peoples around the world. Cultural defense cases breached the national imaginary by suggesting this split anxiety, thereby becoming the spectacles for attracting identifications and disavowals far removed from their limited narrative confines over criminal responsibility. Moreover, the two cultural defense cases discussed proffer two different though related narratives. That they are seen as offering the same "gender-biased message" displaced upon the construct of foreign cultures might suggest that we should dismiss the spectacle and attend to their specificity. But then we would lose an examination of the complex economy the concept of specular politics affords.

The trial of Dong Lu Chen seemed to raise the specter of foreign cultures most clearly in the testimony of Bruce Pasternak. Chinese culture was figured as alien, as a wholly encompassing construct that would drive a Chinese man to commit murder. But, on closer examination, the role of Chinese culture in supplying motivations for action are more suspect. Indeed, the "cracking factor," the "cracks" through which the "victim" (the defendant) fell, was not his Chinese culture but the void of cultural difference, specifically the void created by cultural miscegenation. Pasternak, despite his essentialized rendering of the "shame" adultery would bring in China, asserted that had Chen been living in China, social kin would have acted as a "safety valve" to dissolve and ameliorate the situation. Instead, it was his presence in America, with "nowhere to turn," surrounded by "Americans" whom Pasternak explicitly delineated as not including Chinese that rendered Chen's actions legible. When pressed by the cross-examination over his testimony, Pasternak admitted that he could not recall a single instance in which a man had killed his wife in China over adultery.[89] The volatility of Chinese culture and the volatility of cultural miscegenation were thus constructs of his own "American fantasy."[90] And that fantasy of the dangers of cultural miscegenation allowed access to a disavowed and displaced identification with a form of patriarchal reason as an extrajuridical source of moral propriety and sovereignty. Clearly, Pincus embraced notions of patriarchal honor and familial subjection, notions that were enabled by donning the garb of Chen's "culture." Admonishing Chen over a potential loss of face, folding his daughter's marriage prospects within Chen's ability to rehabilitate himself, Pincus could reinforce archaic and sedimented norms of patriarchal sovereignty and domestic subjection in the guise of toleration and recognition, through the inevitable tragedy of miscegenation. The murder of Jian Wan Chen thus became the tragedy, ultimately, not of Dong Lu Chen but of a juridical climate of miscegenation, and Pincus's patriarchal sympathies with the defendant could rework and actuate Unwritten Law discourses of moral propriety and honor that could assuage those anxieties and restore juridical order.

In a different though connected manner, Fumiko Kimura's trial demonstrates the ghostly, displaced presence of these sedimented norms upon the constraints of criminal law. Both Chen and Kimura ultimately received similar, relatively light sentences, but the legibility of cultural factors in their cases followed diametrically polarized patterns. Chen's sentence reflected a finding of guilt mitigated by reasonable provocation; that provocation, displaced onto his "Chinese culture," was in actuality the reasonableness of patriarchal extrajuridical violence in the face of sexual excess magnified by cultural miscegenation. Kimura's sentence could also have been argued to reflect a finding of provocation. This would have been consistent with its treatment under Japanese law, as the petition argued. But, significantly, the trial proceedings could not admit such reasons; indeed, the court could recognize her *only* as insane. That she received a light sentence reflects the arbitrary sympathies of those individuals involved. Ordinarily, findings of insanity would subject her to state institutionalization. Her actions could inspire no restorative honor, could not be excusably connected to the adultery of her husband, could inspire no affect of tragedy that would question her confinement within domesticity; instead her actions could be read only as involving malicious guilt or irresponsible, irrational insanity. Her actions could find no point of purchase within sedimented norms that shadow the codes of criminal responsibility, that provide the means for parsing the distinctions between provocation and insanity. Instead, her case, like Chen's, became productive of spectacles that allow the amnesiac reworkings of these norms, displaced upon the opaque cloth of foreign cultures, disavowed in the same breath as barbaric, yet reinforced through the tacit identifications among the state, the threat of cultural miscegenation, and the protection of the silen(ced) sphere of domesticity. She was ill, mad, exhibiting "brief reactive psychosis," her madness the result of a "disalienation in patriarchal purity," a "secret thrust of instincts against the solidity of the family institution and against its most archaic symbols" and her juridical status, designed all the more to deliver and "protect [her] as a subject of law."[91]

IMPERIAL SUBJECTION?

> For me, stranger-stranger relations are better than stranger-chattel.
>
> —Patricia J. Williams[92]

Spectacles provide the chimera of intimacy and the surface text that holds the gaze. One sees oneself as a spectator of their dramas as they unfold around us with a sense of immediacy. When noted commentators and experts narrate those spectacles, a form of trust ensues, and one's identifications and disavowals become irretrievably interpolated through them. Even if one disavows those narrations and trust becomes suspicion, our gaze remains held or otherwise inflected by them. Stephen L. Esquith in his *Intimacy and Spectacle: Liberal Theory as Political Education* argues that such spectacles constitute the prevailing mode of political life in corporatist, pluralist forms of American politics.[93] Modern liberal orientations toward citizenship and power, Esquith argues, involve a particular modus vivendi, a form of political education and socialization, in which "citizens . . . are defined in terms of their classification by professional experts, their status as consumers, and their own counterinterpretations of the prerogatives attached to these roles."[94] Political conflicts and, more generally, politics become organized "around the constitution of expert authority by clients, consumers, and professionals in and outside of government," whether through media spectacles, official hearings and court disputes, or behind-the-scenes policy negotiations.[95] These dramas of political conflict thus *educate* citizens in what they can expect of politics, in how they see themselves in relationship to it. Citizens' democratic agency and power become one of specular consumption, guided by the input and action of "experts" and "professionals" within circumscribed domains that exist both inside and outside government, officially visible as well as invisible. They therefore encode and enact "exemplary" scenes of action and identification, providing illusory pathways of trust and intimacy, consumer satisfaction, and governmental responsiveness. And, as a result, the democratic agency of citizens becomes eclipsed, accessible only through the specular dramas between experts and advocates, visible officials and invisible policy actors and bureaucrats.

Esquith's exploration of how contemporary political life in the United States (enabled by liberal theory) is organized around the consumption of political spectacle intersects with Rogin's analysis of specular politics, with which I began this chapter. Primarily, they connect in posing the dimensions of political subjection through which politics in the specular mode reinforces. The arguments of both writers suggest that specular politics bifurcate or split political agency between on the one hand the trusting intimacies of normative identification offered by experts, advocates, or elected officials and on the other the underlying pull toward thorough interpolation through their use and deployment of juridical categories and procedures. Political agency is thus severed from its dialectical relationship with the juridical order, becoming a relationship of consumption between individuals and their respective interpolators, while those representatives enact a drama and contest with each other under rules and regulations that seem both estranged and fully determining.

We can see from this estrangement how the allure of a normative sovereign agency, of a normative extrajuridical agency can serve all the more as a salve for juridical conflicts and anxieties. Of course, Esquith and Rogin deal specifically with the post-'50s and -'60s American milieu. But unless one wants to construct a golden age of political immediacy and authenticity prior to that period, it is likely that the industrializing world of the nineteenth century encountered its own struggles and anxieties over juridical estrangement. If so, the spectacular trials involving the Unwritten Law in the nineteenth century seemed to provide a ready assurance of this sovereign extrajuridical agency. Through them, anxieties over juridical transformations—the increasing property rights of married women, republican discourses over female virtue, fears of widespread libertinage—could elevate all the more counterdiscourses of an originary sovereignty, one that the juridical state of affairs seemed to be undermining and betraying. That discourse both failed and succeeded. In its efforts to win legal juridical recognition—though it influenced the evolution of criminal codes and expanded notions of both provocation and insanity—it did not gain full expression as such within its terms. Yet, as a ghostly form of normative sovereignty, it persisted and succeeded all the more in colonizing that normative agency, particularly in its productive associations with race. And through such a normative, specular, identity politics, it could both excuse acts of extrajuridical violence and spur contesting forms of juridical elaboration and subjection.

The question of the legibility of a "cultural defense," of whether the state should recognize "cultural difference" within its laws, is irretrievably haunted and influenced by these earlier struggles.[96] Implicitly, arguments over the cultural defense, whether or not for formalization, struggle against an inherent hegemonic normative bias in the law. They are caught in the nexus between unwritten political norms that shape the application of juridical laws and the attempt to *write* into the law political counternorms of difference.[97] For example, James Sing argues that the "cultural defense" should be formalized as part of a reconstituted provocation defense, noting how provocation serves as an implicit hegemonic cultural defense while the toleration of cultural difference as generative of irrational activity is objectionable.[98] But Sing does not outline how such a reconstituted provocation defense would mitigate against its continued hegemonic bias. Alison Dundes Renteln argues that a cultural defense should be formalized as a separate entity and that only such a separate standard can ensure that cultural factors will enter into the courtroom. She thus circumscribes her arguments the most in terms of confining them to questions of legal remedy, and yet even her account depends on (without fully exploring) the sources and political consequences of the hostility with which cultural factors are received by American courts. She thus implicitly accepts distinctions between hegemonic norms of "us" and norms of difference.[99] Leti Volpp, in arguing against formalization of the "cultural defense," provides the most nuanced treatment of both the political and the legal "texts" involved in the cultural defense. But in her attempt to argue for a principle of antisubordination to guide the selective ("strategic essentialist") use of cultural factors, it is hard to see how this principle would not be continually contested or yield its own authoritative elisions.

Each of these proposals relies on either the hope for or the specter of political power as guides for or counters against the legible prescriptions they offer. Sing *hopes* that folding cultural difference within provocation will generate a more equitable field. Renteln presumes a congealed "hostility" to cultural factors. She is certainly right on that score, and yet her prescriptions of a separate cultural defense would reinscribe those boundaries into the law, making them the spur for the proliferation of (one hopes conscientious) interpolating expert testimony. Volpp's prescription of a principle of antisubordination is surely the most politically mindful since it seems deliberately offered to contest prevailing antidiscrimination arguments that generate their own elisions. But such a principle is hard to square with the practical constraints of an adversarial court system, and it would not be immune to its own political perversions. After all, Okin's arguments against the cultural defense embody their own antisubordination logic.

My critiques of these arguments should not be viewed as in the service of better prescriptions. The issues raised by the "cultural defense" explode any attempt that tries to work through them strictly in terms of legal remedy. Their specular investments are too deeply entrenched, too prodigious of other political formations, to be treated solely through circumscribed juridical artifice. They call forth and respond to crises of political power and sovereignty caught between the (among others) ongoing struggle over racial "reconstruction" and the growing engagement and preoccupation with the management, toleration, and disciplining of diverse peoples. The argument of this chapter has thus been to situate the spectacle of the cultural defense as caught within that nexus and in a manner that reworks racialized patriarchal discourses of originary sovereignty that can provide an (ultimately illusory) sense of normative agency and identity against fears and anxieties of juridical excess and subversive miscegenation.

Of course, Esquith's understanding of political education or political subjection in contemporary American political life impacts quite differently upon the marginalized. Though that fantasy of a restorative normative sovereign agency may be ultimately illusory with respect to the state, those discourses can still sanction sympathies with extrajuridical, exceptional violence as well as harsher forms of juridical discipline and subjection. Fundamentally, the Unwritten Law discourses sought to develop lines of imaginative identification between citizen and polis through distinguishing exemplary and original bearers of political authority from others who were its proper subjects. The generalized subjection Esquith articulates thus must be set against the racial and sexual normativity of enduring specular forms that differentiate and inflect the impact of that subjection. As with Okin, the specter of cultural miscegenation circulates around anxieties over an exemplary basis for political authority, one wherein her own liberal feminist desires could be identified with the state and thus able to adjudicate the tangle of rights claims of those figured as different. Yet, rather than accept the necessary and ambivalent estrangement between her political desires and the juridical order, she reinforces and redeploys sedimented forms of normativity through her own amnesiac recollections that serve as the basis of assurance. The spectacle of the cultural defense thus legitimates reworked racial and gendered demonologies that can guide and present the limits within the toleration/aversion calculus[100] confronting the juridical management and discipline of cultural difference.

The prodigious colonizing effects of such specular politics can likewise extend to the forms of resistance and counternarratives that develop in reaction to them. Two possibilities show the perils of specular politics and demonstrate how the spectacles over the cultural defense can colonize both the embrace of and the resistance to the cultural defense. Renteln's embrace of the cultural defense is based upon the injustice inflicted on cultural minorities who are denied the full possibilities of defending themselves before the court. And yet her desire rests on the reification of difference—through which cultural minorities must then depend upon interpolating experts. We can see the problematic dimensions of this most clearly in efforts to develop the so-called black rage defense.[101] During the early phases of Colin Ferguson's trial in 1994 (Ferguson shot and killed six and wounded nineteen on the Long Island Railroad), his lawyers, William Kunstler and Ronald Kuby, attempted to advance a "black rage" defense. They argued that Ferguson's impoverished background and the lack of racial equality drove him to become enraged and that therefore he did not have full rational control of his actions on that fateful day.[102] On some level, the attempt to introduce social and economic factors into criminal cases is laudable, and yet Kunstler and Kuby packaged those dimensions within a reified psychological state.[103] Even if Kuby and Kunstler were, like Darrow, Delmas, and the other Unwritten Law articulators, playing an inverse ironic game of (racial) political sympathy and legal insanity, it was unlikely that the general public would sympathize with the nuances of such a dance. Instead, like other cultural defenses that are parasitic on notions of temporary insanity, the black rage defense folded factors that point toward cultural, social, and economic context into a racially essentialized instability, thereby eliding the complexity of those factors in the same gesture. This gesture colonizes our sympathies and identifications with such defendants (perhaps not Ferguson but others with similar backgrounds).[104] Insofar as we seek their recognition within the law, we in effect sanction the legibility of inverse racial essentialisms.

Even those who seek political possibilities to contest the law can be drawn into these colonizing specular investments. For example, consider attempts to encourage black jurors to utilize forms of jury nullification (the right to judge both law and facts) to disrupt and shut down an unjust criminal justice system that has led to skyrocketing rates of incarceration for African Americans.[105] Paul Butler, a former District of Columbia assistant attorney, recounts how in 1990 he and other fellow district attorneys participated in a training session preparing them for an eventuality they would likely face. Their trainers warned them that there would be cases that they would lose "despite having persuaded a jury beyond a reasonable doubt that the defendant was guilty. We would lose because some black jurors would refuse to convict black defendants who they knew were guilty."[106] During the same time, Butler was on hand to witness the much-publicized trial of Mayor Marion Barry of Washington, D.C., for drug possession and perjury. According to Butler, many fellow black prosecutors hoped that Barry would be acquitted because they believed that in singling out (and apparently entrapping) Barry, the FBI investigation and indictment were racist.[107] On the basis of this episode and the realization that jurors have a very powerful though largely unknown right to judge law,[108] Butler develops an argument that black jurors should utilize this in certain cases, specifically those involving nonviolent offenses.

As a form of juridical protest and a refusal to participate in a racist criminal justice system, black jury nullification seems to me largely unobjectionable. Indeed, the way in which such occurrences are likely overblown and themselves specularized by racist criminal legal practitioners demands that one not overreact to its possibilities. Still, Butler's defense of black jury nullification as a *political strategy* seems to me to be fully confined within its own specular investments over black identity. Specifically, Butler confines his appeals to *only* black jurors—he repeatedly uses the term "just 'us' " as a play on justice—as if the critiques of the criminal justice system and its overwhelming impact on young African American males could not be identified with, could not be sympathized with, by others. Butler also seems to presume that a single mind and vision would underlie such disparate nullifications among African Americans. Besides offering the distinction between violent and nonviolent offenders, Butler offers no suggestions about how such a strategy would cohere or how it might be the basis for transforming the law. Perhaps as tool of a movement, like other forms of civil disobedience during the civil rights era, jury nullification could serve a larger purpose, but that is precisely what seems lacking and what is presumed by Butler. Instead, Butler seems to engage in a fantasy of black sovereign autonomy, one that assumes identifications between different instances of black jury nullification, one that forecloses those identifications for others, one that deploys its own specular image of black normative agency. In refusing the law, Butler assumes a prior and restorative form of community, thereby echoing the specular appeals of Unwritten Law discourses.

What then might constitute nonspecular forms of political resistance? In tentatively answering this question, we might perhaps turn back to Hawaii, turn back to its response to the Massie trial as a source of inspiration, a source of expansive identification. Recall that the Massie affair impugned the ability of Hawaii's racialized population (indigenous Hawaiians, Japanese, Chinese, and Filipinos) to democratically govern itself. Specifically, the perception of Hawaii in the continental United States was that the local white hegemonic establishment had given its racial laboring classes too big a role within its juridical structure. In fact, Hawaii was still largely a colony with some of the worst plantation labor conditions in the Western Hemisphere. Prior to the Massie trial, the explicit designs of Hawaii's plantation owners were to keep their laborers separate and isolated from one another on the basis of race and nationality, indeed to pit them against each other as they sought favor and advantage. Even the sporadic riots and strikes that dotted Hawaii's history prior to the Massie trial largely represented the efforts of a single group and were met with violence and the importation of new racial groups to break up strikes. Such patterns of segregation and alienation persisted even after plantation workers had accumulated enough savings and moved on to the city. This separation was reflected in the creole dialects for each group, with each group possessing its own distinct dialect.

But during and after the Massie trial, a young teacher named John Reinecke began noting the formation of a common creole dialect, particularly among the younger generation of Hawaiians and Asians. This common language, he wrote, reflected both a "class dialect and a local dialect in one" that provided a "mark of a large we-group of racial and class origin."[109] Such forms of developing linguistic solidarity were also traceable in English slang designations such as the term "local." Stannard argues that "local" had always referred to longtime residents of the islands and bore no racial or national mark. But beginning in the fall of 1931 and to this day, "local," initially deployed in reference to the accused young men, began to stand for Hawaiians and Asians collectively.[110] By the summer of 1933, "confidential navy intelligence reports were warning of growing interracial solidarity in even the most remote parts of the outer islands."[111] Still, in themselves, developing forms of linguistic and cultural solidarity may signal little beyond their own specular reactions to the unifying racism brought out by the Massie trial. It is what they did with those common forms of identification and expression that becomes truly inspiring.

For in acts both juridical and extrajuridical, native Hawaiians and diverse Asian groups began hybrid efforts to transform Hawaii's rigid class oligarchy into a more democratic, labor-active, and politically equitable society. Starting with the elections of 1932, Hawaii began an electoral realignment that persists to this day. Labor unionizing reached new heights in both numbers and in its interracial basis, as even more experienced and radical white labor leaders were recruited from the mainland and a common newspaper, the *Voice of Labor*, was produced. The strikes of 1938, again met by police fire, were distinct from previous strikes in that they were interracial, sparking supporting strikes and marches on different islands. Martial law during the war temporarily disrupted this activity. But by 1947, the International Longshoremen's and Warehousemen's Union had grown to thirty thousand members from nine hundred in the closing months of the war and began to agitate for laborers in the agricultural industry. But perhaps what shows the nonspecular nature of their politics, the *capaciousness* of their identifications and political sympathies, is how they responded to the pressures of World War II. Stannard notes that while anti-Japanese paranoia was sweeping the West Coast, in Hawaii, where thousands, including civilians, had been killed in the Japanese attack on Pearl Harbor, an aggressive anti-internment movement arose among Hawaii's non-Japanese population. In fact, a plan had been developed to move all of Hawaii's Japanese population to a remote and isolated location. That the plan was never implemented might simply reflect the realization that the Japanese on Hawaii were too integral to the functioning of the islands for such a plan to be workable. Still, in both highly visible and less visible ways, Hawaii's residents showed their solidarity with their Japanese neighbors. For example, they reelected four Japanese incumbents to the territorial legislature and the county board of supervisors, although they were subsequently forced to step down because of a national uproar. But, more telling, Stannard relates how groups of "large and powerfully built Hawaiians" began to ride shotgun with predominantly Asian streetcar drivers who were constantly being harassed and pushed around by soldiers, especially late at night when the soldiers were drunk.[112]

Nor were such sympathies and identifications limited to the local inhabitants of the islands. They were also extended to black servicemen, who were themselves frequently subjected to harassment and racism while stationed on the islands. Indeed, a military intelligence report in 1943 titled *The Negro Problem in the Fourteenth Naval District* devoted a quarter of its contents to the suspicious friendliness between Japanese civilians and African American soldiers.[113] Apparently, the report noted, Japanese families would often invite black soldiers to their homes at night. The report concluded, "While there is evidence indicating a genuine and legitimate common interest among Japanese and Negro leaders in the advancement of minority groups generally, the motives actuating Japanese leaders remain obscure." If such "motives" were inscrutable to military intelligence, they were clear for black soldiers. When the war ended, the black civilian population increased tenfold.

This movement—its coalitions and solidarities, its sympathies and expansive identifications—began to dissolve in the '60s and '70s. Statehood brought with it what the *Time* magazine article predicted, a flood of tourist visitors and tourist dollars. The resulting wealth formed new class divisions, new concentrations of power. Labor unionism declined as elsewhere, and the interest-group pluralism that the article misrecognized in the '50s was realized in the resulting concentrations of wealth and power. Japanese and Chinese inhabitants capitalized on the changes the most, while native Hawaiians remain the most impoverished people on the islands, possessing "far and away the worst health and the shortest life expectancy of any ethnic group."[114] But, for almost three decades, a generation of "locals" acted to transform Hawaii's racist, oligarchic, and oppressive regime. That they were motivated by the spectacle of the Massie case, by an imperial specular politics fixated around a certain sedimented normativity, did not propel them into advancing a counterspecular politics or propel them into reinvestments into counternotions of organic or sovereign normativity. Instead, the case became the occasion for them to open the doors to their identifications and their sympathies—indeed, to develop new languages for connecting and living with one another.

NOTES

1. Alexis de Tocqueville, *Democracy in America* (New York: Harper Perennial, 1988), 620.
2. Jacques Derrida, "Force of Law: The 'Mystical Foundation of Authority,'" in *Deconstruction and the Possibility of Justice*, ed. Drucilla Cornell, Michel Rosenfeld, and David Gray Carlson (New York: Routledge, 1992), 33.
3. Michael Rogin, "'Make My Day!': Spectacle as Amnesia in Imperial Politics," *Representations* 29 (Winter 1990): 99–123.
4. Ibid., 107. Reagan's citation of "Make my day!" came in a threat to Congress to veto a proposed tax increase.
5. Ibid.
6. Ibid.
7. This connects with Judith Butler's analysis of the category of hate speech and homosexuality in her *Excitable Speech* (New York: Routledge, 1997). For Butler, the discursive politics of normativity actively constitutes even as it disavows the abject identities it requires to maintain its own coherence.
8. Rogin, "Make My Day!," 118.
9. Ibid., 105.
10. Ibid., 106.
11. Ibid.
12. The three most prominent cases are *People v. Dong Lu Chen*, Supreme Court of the State of New York, Kings County, Indictment no. 7774/87, 1989; *People of the State of California v. Fumiko Kimura*, Case no. A091133, 1985, and *People v. Helen Wu*, 286 California Reporter 868, 1991. Other nonhomicide cases often discussed in relation to the cultural defense include a number of incidents of alleged rape by Hmong males in "marriage-capture" rituals. See *People v. (Kong) Moua*, 1986, and Alison Dundes Renteln, *The Cultural Defense* (Oxford: Oxford University Press, 2004), 126–128.
13. Since there exists no officially recognized "cultural defense," the attempts by defendants to introduce cultural evidence must be indirect or parasitic upon other established defenses and are subject to the discretion of trial judges.
14. See Susan Moller Okin and respondents, in Joshua Cohen, Matthew Howard, and Martha Nussbaum, eds., *Is Multiculturalism Bad for Women?* (Princeton: Princeton University Press, 1999).
15. For a different analysis of the "cultural defense" as manifesting colonial and imperial discourses and projects, see Kristin Koptiuch, "'Cultural Defense' and Criminological Displacements: Gender, Race, and (Trans)Nation in the Legal Surveillance of U.S. Diaspora Asians," in *Displacement, Diaspora, and Geographies of Identity*, ed. Smadar Lavie and Ted Swedenburg (Durham: Duke University Press, 1996), 215–233.
16. Alison Dundes Renteln's *The Cultural Defense* is distinctive in attempting to provide a comprehensive treatment of the different arenas in which individuals in court attempt to have their cultural background taken into account by the legal system. Her book is thus divided thematically among different areas of such conflict including the care of children, the treatment of animals, customs concerning the dead, attire, marriage customs, and of course, homicide. As she argues, "This study is predicated on a broader interpretation of the cultural defense than is found in the usual debates . . . our understanding of this pervasive phenomenon ought not to hinge on the same few U.S. homicide cases . . ." (7).
17. See for example, Kimberle Crenshaw's "Introduction" in her edited collection *Critical Race Theory: The Key Writings That Formed the Movement* (1995),

as well as Patricia J. Williams's *The Alchemy of Race and Rights* (Cambridge: Harvard University Press, 1991). Leti Volpp's work on the cultural defense are exemplary instances of this balanced ambivalence. See her articles "(Mis)identifying Culture: Asian Women and the 'Cultural Defense,'" *Harvard Women's Law Journal* 17 (1994): 57–101; "Talking 'Culture': Gender, Race, Nation, and the Politics of Multiculturalism," *Columbia Law Review* 96 (1996): 1573–1617; and "Feminism versus Multiculturalism," *Columbia Law Review* 101: 5 (June 2001): 1181–1218.

18. Rogin, "Make My Day!," 106.
19. For an interesting account of such forms of the "juridical unconscious" see Shoshana Felman's *The Juridical Unconscious; Trials and Traumas in the Twentieth Century* (Cambridge: Harvard University Press, 2002). Felman discusses as well the O. J. Simpson case and the unconscious, unspeakable void between race and gender that determined the shape of that trial.
20. Wendy Brown calls these forms of discourse "protection codes." See her chapter "Finding the Man in the State" in Brown, *States of Injury* (Princeton: Princeton University Press, 1995).
21. Itself an unstable, shifting discourse, the Unwritten Law was invoked through the narratives of defense attorneys in a number of sensational murder trials in the mid- to late 1800s and then as the sympathetic, ironic construction of "Dementia Americana" in the 1907 trial of Harry K. Thaw for shooting Stanford White, the famous architect and designer of Madison Square Garden. Yet its resonances travel far beyond the dramas of their particular trials. As will be clear later, characterizing the Unwritten Law as a legal artifact poses symptomatic difficulties, for it was not recognized as a sanctioned defense; indeed, its sympathetic power lay in refusing legal categories in appealing to a "higher law." Nevertheless, I will argue that its underlying discourse has actually influenced the elaboration of legal categories of criminal defense, including the distinctions between such *legible* defenses as provocation, insanity, and their hybrid mixture of temporary insanity. For treatments of the Unwritten Law as it was evoked in the nineteenth century, see Hendrik Hartog, "Lawyering, Husband's Rights, and the 'Unwritten Law' in Nineteenth-Century America," *Journal of American History* 84, no. 1 (June 1997): 67–96; Robert M. Ireland, "The Libertine Must Die: Sexual Dishonor and the Unwritten Law in the Nineteenth-Century United States," *Journal of Social History* 23, no. 1 (April 1987): 26–44, and Ireland, "Insanity and the Unwritten Law,"*American Journal of Legal History* 32, no. 2 (April 1988): 157–172. For treatments that extend it into the early twentieth century see Susan Gillman, "'Dementia Americana': Mark Twain, 'Wapping Alice' and the Henry K. Shaw Trial," *Critical Inquiry* 14, no. 2 (Winter 1988): 296–314; Martha Merrill Umphrey, "The Dialogics of Legal Meaning: Spectacular Trials, the Unwritten Law, and the Narratives of Criminal Responsibility," *Law and Society Review* 33, no. 2 (1999): 393–423. For historical arguments over the Unwritten Law and attempts to situate it in relation to Progressive-era struggles over "folkways" and "stateways," see Lewis H. Machen, "Should the Unwritten Law Be Written?," *Virginia Law Register* 13,no. 2 (June 1907): 107–113; Note, "Recognition of the Honor Defense under the Insanity Plea," *Yale Law Journal* 43 (1934): 809–814; and Rupert B. Vance and Waller Wynne Jr., "Folk Rationalizations in the 'Unwritten Law,'" *American Journal of Sociology* 39: 4 (January 1934): 483–492.
22. Cited in Gillman, "Dementia Americana," 297.
23. "The Brown & White Mosaic," *Time*, February 18, 1952. Hawaii would not be admitted formally until 1959.

24. The previous year, the Supreme Court gave its approval to the Smith Act (making it illegal to advocate the violent overthrow of the government), and the "Hawaii Seven" would subsequently be charged with and convicted of its violation.
25. For general accounts of Hawaiian history, see Lawrence H. Fuchs, *Hawaii Pono: A Social History* (New York: Harcourt Brace, 1961), and Gary Y. Okihiro, *Cane Fires: The Anti-Japanese Movement in Hawai'i, 1865–1945* (Philadelphia: Temple University Press, 1991).
26. Much of my treatment of the Massie case follows David E. Stannard's *Honor Killing: How the Infamous 'Massie Affair' Transformed Hawai'i* (New York: Viking, 2005).
27. Stannard, *Honor Killing*, 3–4. As Stannard notes, 1931–1932 was not lacking in newsworthy items, including the election of FDR, the kidnapping of the Lindbergh baby, the imprisonment of Al Capone, and the worst days of the Great Depression.
28. For the trial particulars and the later Massie-Fortescue trial, see Stannard, *Honor Killing*, and the 2005 PBS documentary "The Massie Affair."
29. Stannard, *Honor Killing*, 231–232. Stirling would later specify his views to the investigative team sent by Congress, calling for "limited suffrage" in the islands and a military commission type government akin to how "ships at war" are governed. Stannard, *Honor Killing*, 322.
30. Ibid.
31. United States Senate, Seventy-second Congress, Committee on Territories and Insular Affairs, Hearings on Joint Resolution 81 (1932). Cited in Stannard, *Honor Killing*, 276.
32. See bills S. 4309, S. 4310, S. 4311, S. 4312, S. 4314, S. 4315 and S. 4375, United States Senate, Seventy-second Congress, Second Session, Committee on Territories and Insular Affairs, Hearings on Bills Relative to the Administration in Hawaii (January 16, 1933).
33. Though he usually seemed to favor the challenge of evoking populist sympathy for the underdog. See also Arthur Weinberg, *Attorney for the Damned: Clarence Darrow in the Courtroom* (Chicago: University of Chicago Press, 1989).
34. Stannard sees a modern-day equivalent of Darrow with the late William Kunstler.
35. Stannard, *Honor Killing*, 314.
36. Ibid., 370.
37. Ibid., 369.
38. Ibid., 372. Darrow's efforts to elicit the sympathies of a racially mixed jury here are suggestive of an early instance of "amnesiac representation" since he was essentially calling for a kind of white "cultural defense" disguised as the pathos of *human* tragedy.
39. Indeed, *in flagrante delicto* became written law in Texas, Utah, and New Mexico, with some variation related to whether such a defense would mitigate to manslaughter or be exculpatory altogether. See Hartog, "Lawyering, Husband's Rights, and the 'Unwritten Law' "; Ireland, "Insanity and the Unwritten Law"; Umphrey, "The Dialogics of Legal Meaning."
40. Hartog, "Lawyering, Husband's Rights, and the 'Unwritten Law,' " 67.
41. Relatedly, the proliferation of antimiscegenation statutes and cases after the Civil War was a similar symptomatic expression.
42. Defense attorneys would sometimes read from appropriate scriptural passages.
43. Many of the most famous cases, such as the trials of Daniel Sickles (1859), George Cole (1867), Daniel McFarland (1869), James Nutt (1883), and Harry K. Thaw (1907), were closely covered by newspapers. It is also important to note that such trials were not confined to the South.

44. The trials of Singleton Mercer (1843) and James Nutt (1883). See Ireland, "Insanity and the Unwritten Law."
45. The trial of Mary Harris (1865). See "Insanity and the Unwritten Law," 158. Hartog's article seeks to restrict and distinguish such cases from those involving the honorable rights of husbands, arguing that only the latter are truly cases of the Unwritten Law. This is ostensibly for the purpose of isolating the roots of its appeal to archaic notions of husband's rights and to draw parallels with modern-day father's-rights discourses. Both views seem reconcilable in that other expansions of the Unwritten Law may still be parasitic on the archaic rights of husbands even as they are semantically expanded and generalized to affronts of sexual dishonor upon the community at large.
46. Umphrey, "The Dialogics of Legal Meaning," 393.
47. An analogy can be drawn to evidentiary rules in rape trials that seek to restrict the introduction of evidence that would impugn the sexual history and character of the rape victim.
48. Texas Penal Code Ann., sec. 1220 (1861). Cited in Umphrey, "The Dialogics of Legal Meaning," 410.
49. Umphrey, "The Dialogics of Legal Meaning," 410.
50. Provocation defenses today require a "reasonable" standard of emotional distress, which feminists have long attacked as the "reasonable man standard."
51. Ireland, "Insanity and the Unwritten Law," 159.
52. It should be noted that insanity, though exculpatory, generally leads to state institutionalization. Nothing could be further from the dignity and freedom of honorable action than to be committed by the state as insane. Though defense attorneys used the legal fiction of insanity to introduce counternarratives of criminal responsibility, ideally their appeals were for juries to sympathetically nullify the law rather than actually find their defendants insane. Indeed, decisions of insanity could lead to longer even interminable terms of imprisonment than a guilty plea.
53. Much was made during jury selection of one juror who when asked for his ethnicity answered that he was a mixture of Hawaiian, Tahitian, French, Scotch, and Irish as well as being able to speak Japanese and Hawaiian. The *San Francisco Examiner* headlined a story the next day: "Juror Belongs to Six Races!" Stannard, *Honor Killing*, 326.
54. Ibid., 364.
55. Ibid., 385.
56. These changes will be discussed in the conclusion to this chapter.
57. Foucault, *Madness and Civilization; A History of Insanity in the Age of Reason* (New York: Vintage, 1965), 253–254.
58. This is the argument found in Note, "The Cultural Defense in the Criminal Law," *Harvard Law Review* 99 (1986): 1293–1311.
59. This defense can be found in Renteln, *The Cultural Defense*, and James Sing, "Toward a Synthetic View of Provocation and Culture in the Criminal Law," *Yale Law Journal* 108, no. 7 (May 1999): 1845–1884. This of course gets into notorious disputes between equality-of-sameness and equality-of-difference formulations.
60. Critical race theoretic accounts generally adopt this view of the cultural defense, though, as noted previously, with a certain ambivalence especially with regard to the re-essentializing possibilities of asserting cultural difference. Examples include Volpp, "(Mis)Identifying Culture: Asian Women and the 'Cultural Defense' "; Holly Maguigan, "Cultural Evidence and Male Violence: Are Feminist and Multicultural Reformers on a Collision Course in Criminal Courts?," *N.Y.U. Law Review* 70, no. 36 (1995);, and Sing, "Toward a Synthetic View of Provocation and Culture in Criminal Law." It should be noted that feminists have long contested and exposed the masculinist

presuppositions of Western criminal jurisprudence, particularly the mens rea standard of the "reasonable man."

61. Such distinctions can vary considerably in their relative emphasis depending upon state statutes. For a more general discussion of mens rea, see R. Perkins and R. Boyce, *Criminal Law*, 3rd ed. (Mineola: Foundation Press, 1982), 828–831.
62. For a discussion of provocation and the Battered Women's Syndrome defense, see Victoria Nourse, "Passion's Progress; Modern Law Reform and the Provocation Defense," *Yale Law Journal* 106 (1997): 1331–1438.
63. This presupposes that cultural factors are admitted in court. In general, American courts have been hostile to their introduction, whether or not they are based on insanity. It is out of objections to this propensity as well as objections to the arbitrariness of whether cultural factors "make it" into the courtroom that some defenders argue for its formalization. See Renteln, *The Cultural Defense.*
64. *People v. Dong Lu Chen*, Supreme Court of the State of New York, Kings County, Indictment no. 7774/87 (1989). The essentializing problems of this case are most fully addressed by Volpp in her article "(Mis)Identifying Culture: Asian Women and the 'Cultural Defense.'"
65. Celeste Bohlen, "Holtzman May Appeal Probation for Immigrant in Wife's Slaying,"*New York Times*, April 5, 1989, B3.
66. Volpp, "(Mis)Identifying Culture," 69.
67. Bohlen, "Holtzman May Appeal."
68. Volpp discusses in detail the way Jian Wan Chen was made invisible in the course of the trial.
69. Shaun Asseal, "Judge Defends Sentencing Wife-Killer to Probation," *Manhattan Law*, April 4–10, 1989, 4. Also found in Volpp, "(Mis)Identifying Culture," 73–74.
70. Volpp, "(Mis)Identifying Culture," 73.
71. A sampling of articles includes Alexis Jetter, "Fear Is Legacy of Wife Killing in Chinatown, Battered Asians Shocked by Husband's Probation," *Newsday*, Nov. 26, 1989, 4; Linda Anthony, "Women Discuss Protection for the Battered Following Controversial 'Cultural Defense' Verdict," *Korea Times*, July 14, 1989; Julia P. Sams, "The Availability of the 'Cultural Defense' as an Excuse for Criminal Behavior," *Georgia Journal of International and Comparative Law* 16 (1986): 335–354; Nilda Rimonte, "A Question of Culture: Cultural Approval of Violence against Women in the Pacific-Asian Community and the Cultural Defense," *Stanford Law Review* 43 (July 1991): 1311–1327.
72. Bohlen, "Holtzman May Appeal."
73. Cited in Deborah Woo, "The People v. Fumiko Kimura: But Which People?," *International Journal of the Sociology of Law* 17 (1989): 423.
74. As well as the Anita Hill-Clarence Thomas controversy. For treatments of the Simpson trial, see Toni Morrison and Claudia Brodsky Lacour, eds., *Birth of a Nation'hood; Gaze, Script, and Spectacle in the O. J.Simpson Case* (New York: Pantheon, 1997). For the Thomas hearings, see Toni Morrison, ed., *Race-ing Justice, En-gendering Power* (New York: Pantheon, 1992).
75. See Tamar Lewin, "What Penalty for Killing in Passion?," *New York Times*, Oct. 21, 1994, A18.
76. I am indebted to Victoria Hattam for the language of associative chains. See her *In the Shadow of Race: Jews, Latinos, and Immigrant Politics in the United States* (Chicago: University of Chicago Press, 2007).
77. Okin, *Is Multiculturalism Bad for Women?*, 118.
78. Indeed, Okin's book has silenced not only contrary and heterodox views on multiculturalism but also generations of contention between feminists of color and a hegemonic liberal feminism. Not only must we refuse the opposition

between feminism and multiculturalism, but we must also contest the boundaries and historicism of feminist struggle. See Audre Lorde, *Sister Outsider* (Freedom, CA: The Crossing Press, 1984); Gloria T. Hull, Patricia Bell Scott, and Barbara Smith, *All the Women Are White, All the Blacks Are Men, but Some of Us Are Brave* (New York: The Feminist Press at CUNY, 1982); bell hooks, *Ain't I a Woman?: Black Women and Feminism* (Boston: South End Press, 1999).

79. The details of the case are discussed most fully in Woo, "The People v. Fumiko Kimura; But Which People?"
80. Ibid., 404.
81. The petition is documented in ibid., 404.
82. Ibid., 425–426, note 2.
83. Okin, *Is Multiculturalism Bad for Women?*, 19.
84. Woo, "The People v. Fumiko Kimura; But Which People?," 412.
85. Ibid., 405.
86. Ibid.
87. Apparently, a large contingent of Japanese Americans attended the trial proceedings, sometimes expressing dismay over the competency of the translations.
88. Woo, "The People v. Fumiko Kimura; But Which People?," 406.
89. Volpp, "(Mis)Identifying Culture," 70.
90. Ibid.
91. Quotes are from Foucault, *Madness and Civilization*, 253, 254, 252.
92. Patricia J. Williams, *The Alchemy of Race and Rights* (Cambridge: Harvard University Press, 1991), 148.
93. Esquith, *Intimacy and Spectacle: Liberal Theory as Political Education* (Ithaca: Cornell University Press, 1994).
94. Ibid., 4.
95. Ibid.
96. My identification of the Unwritten Law as part of these earlier struggles should not be taken as sui generis. Those discourses, themselves, were shaped, both synchronically and diachronically, with others.
97. It is out of this nexus that Habermas can reply that rights of recognition for cultural minorities are redundant. The democratic constitutional order implicitly relies on and reflects intersubjective elaboration. See his "Struggles for Recognition in the Democratic Constitutional State," in *Multiculturalism and the Politics of Recognition*, ed. Amy Gutmann (Princeton: Princeton University Press, 1994), 107–148.
98. Sing, "Toward a Synthetic View of Provocation and Culture in the Criminal Law." Provocation defenses have been accepted in Australia for some trials involving homophobic violence. See Santo de Pasquale, "Provocation and the Homosexual Advance Defence: The Deployment of Culture as a Defence Strategy," *Melbourne University Law Review* 26 (2002): 110–143.
99. Renteln, *The Cultural Defense*. In thus treating it wholly within the realm of legal remedy, Renteln seems to me to further the juridical subjection of "difference" since her prescriptions would expand the interpolations between defendants and expert testimony (presumably by reputable anthropologists).
100. Wendy Brown's *Regulating Aversion: Tolerance in the Age of Identity and Empire* (Princeton: Princeton University Press, 2006) argues that this disciplinary frame is the key to redeployed "civilizational discourses" in contemporary imperial politics.
101. See Paul Harris, *Black Rage Confronts the Law* (New York: New York University Press, 1997), and Judd F. Sneirson, "Black Rage and the Criminal Law: A Principled Approach to a Polarized Debate," *University of Pennsylvania Law Review* 143, no. 6 (June 1995): 2251–2288.

102. Ferguson subsequently fired his defense team and represented himself, arguing that he was not the real shooter.
103. They would of course argue that those were the constraints given to them by the law.
104. Prohibiting the kinds of complex affects suggested in the communal reaction to Kimura's case.
105. See Paul Butler, "Racially Based Jury Nullification: Black Power in the Criminal Justice System," *Yale Law Journal* 105, no. 3 (Dec. 1995): 677–725.
106. Ibid., 678.
107. Ibid.
108. Jury nullification has had a long and sporadic history: from jury nullification of seditious libel charges against British rule during the colonial period to nullification of trials involving the Fugitive Slave Act. The 1895 Supreme Court case *Sparf v. United States* established what is still largely the ambiguous rule governing jury nullification: juries have the "physical" power to nullify since their deliberations are secret and their verdicts cannot be set aside, but courts do not have to inform juries of this implicit right to judge law—a kind of "don't ask, don't tell" policy.
109. Cited in Stannard, *Honor Killing*, 414. John Reinecke, *Language and Dialect in Hawaii: A Sociolinguistic History to 1935* (Honolulu: University of Hawaii Press, 1969).
110. *Honor Killing*.
111. Ibid., 415.
112. Ibid., 417.
113. Ibid.
114. Ibid., 422.

5 The Uncanny Compensations of Culture over Class

CIVIL RIGHTS CRYPTS AND THE INCLUSION OF ETHNICITY

> The memory is of an idyll, experienced with a valued object and yet for some reason unspeakable. It is a memory entombed in a fast and secure place, awaiting resurrection . . . a crypt in the ego. Created by a self-governing mechanism we call *inclusion*, the crypt is comparable to the formation of a cocoon around the chrysalis. . . . Inclusion attests to a painful reality, forever *denied*: the "gaping wound" of the topography.
>
> —Nicholas Abraham and Maria Torok[1]

If multiculturalism engenders a certain contemporary way of being that is sensitive to the consequences of cultural difference, surely one of its prime objects has been the concept of ethnicity. As a lynchpin in multicultural "technologies of the self," ethnic cultural difference has been an object malleable and far reaching, able to rationalize the formations of one's surroundings, able to incite one's own practices and the practices of others. But, paradoxically, its ability to do so rests in its given-ness—an object beyond the contingencies of the world, an irreducible object shared by others in their own particular ways. Each to his own, naturally equivalent, if not constructively or productively so, ethnicity can serve as an overarching principle or bounded space where one can understand the world *anew* or *return* to the world, thereby bridging the gulf between one's will to know and will to power and creating a new set of relations of truthful practices.[2] However, precisely because of its presumed given-ness, such authentic practices can never be simply self-authorizing. If they are to be worthy of the name, that is, worthy of trust, reliance, and belief or of an authorized origin, they must spring from another ground, respond to the call of something beyond. And to the extent that this origin remains problematic or retains its problematizing call, then the bounds of such truthful practices will remain tied to a problem of memory, will remain confined in the shape of an uncertain and imperiled memorial. How then should one remember one's ethnic origins? How then should one ascertain their compensations as a link between one's present practices and a past that is never quite left behind? And what of those links that lie on the fringes of this return, remainders of a spectral presence, of race and class, among others, that retain all the more their constituting and haunting quality? How then might we illuminate these constitutive links without remaining bound to their configuration?

Two books, Matthew Frye Jacobson's *Roots Too* and Marilyn Halter's *Shopping for Identity*, attempt to document this apparent plenitude of ethnicity's reach as an organizing principle of contemporary practice in the United States but also something of its haunted history.[3] In speaking about the origins of his project, Jacobson recounts how, after an early presentation of his work, Werner Sollors walked up to him and handed him "a very fat file of newspaper clippings, magazine articles, and other 1970's ephemera," saying simply, "It's your project now."[4] Jacobson called this his most "difficult project" because it "sent me back into my own past," and his remarks and the book itself reveal how the ethnic revival and its legacy are fundamentally about the pervasive construction of memory, about the *need* for memory retrieval as a *national* project. For Jacobson, this need should not be understood in any individual sense but probed in its collective dimensions. Jacobson states, "these developments mark the emergence of a wholly new syntax of nationality and belonging. . . . It was not the interiority but the *collectivity* of the ethnic revival whose reach in American political culture was most important—not the politics of 'identity' for individuals, but the politics of 'heritage' for the nation at large" (original emphasis).[5] Jacobson thus organizes his exhausting attempt to catalogue the prodigious artifacts of this ethnic revival—from novels, films, and social science tracts to speeches, exhibitions, and advertisements—arranging them according to such collective political shifts. Though his overarching argument often gets buried under the weight of all this classifying, Jacobson seems to emplot their trajectory within the familiar parasitic backlash of white ethnics, who, in appropriating the affirmation of group difference during the late civil rights era, enacted a new nationalist memory of the primacy of the nation's immigrant origins. And in this *politics* of memory, the Statue of Liberty and the restoration of Ellis Island became fused as *the* emblems of contemporary American national identity.

Halter's book as well documents the pervasiveness of ethnic difference as an organizing principle of contemporary American life. But where Jacobson focuses on the representational or discursive currents of the ethnic revival, Halter's text discloses the activities or practices that the primacy of ethnic cultural difference has engendered. Depicting not just a world of consumption but also ethnic entrepreneurial activity, she shows how ethnic difference became not just a cathected object of desire but also a modality of capitalist practice. Further highlighting the integration of ethnicity with capitalist activity, she points out how ethnic identification seems to *increase* with one's socioeconomic class.[6] From Dunkin' Donuts ads that feature Yiddishisms like "It's Worth a Schlep" to ads created by sophisticated multicultural marketing consultants like YAR Communications, whose worldwide clientele includes Mack Trucks and Merrill Lynch, ethnicity has become a form of "cultural capital" to be exploited, circulated, and commodified.[7] And as she concludes her book, ". . . the children, grandchildren, and great-grandchildren of the immigrant generation have realized that *in order to move forward* into the future, they cannot completely let go of the past . . . whether we like it or not, we are all deeply immersed in a commodity-driven, consumer culture that daily shapes who we are and how we define ourselves" (emphasis added).[8]

Yet, besides the difference in emphasis between these two books, Halter's conclusion signals another, subtler difference between the two. Note how there is a curious passivity attributed to the "immigrant generation." Note also the boundedness of the subject—the descendants of the immigrant generation. Yet, from beginning to end, the world she depicts in her book shapes the lives of all American inhabitants, not just as consumers but also as capitalist producers, whether white ethnics or racial minorities. Nevertheless, Halter subtly imbues her analysis with a narrative of nostalgic loss, anchored in the experience of the "immigrant generation," by which she clearly means the Southern and Eastern European immigrants of a century ago. Indeed, in her introduction, she locates the origins of her analysis in the transformations of two legacies from the '60s, neither of which attributes any agency to the descendants of these immigrants: first, "the quiet passage of the Immigration Reform Bill of 1965" and second, "the movements by traditionally oppressed groups for recognition and self-determination . . . spearheaded by black nationalism and then quickly followed by the American Indian Movement and the stirrings of a new Chicano militancy."[9] In fairness, Halter then includes the "backlash against minority group movements for racial power, [by] white descendants of immigrants."[10] But even then, these later developments are construed "largely as a defense against perceived threats of black power" and were "reactive."[11] Whereas Jacobson strongly grounds his narrative in the agency of white ethnics in fashioning the ethnic revival and ultimately reshaping the politics of national identity, Halter presents that ascendance of ethnicity as a passive reaction and ultimately a kind of melancholic loss for the "immigrant generation," who "cannot completely let go of the past" if they are "to move forward" into this brave new world.

We might attribute these differences between Jacobson's and Halter's recollections as simply stemming from their political affinities. Where Jacobson speaks from the position of an antiracist critic of the white ethnic revival, Halter takes a mildly conservative position, reflecting on the ironies confronting white ethnics who were first forced to assimilate and whose descendants are now compelled to differentiate. And certainly this fault line, coded within the bounds of agency and passivity, is quite common within the debates on multiculturalism, coloring one's position in a number of domains and politically charged issues. Rather than choose a side, however, perhaps it might be more fruitful to examine their commonalities. Indeed, both can be said to be mild critics of the artificiality of ethnic recovery in its capitalist- and consumerist-driven modes of activity; both point to its artifice. But, more important, both locate the origins of cultural group affirmation during the civil rights era, and both attribute this shift to the claims advanced first by blacks and then spread among other minority groups.[12] Whatever one's position on the salutary and salient dimensions of the inclusion of ethnicity in American life then, its transformative ascendance is commonly pinned upon this shift from an integrationist politics of the early civil rights era to a pluralist and affirmative politics of racial group difference, and this in turn is largely attributed to the shifting agency and strategy of black political groups and their subsequent spread among other minority, feminist, and subaltern groups. Problematizing the inclusiveness of ethnicity (fundamentally to question our own present inclusion within the space of ethnicity) therefore remains tied to the contagion of the civil rights era, to the civil rights era as a problematic origin, and consequently the need to question the present in its memorializing configurations.

We might call this the Contagion thesis, and it is a surprisingly resonant undercurrent within many quarters reflecting on the vicissitudes of identity in early twenty-first-century America. It is in this fractured narrative, therefore, that John Skrentny's much-addressed *The Minority Rights Revolution* illuminates and intensifies this understanding of the civil rights era as *the* archive of the present.[13] Though Skrentny's text is concentrated on the decision-making processes that shaped minority rights policies during the civil rights era rather than the overall scope of the years after the civil rights era, it is clear that the arguments he advances are meant to incite far more. In his preface, he states forthrightly the larger context of his aims: "I want to understand modern American political and *moral* culture and the meaning of 'Left' and 'Right.' I want to show how weak groups often win big in American politics. I want to trace the genesis of various controversial policies and America's current tendency toward 'identity politics.' In doing so, my aim is to cut through the shrillness of political rhetoric and improve American democratic deliberation by informing participants in policy debates how we arrived at our current situation" (emphasis added).[14] But if Skrentny's ultimate aim is to "cut through the shrillness" and inform us of the nature of identity politics and "our current situation," he is unlikely to succeed. This is because Skrentny's book is highly polemical, indeed, likely to tighten the screws as we rail with suspicion about the origins of who we are.

For Skrentny, if the civil rights era's legacy resides in its confrontation with the pervasiveness of discrimination in American life, then the ensuing "minority rights revolution" constitutes something of an illegitimate offspring. Repeatedly demonstrating the arbitrariness of policymakers seeking to codify and instantiate the efforts to redress discrimination, Skrentny argues that the "minority rights revolution" was the result of an incoherent logic by elite policymakers seeking to apply a "black analogy" to other subaltern groups, paradigmatically those of other minorities (most egregiously those minority immigrants that arrived as a result of the 1965 immigration reforms) but also to women, the disabled, and, potentially, homosexuals. Indeed, for Skrentny, the incoherence of this political logic of compensation is underscored by the fact that such policymakers extended the "black analogy" to categorical groups even in the minimal presence of agitating demand on the part of such groups. He states, "Politicians simply *anticipated* that they would like them, and pushed them through based on this perception" often with little or no public debate or demand." (emphasis added).[15] Collectively, such "decisions" therefore constituted the minority rights revolution whose legacy has been an arbitrary legal edifice perverting the effort to redress black racial discrimination as well as clouding the attention to other, more salient forms of discrimination such as those involving class.

Skrentny therefore focuses our attention to the *event* of the civil rights era, what he calls, following Hugh Davis Graham, a "rare American epiphany."[16] But rather than seeing the primal emergence of social movements and social demands, he depicts a world that centers on exchanges and negotiations, shaped by analogies and anticipations, conducted in memos by elite policy makers. Skrentny's exercise thus constitutes something of a genealogy, tying not only the political and legal categories of the present but also its moral categories to what turns out to be not the myth of social movements seeking just compensations during the civil rights era but to the incoherent and arbitrary origins of elite rationale. Perhaps it might be argued that Skrentny's overall aim is to recover and purify a more legitimate compensatory logic grounded in the paradigmatic case of African American discrimination before it was analogized and anticipated, before its contagion generated the contemporary world of identity politics. But even this is clouded by Skrentny's own genealogical sympathies. For example, he forthrightly states that he believes that "white ethnics . . . got a raw deal."[17] Documenting their tentative mobilizations as claimants for discriminatory compensation, Skrentny devotes a chapter to how their appeals fell on deaf ears. Yet even by his own analysis, white ethnic mobilization never reached a certain threshold presence, remaining for the most part a nascent potential possibility. And while this operates as a profound critique in his analysis of minority rights extension, here it possesses no such force.[18] Hence, Skrentny simultaneously indicts and *appeals to* the analogizing and anticipatory possibilities of the civil rights epiphany. Paradoxically judging the minority rights revolution as an origin both too anticipatory and not anticipatory enough, Skrentny offers a genealogical critique whose force thus rests solely in casting suspicion at the *arbitrariness* of our origins. And rather than estranging this origin in the service of freeing possibilities of transforming the present, Skrentny's sympathies remain tangled up within that problematic origin, repeating its failures of compensation, its wounds seeking redress.

Each of these three texts then seeks to problematize and document the ascendance of ethnic cultural difference within contemporary American life and, in the process, something of the fraught lines between race and ethnicity that lie just below its pervasive surface. And certainly all three more or less explicitly tie these lines to something of the transformative shifts carried out during the civil rights era. This attribution alone might not be significant if it were not for the fact that all three circumscribe very different remembrances of its transformative quality. Jacobson tells the story of the politically discursive hegemony enacted by white ethnics through cultural productions enabled by the "contagious" and perverted affirmation of group difference, transposed from their racially antidiscriminatory contexts. Halter discloses a largely new world of entrepreneurial activity and consumption where ethnic cultural difference becomes a technology for capitalizing upon *oneself* as much as on others. Yet her story is imbued with a certain ironic pathos for descendants of immigrants who are now *forced* to adopt such technologies of the self through the contagions of the recognition of racial group difference. And though Skrentny complicates the origins of the affirmation of cultural group difference, he too indicts the present in its moralizing identity politics and its uncertain and vulnerable commitment to antidiscrimination by attributing it to the arbitrariness of elite rationale during its seminal period. Ethnic cultural difference seems thus to be a many-sided space, both actively embraced and passively adopted, and for all three, more or less explicitly, beneath its surface forms lies interred a contentious terrain located in a generative civil rights era.

Nor have they been alone. Many have been critical of both the evasive superficiality of cultural difference and its overloaded debts in contemporary American politics. Mary Waters in her *Ethnic Options* identifies within it the dream of a "cost-less community" and concludes her study with reflections on its racially evasive politics, on the invisibility thereby enacted upon those forms of community that are inextricably bound with costs.[19] From the opposite end, Wendy Brown cautions against those forms of identity politics fully invested in its wounds, whose demand for an impossible compensation can lead only to a nihilistic *ressentiment* and a paralyzing repetition of its wounds.[20] But whether they conceive of identify politics as a utopian dream or a perpetual nightmare, both likewise tie their critiques to a problem of memory, either to a groundless memory that evacuates the ground of other politics or an overloaded memory unable to relinquish itself and conceive of an alternative future. The "gaping wound" of the civil-rights-era landscape continues to beckon.

If on the edges and behind the surface bounds of ethnic cultural inclusion therefore lies a problem of memory, particularly of civil-rights-era memory, then the political possibilities for breaking free of their fraught shackles seem to be similarly bound in a question of confronting the debts of the present in that conflicted generative past. Judging from Abraham and Torok's analysis of mourning and melancholia in the opening epigraph, inclusion attests *not* to the integration of a conflicted or traumatic experience but rather to its paralysis in an idyllic space, a sacred utopia with all the requisite appeal of an exquisite corpse. Instead of generating a transformative acceptance of an ambivalent experience, inclusion and incorporation are bellwethers of an amnesiac remembrance of conflict, a false remembrance that splits the elements of a conflict into compensatory spaces displaced elsewhere. But, as Jacobson and Halter show, such spaces are not merely fantasies; they coalesce into actual practices, shape and propel a world in its many transactions. Michael Rogin was perhaps *the* theorist of the amnesiac investments of race in our newfound inclusionary post-'60s American milieu, and, concomitantly, Rogin was ever ready to pierce those veils in their logics of compensation and reveal, following Nietzsche, that there was a price of cruelty enacted on a body somewhere.[21] But even if we approach our inclusionary age with a hermeneutics of suspicion rather than trust, such approaches might still seek solace in pushing back to find a more truthful archive, a more truthful set of compensatory spaces. Still locked in its own hermeneutic circle, such compensations inevitably spiral in as intensifiers of both melancholia and ressentiment. Such efforts might, for example, fold the civil rights period back into American history only through the primal lens of a "metalanguage" of race, whiteness, and white supremacy or, alternatively, as a massive evasion of class, or, perhaps the most persistent of them all, as a vessel for reaffirming the promise of the American dream of autonomous freedom and its corrupted history. For Nietzsche as well as for Abraham and Torok, the efforts to construct compensating spaces had their roots in the *problem* of deriving sense out of senseless suffering—in guaranteeing the promissory note of an inaugural traumatic event.

Instead, we might try to resist narrowing the narratives of our civil-rights-era crypts in the interest of estranging ourselves from what "what we are,"[22] that is to say, in the interest not of legislating our politics *through* interpreting that seminal period but of opening up the possibilities of political practice *out* of the acknowledgment of the civil rights period as a heterogeneous event. For the counterpart of the post-'60s inclusionary spirit has been the proliferation of claims and counterclaims of resentment, as amply demonstrated by the continuing "culture wars", whose overarching principle perhaps is that there can be no intermingled space between competing resentments, competing compensations. If the hallmark of multicultural discourse lies in the uncanny fracture between the utter banality and ubiquity of multicultural hyphenated identity and the simultaneously embittered and heavily freighted nature of some of these debates, then this suggests that we remain tied and marked to a set of transformations whose definitive contours fundamentally lie beyond reproach and recompense. In the face of this, we might find possibilities not in searching for a more definitive ground out of that period but in enlivening its many-sidedness and dissolving some of the demand for equivalent compensations over a failed forebear or a futile search for a more trustworthy one.

The guiding ethos of Foucault's theorizing was precisely in the effort to shatter the impasses of "what we are," and for that reason I draw upon his work in this chapter. Conducting genealogical histories of "the present," Foucault focused his efforts less on the nature of a slow accretion of a unifying theory or even on establishing a single interpretive "truth" of the present but ever on pluralizing the precursors and origins of what we take to be our most cherished and settled truths. For this very reason, the charges of "normative confusion" or of the systematic inadequacy of his contributions regarding power are off the mark.[23] They presume that he was engaged in a project of denying his own present or else erecting an overarching ontological theory that would allow us to replace the present rather than the persistent effort to pluralize the dynamism underlying it. From his early works on madness and the accumulation of the human sciences to his more politically focused middle works on discipline and sexuality to his late works on self-discipline and the "care of the self," there is a common thread—the struggle to estrange our truths as "games of truth" with discontinuous and often politically unsettling origins and what it would ethically involve to constitute ourselves in the effort to move *out* of the present.[24] But even in his late efforts, Foucault's paradoxically *antitheoretical* impulses could look only to the past for possibilities.[25] Always with a foot in the present, Foucault explored "lines of fragility" that could lead one to comprehend our plural pasts in the effort to freely practice different futures.[26]

Of course, even though I claim Foucault's work was animated by a coherent concern over pluralizing the fractured spaces of "what we are," nevertheless, he did employ a variety of shifting tools and terminologies in those efforts. And befitting the concern to pluralize the dynamic spaces of the present, the domains of Foucault's investigation themselves were quite heterogeneous without any final ordering of their relationships with one another. These are not weaknesses of his contributions, however, but speak to their strength and their purpose. Genealogy was an effort not to oppose or replace historical narrative but rather to show the heterogeneity and discontinuity out of which our own historical a priori were fashioned and thus to situate our own understanding of ourselves in a different light. There was no corresponding move to then fix these genealogical insights into a new ground out of which a discursive knowledge or truth could be found to which we would submit our own will in the present. Neither would it be a simple question of refusing the discourses we have inherited.[27] Knowledge, thought, and reason could be seen as compensating spaces for "reality." Within their imaginative bounds, they constitute and intensify our memorials of reality, the modalities of truth through which those memories are organized, the subjectivities thereby called into being, and the technological practices fashioned that mediate both the conduct and the nature of subject-subject relationships within and between these spaces—and always, of course, knitting together relations of power. Yet such compensating spaces are neither sui generis nor self-enclosed; they should not be "taken at face value" but are themselves problematic fractures of prior problematizations.[28]

Confronting sequences of cocoons and internments, the task Foucault set for himself was in exploring not just the diverse networks out of which they were cast but also something of their cathected nature. Foucault would have resisted psychoanalytic terminology to characterize his work, preferring the nonmoralizing, nonpathologizing language of strategy, tactics, and problematization, but clearly the effort of effecting a transformation of "what we are" in its paralyzing fractures by diffusing its given boundaries and abstaining from (or at least minimizing) a moralizing vantage point has clear psychoanalytic affinities.[29] Indeed, it might not be such a stretch to characterize Foucault as fundamentally an antimelancholic thinker, certainly inspired by Nietzsche but giving that animus a level of detail and concreteness where Nietzsche at best could be profoundly suggestive.[30]

In a Foucauldian vein, then, we might begin to seize the lines of fracture in our present by following the lines of fragility on the surface of Jacobson's, Halter's, and Skrentny's accounts. Both Jacobson and Halter identify the plenitude of ethnicity as a technique of cultural, economic, and political activity, and both situate it as something of a troubled compensation out of the shifts of the civil rights era. And Skrentny draws our attention to political elites who, in confronting a problem of liberal compensation for the pervasiveness of discrimination and inequality, crafted forms of legal redress but also imposed limits on those efforts, reinforcing a division between racial minorities and white ethnics that persists to this day. Skrentny argues that this division was arbitrary, thereby tacitly arguing that the legal categories of affirmative action and the moralizing of identity politics today are themselves arbitrary.

But perhaps there was a deeper normalizing cultural logic underlying that dividing rationale.[31] Perhaps racial difference and ethnic difference were linked as a form of triage[32] over the possibilities and limits of a specifically *liberal* problematic of compensation, where racial cultural difference could be seen as a pathology requiring governmental intervention while treating white ethnics in this way would carry liberalism beyond its promise of limited government, beyond its promise of the economic sphere as the primeval compensating mechanism. If so, then the political effort to confront inequality and discrimination would increasingly morph into the calculus for *potentials* of equality of opportunity, freeing ethnic cultural difference as a marketable technique, as a rationale for the recovery of the economic sphere as the ultimate basis of compensation, while isolating racial cultural difference as a pathologized category of normalizing governmental concern, an impediment and incitement of liberalism's promised autonomy and mobility.

Certainly this way of viewing race and ethnicity as part of a developing triage formulated in response to the crisis of liberalism's promise in the 1960's is suggested by the arc of Daniel Patrick Moynihan's involvement during this period. Coauthor with Nathan Glazer of one of the first comparative social scientific treatments of ethnicity, *Beyond the Melting Pot*, in 1963 Moynihan was already asserting the category of ethnicity as an indispensable comparative analytic for understanding the social and cultural forms underlying political formations and problems.[33] This, along with his interest in the analytic concepts of epidemiology, would shape his use of social science as a means of crafting judicious governmental policy in a variety of domains.[34] As assistant secretary of labor he played a key role in drafting Johnson's War on Poverty legislation, where he battled other drafters against allowing politically oriented community action initiatives to take precedence over more economically geared proposals such as job training. Generally credited with writing the first draft of Johnson's famous 1965 Howard University speech,[35] he also authored the infamous Moynihan Report, released to the public later that year. But, despite the speech's emphasis on equality as a "fact and a result" (an assertion also made in the Report), both also signal the special challenge raised by "Negro poverty." In other words, both need to be seen as sharing a growing ambivalence over the nature of the means and the possibility of their success in achieving equality. As is well known, Moynihan's document, *The Negro Family: The Case for National Action*, argued that a "culture of pathology" within the Negro family posed particular challenges to purely economic forms of assistance, much less more radical political forms of transformation. Explicitly comparing black family structure to the "unusually strong family bonds" of "a number of immigrant groups," the Report thus argued that governmental efforts should be aimed at stabilizing "the highly unstable" black family.[36]

Though often critiqued for "blaming the victim," the Moynihan Report may be most important for documenting a still-ambivalent but distilling shift over the limits of a specifically *liberal* form of governmental compensation, from the political indictments of inequality, to ameliorative measures working within the economy, finally to addressing the comparative *cultural* rather than biological precursors of economic activity. By the time of his joining the Nixon administration as assistant to the president for urban affairs, Moynihan had become thoroughly disenchanted with the politicization of racial inequality. In his *Maximum Feasible Misunderstanding*, he blamed urban rioting and the radicalization of racial-ethnic politics on the community action programs of the War on Poverty and "utopian" white liberal elites for whom racial guilt dictated a black/white Manichean messianism.[37] Along with the growing ranks of neoliberals whose positions were hashed out in journals such as *The Public Interest*[38] and *Commentary*, Moynihan would thus famously advise Nixon to adopt a position of "benign neglect" toward issues of racial inequality, not so much because Moynihan had abandoned his concern for addressing racial economic deprivation but because he believed explicit governmental interventions were fanning the flames of political radicalism, fomenting unrealistic political hopes, and jeopardizing the faith in and the stability of the economic sphere as the ultimate solvent of political problems. And from the 1970s on, Moynihan would "presciently" continue to see the salience of ethnicity not only as a principle of American political and economic understanding and strength, but also as a vector for his increasingly international concerns; as a defender of Israel during his time with the U.N. and in "predicting" the collapse of the Soviet Union over its volatile mix of economic downturn structured by ethnicity.[39]

As a consummate liberal public intellectual who embraced the skepticism of governmental folly and the principle of limited government, as a prescient innovator of both the possibilities and the limits of the intersection of social scientific knowledge and government policy, and as a reaffirmation of the image of the classically humanist benevolent paternal legislator, Moynihan and his role in negotiating a liberal governmental problematic out of the crisis of the civil rights era fairly cry out for a Foucauldian "interpretive analytics."[40] And throughout this period, Moynihan continued to develop and assert ethnicity and race as part of an analytic continuum, no longer understood as rooted in biological propensities but seen through cultural practices causative of differentials in economic autonomy and prosperity, whose specifically liberal compensations must likewise be differentially calibrated. Like a Benthamite figure, Moynihan can serve as a key contributor for revealing the shifts of that period, the problematizations out of which they arose, the techniques and rationales developed to isolate, respond, and rework those problematics. In *Discipline and Punish*, Foucault placed special emphasis on Jeremy Bentham not because his panopticon was widely instituted but because he captured something of the rationalizing, disciplinary dreams of that era and the problematic of amplifying a nonintrusive, corrective *humane* governmental power. Moynihan likewise serves as a pivotal figure in the transformations of this period not because his prescriptions and solutions were universally accepted but because his writings in and out of government service reveal the knitting links that connect ethnicity as a new analytic tool, the confrontation with a liberal crisis and problematic of compensation for the many indictments of that period, and a developing technological rationale that could reaffirm the promise of liberal limited government; setting race and ethnicity on diverging paths—the first toward governmental normalization and surveillance, the second as a new modality of economic autonomy. And between these lines, ethnicity and race could encrypt the memory of inequality and economic grievance, could serve just as well as the melancholic substitute *for* economic mobility, returning to oneself the means of narrating both its successes and its failures, enlivening the pathos of its underlying sacred promise.

But to articulate cultural difference of race and ethnicity as part of a developing logic mediating a crisis of liberal compensation might be viewed as an effort to capture *the* truth of this seminal period.[41] And, as such, it would serve to spiral inward the interpretations and judgments of which this truth would become its own bounded compensating space for the fractures of our present, an archive able to serve as the guarantor of our own "undecidability."[42] Certainly, Foucault's most famous books, *Discipline and Punish* and *The History of Sexuality, Volume One*, as well as his articulations of such concepts as liberal governmentality and biopower, seem to suggest an overarching truth of the present, one in which social scientific knowledge and governmental power increasingly combine to form an all-pervasive iron cage. But this would discount his own conceptualization of these efforts as genealogies. Likewise, my attempts in this chapter to offer a different generative logic of the contagions of racial and ethnic cultural difference should not be seen as the *only* truth to be found in the archive of "what we are." For to do so would be to foreclose the heterogeneity of ethnic-racial inclusion only in terms of its ability to serve as a liberal form of compensation—an impossible task always already interring its excessive voices on the margins *within* its prodigious problematic. For Foucault, the task was to illuminate such problematizations as *events* and thereby to spiral outward rather than inward our own attempts to conceive of the present as an ongoing *tensile* event, in all the senses of that word. But to appreciate these negotiations and to sharpen the need to move beyond ethnic-racial inclusion as an encrypted monument to a governmental problematic of compensation, we need to see something of the troubled methodological trajectories through which Foucault himself scaffolded his later "memorials" to liberal governmentality, troubled not in a moralizing sense but out of an obstinate antimelancholic need to "get free of oneself."[43]

THEORETICAL EXCURSIONS: PSYCHOANALYSIS, THE CONSOLATIONS OF DISCOURSE, AND THE HETEROTOPIC SPIRAL

> . . . if this subjectivity of the insane is both a call to and an abandonment of the world, is it not of the world itself that we should ask the secret of its enigmatic status? Is there not in mental illness a whole nucleus of significations that belongs to the domain in which it appeared—and, to begin with, the simple fact that it is in that domain that it is circumscribed *as* an illness?
>
> —Michel Foucault[44]

> On the other hand, I believe that the concept of governmentality makes it possible to bring out the freedom of the subject and its relationship to others which constitutes the very stuff of ethics.
>
> —Michel Foucault[45]

These quotes bookend Foucault's corpus, from his first disavowed book in 1954 to one of his last interviews mere months before his death, in 1984. How to reconcile them? How to reconcile the transition from mental illness to ethical freedom? How to reconcile the focus on a "domain" that circumscribes and produces "subjectivity" and an approach to that domain that can "make possible" the freedom of the subject?

In the first epigraph, the space between a "whole nucleus of significations" and the question of the subjectivity of the mentally ill seems to signal the unique advent for a psychoanalytic inquiry. Indeed, Stuart Hall, in his introduction to the edited collection *Questions of Cultural Identity*, articulates the continuing need to theorize the lack opened by the Althusserian problematic of interpellation and the speculary structure of ideology, namely a theorization of identity or identification as the mediating term between subjects and discourse.[46] Yet, in discussing the advancements offered by Foucault's work on this problematic of accounting for identification, Hall nevertheless identifies in him both an increasing movement towards but also a limit in his theorizing over psychoanalysis. He states,

> . . . what remains is the requirement to think this relation of subject to discursive formations *as an articulation*. It is therefore all the more fascinating that, when finally Foucault *does* make the move in this direction, he was prevented, of course, from going to one of the principal sources of thinking about this neglected aspect—namely, psychoanalysis; prevented from moving in that direction by his own critique of it as simply another network of disciplinary power relations. What he produces instead is a discursive *phenomenology* of the subject . . . which is in danger of being overwhelmed by an overemphasis on intentionality—precisely because it cannot engage with *the unconscious*. For good or ill, that door was already foreclosed. [original emphasis][47]

At the end of his life, the preoccupying concerns Foucault left us were the analysis of biopower and governmentality, of the pervasive stitching together of governmental power in its biopolitical productive sense, and paradoxically an increasing focus on what might appear to be a solipsistic self-subjection, a focus on the moral and ethical "arts" of *askesis* by which individuals from antiquity to the rise and dominance of Christianity came to exercise their own practical subjection.[48] And, hence, it would seem that Hall's judgment undeniably carries force. How could Foucault relate these two concerns? By "foreclosing" psychoanalysis, how could he theorize that mediate space as other than a positivism, that space by which individuals would either be wholly subsumed within larger discursive currents or possessing of a transcendental agency, ethical or otherwise?

Hall's pronouncement is neither the first nor the last in judging a limit in Foucault over his foreclosure of psychoanalysis. Certainly, Judith Butler has made the intersection of Foucault and psychoanalysis a central thematic for her theorizing. Jacques Derrida titled his memorial to Foucault "To Do Justice to Freud."[49] More reductively, Joel Whitebook critiques Foucault's rejection of psychoanalysis, attributing it to "rivalry," among other factors.[50] Clearly, Foucault had a troubled relationship with psychoanalysis not just on the level of ideas but also on a personal level during his graduate studies.[51] But, rather than psychoanalyze Foucault or defend Foucault against psychoanalysis, perhaps it might be better to resituate Foucault's "foreclosure" and ask where we might *locate* this foreclosure. Hall's passage presumes that psychoanalysis became an increasingly latent concern for Foucault, a concern he could not engage because he had already excluded psychoanalysis, placing it as an object *outside* his own theorizing. Instead, we might see how psychoanalysis was an *interior* concern for Foucault from the beginning, an internal/interred problematic that propelled Foucault progressively outward even as his theorizing took on/incorporated something of an *ethos* opened by psychoanalysis.

Certainly, from beginning to end, Foucault exhibited a productive uneasiness in thinking about psychoanalysis. His first book, *Mental Illness and Psychology*, attempted to push beyond psychoanalysis, arguing in the original version for locating the understanding of the mentally ill within a Marxist-inspired account of the social and economic context. In the second edition, Foucault dropped the Marxist optic, locating instead the account of the mentally ill within a Heideggerian existential analysis of the cultural conditions of possibility for the very idea of mental pathology. This second edition, revised in 1962, brought the analysis of *Mental Illness and Psychology* in line with his just published *Madness and Civilization*, in which he charted the emergence of madness as Reason's interred Other. Yet even this revised edition left him unsatisfied, and Foucault refused the reprint rights to the first edition as well as unsuccessfully trying to block the translation rights to the second edition.[52] Indeed, Foucault's dissatisfaction with his theoretical formulations in these early texts would continue on to the very end of his life. In the original preface to his *History of Sexuality*, Volume 2 (published in 1984), Foucault would return to these early steps, confessing his own dissatisfaction with the "theoretical weakness" of his "earlier project" over the "notion of experience."[53] Moreover, in retracing this earlier problematic in his thinking, Foucault seems to signal its link to the lengthy publication delay between the first two volumes of *The History of Sexuality*, suggesting its connection for him to the dramatic change in emphasis between those two volumes. For if the first volume depicted psychoanalysis as part of a network of power relations constituting sexuality, the second can be said to reconsider the implications of this "present," rummaging around in antiquity for the degrees of freedom leading up to that present.

Clearly, in this characterization, we can see the elements of Foucault's refocused genealogical method. But in his relationship to a certain psychoanalytic problematic, one can see also the unique contributions Foucault made in sharpening something of the cathected structure of his own genealogical approach. For if Nietzschean genealogy became something of a "revelation" for Foucault sometime around 1953, it could do so only by way of an already existing problem that confronted Foucault—in other words, genealogy became a means of return rather than a free-floating method.[54] We might venture to encapsulate this earlier problem as the question of mental illness's *present* and, along with it, the "enigmatic" status of its isolation and internment.

The great quarrel Foucault had with psychoanalysis, psychiatry, and psychology was their impulses to drive whatever insights they yielded *inward* into a metaphysical space of individual interiority, that is, their presumption of crafting an objective *knowledge* of the individual psyche.[55] From his first book and some of his earliest publications, however, Foucault's interest in mental illness was always in pushing the other way, in expanding the "secret of its enigmatic status" outward as yielding insights into a larger domain of significations.[56] But exactly how to conceptualize that outwardly disclosing enigmatic secret of the mentally ill and, later, the criminal, the delinquent, and the deviant would become a productive problematic for Foucault in what seems to me to be a specifically antimelancholic Nietzschean *and* psychoanalytic ethos.[57] For if in "Dream, Imagination, and Existence," Foucault would argue that the experience of "time is in essence nostalgic," circularly reiterative in which "absence is always a pledge of return," Foucault would return again and again throughout his life to what might be called the compensating consolations of experience—its capacity to reflect, remember, and reconstitute prior experiences and meanings—of both a "whole nucleus of significations" and his own attempts to grapple with them.[58] And in these returns, one can see once again his impulse in expanding outward his appropriation of the psychoanalytic import attached to fantasy and dreams, extending its purview to include discursive formations more generally and the development of scientific knowledge. Foucault's famous quote at the very end of *The Archaeology of Knowledge* therefore evinces something of Foucault's own Nietzschean and psychoanalytic debts, something of an admonition against his own theoretical consolations:

> Discourse is not life: its time is not your time; in it, you will not be reconciled to death; you may have killed God beneath the weight of all that you said; but don't imagine that, with all that you are saying, you will make a man that will live longer than he.[59]

Nietzschean genealogy, therefore, revealed for Foucault a means of breaking a stalemate in his thinking on mental illness and psychoanalysis. Not only did it yield a path toward broaching the divide between psychoanalytic concepts of interiority and his outward aims of linking them back into a larger world; it also gave him a conceptual engine with which to critique and understand discourse. But it needs to be remembered that Foucault's own methodological negotiations were neither smooth nor untroubled, both in how he was perceived and in his own compensating obfuscations. *The Archaeology of Knowledge* was, after all, a clarifying response to how *The Order of Things* was misread. That text had been perceived by many as part of the structuralist deluge then ascendant. And, paradoxically, Foucault's attempt to comprehensively show the discontinuity in the rise of the human sciences easily lent an obfuscating totalizing coherence against the book's very aim. More important, Foucault's lifelong interest in "recovering" something of the "enigmatic secret" of the interred Other often led to flirtations with twin compensations: on the one hand the quest to recover/liberate the truth of the interred other in its own right and on the other hand the propensity to give a discursive formation in which the interred other becomes its condition of possibility, a totalizing, paralyzing coherence. Whether in the desire to recover the subjectivity of madness before the advent of the Age of Reason as in *Madness and Civilization* or in what is often perceived as his totalizing accounts of the rise of networks of power oriented around disciplinary biopower or governmentality, Foucault revealed genealogical antimelancholic impulses that could be effaced through his own rhetorical desires. Though Foucault's desire to recover some innate or original truth of the interred Other was disabused fairly early on,[60] certainly the perception of Foucault as painting a pervasive iron cage persists. Perhaps one could say that even if Foucault developed an "interpretive analytics" that sought to go "beyond hermeneutics and structuralism," he was not immune to the consolations of a hermeneutics of suspicion.

Foucault's work, especially prior to *Discipline and Punish*, is thus rife with shifting, clarifying methodological forays and experiments, a journey that was as much an exploration of Nietzsche as it was a work on his own psychoanalytic attachments. One of the more important "scaffolds" of his theorizing was a short article, "Of Other Spaces," first given as a radio broadcast, then as a lecture to a group of architects in 1967. It was not published until after his death and then translated into English in two versions.[61] Despite its brevity, many commentators over the years have found it highly suggestive, particularly in its conceptualization of "heterotopia" as a different kind of space, a conceptualization that suggests a space of resistance and an emancipatory promise.[62] Yet Foucault's discussion of heterotopic spaces remains elusive and confusing in this text, further borne out by the divergences in its treatment by commentators. Indeed, Foucault himself dropped further mention of the term subsequently. Still, its dilemmas document something of Foucault's developing methodological concerns and yield an important cautionary insight for any attempts to interpret from a Foucauldian position. In it one can see the increasing specification of his Nietzschean and psychoanalytically inflected approach to discourse in three dimensions: first, in pushing outward the interiority of fantasy and dreams onto the register of discursively constituted space; second, in conceptualizing the problematizing links between such spaces and "reality"; and third, in flirting with the possibility of finding a space that would not adhere to a compensating fiction or a sacrelizing desire.

Perhaps the most important conceptual move of this article is his attempt to think the specificity of our historical epoch in terms of space and this in a clearly psychoanalytic sense. He states, "Our epoch is one in which space takes for us the form of relations among sites. In any case I believe that the anxiety of our era has to do fundamentally with space."[63] Clarifying what he means by anxiety, Foucault describes how emplacement becomes the means to express a kind of psychoanalytic splitting driven by a Nietzschean form of sacrelizing desire. Hence, "our life is still governed by a certain number of oppositions that remain inviolable, that our institutions and practices have not yet dared to break down. These are oppositions that we regard as simple givens: for example between private space and public space, between family space and social space, between cultural space and useful space, between the space of leisure and that of work. All these are still nurtured by the hidden presence of the sacred."[64] Calling them "thoroughly fantasmatic," Foucault nevertheless distinguishes his approach to these oppositional spaces not primarily in terms of their interiority but in terms of their implications in "external space." He states, "the space in which we live, which draws us out of ourselves, in which the erosion of our lives, our time and our history occurs, the space that claws and gnaws at us, is also, in itself, a heterogeneous space."[65] Hence, whatever may be said about the fantasies expressed in and internalized by such spaces, Foucault's concern is also how such spaces are imbricated within a heterogeneous reality. Hence, like his studies of the birth of the asylum, the interring of the mentally ill is not simply exhausted in its productivity for elaborating a discourse of normalized reason but also serves as an actual external space with heterogeneous implications.

It is in the interest therefore of analyzing the spacings of our historical epoch, both fantasmatic and heterogeneously external, that Foucault introduces the concept of heterotopia and this in opposition to utopian spaces. Certain sites, he tells us, "have the curious propensity of being in relation with all other sites, but in such a way as to suspect, neutralize, or invert the set of relations that they happen to designate, mirror or reflect."[66] Such sites hold a central importance because they serve as a lynchpin for understanding the spatial relations of many other sites. One could conceive of these central sites as utopian, Foucault goes on, because they themselves have "no real place" even as they serve to shape the relations of many other spaces. And, like utopias, they exist in complex relations with the actual world, allowing one to "suspect, neutralize, or invert" one's relation to the actual world. Utopian spaces therefore serve as a kind of "mirror" that presents "society itself in a perfected form, or else society turned upside down."[67] Bentham's panopticon could therefore be a kind of utopian dreamspace, encapsulating within itself a space that could shape one's view of society. Continuing the mirror metaphor, however, Foucault dispenses with the analysis of such central spaces as utopian. This is because to do so would be to concentrate solely on the reflection enabled by a mirror rather than on the space of the mirror itself. And for that, Foucault introduces the term "heterotopia." For even if the mirror allows a "placeless place," the mirror itself "exists in reality." "Heterotopology," therefore, becomes the term by which Foucault attempts to understand such central spaces not just in terms of the organizing reflections they enable for society at large but also something of their actual locations in society.[68] A "reading" of this kind therefore analyzes such central spaces as "simultaneously mythic and [involving] real contestation of the space in which we live."

Foucault goes on to develop five general principles about heterotopias. He states that heterotopias can be found in all cultures and that the same heterotopias can function differently in other cultures depending as they do on the "synchrony of the culture in which it occurs." He therefore gives the example of the cemetery whose interred space is "unlike ordinary cultural spaces" and has undergone important changes. For instance, he notes how "it is from the beginning of the nineteenth century that everyone has a right to her or his own little box for her or his own little personal decay" but also notes how this corresponds to a geographic shift as cemeteries were placed "at the outside border of cities" and through the bourgeois "individualization of death . . . as an 'illness.'"[69] Further developing the synchronic functions of a heterotopia, Foucault states as his third principle the capability of a heterotopia to juxtapose "in a single real place several spaces, several sites that are in themselves incompatible."[70] He suggests that the garden is perhaps the oldest example of a heterotopia that juxtaposes contradictory sites, discussing how the ancient Persians saw the garden as a "sacred space that was supposed to bring together inside its rectangle four parts representing the four parts of the world" and how carpets were originally reproductions of gardens housing this same juxtaposed symbolism.[71] Befitting their involvement in enabling a sense of the sacred, Foucault then discusses as his fourth and fifth principles the ability of heterotopia to organize chronicity (with the museum and library as his prime examples) and its bounded systems of openings and closings, permitting the terms and rituals of entry.

As a "countersite" allowing discriminating commentary and reflection on society and in its contradistinction to utopian propensities, Foucault's notion of heterotopia could easily be seen as an attempt to find those interred hybrid spaces of a society through which resistance can be imagined. Certainly, the notion of recovering heterotopic sites in society as resources for resistance has figured large in the reception to Foucault's article. Indeed, Foucault does valorize heterotopia, concluding his article by discussing how the "ship is the heterotopia *par excellence*. In civilizations without boats, dreams dry up, espionage takes the place of adventure, and the police take the place of pirates."[72] And, hence, the search for heterotopia could be interpreted as the search for *spaces* of resistance and therefore the attempt to valorize such spaces as implicitly resistant and, more important, implicitly *utopian*.

If one senses a trap here, it is because Foucault's discussion of heterotopia is far more complex and ambivalent. Many of the examples he gives (e.g., the museum, the military, the colony) are clearly unsavory in their relevance for organizing Western modernity. What I argue Foucault valorizes in his use of heterotopia is a certain approach to such spaces, rather than the inherent qualities of the spaces themselves. This is clear when we consider his concluding remarks on the two "extreme poles" toward which heterotopia can function in relation to all other spaces. As in his early discussions of utopian spaces as placeless places of illusion, heterotopias also encompass a space of illusion. Indeed, his last sentence about civilizations in which "dreams dry up" indicates the valorized importance for Foucault of such illusory spaces. But, as with his use of the metaphor of the mirror, one must see heterotopic spaces not solely in the illusory reflections they enable, in the escape routes they enliven but also in terms of the actual relations out of which they emerge, of the relations between the actual space of the mirror and the society that valorizes that space. But this move does not then displace illusion in favor of a more truthful "reality" but *spirals* out to see such actual relations as themselves illusory, the residuum of prior illusions. One must set them alongside one another, analyze the point of their tense connections. Heterotopology seeks to recover the illusory imaginative qualities of these central organizing sites of a society but sees them in a complex problematizing relation to the "reality" of that society—and this in a way as to enable one's imagination not to remain fixated on the utopian "placeless places" they call forth but to imagine those problematizing relations as themselves capable of change. The problem, Foucault's article eventually identifies, is what he terms the heterotopia of *compensation*:

> Heterotopias . . . unfold between two extreme poles. Either their role is to create a space of illusion that exposes every real space, all the sites in which human life is partitioned, as *still more illusory*. . . . Or else, on the contrary, their role is to create a space that is other, another real space, as perfect, as meticulous, as well arranged as ours is messy, ill-constructed, and jumbled. This latter type would be the heterotopia, not of illusion, but of compensation. . . . [emphasis added][73]

If, from Nietzsche, Foucault saw heterotopias as nurturing the "hidden presence of the sacred," perhaps the key word for Foucault was "hidden." In other words, perhaps the task of imagining such heterotopias differently was not to eliminate the dividing practices through which the sacred is enabled (as if this were possible) but to free the ability for a society to dissolve its hidden melancholic attachment to a particular conception of the sacred, thereby freeing its potential imaginative possibilities in the finitude of the life we breathe into them. And likewise if, in a psychoanalytic sense, heterotopias of compensation result in a paralyzed fracture of the imagination, one must reimagine and rework those spaces and their imaginative content in such a way as to dissolve the originating nexus of their fracture. But both, for Foucault, must be brought back in relation to the problematizing link that propels the illusory compensations of discourse with the actual relations synchronizing society. And both must then do so in such a way that does not then fall back on merely a more foundational compensation or on privileging either the domain of discourse or the domain of "reality."

Ultimately, what I argue Foucault meant by the concept of heterotopia was to link the imaginative dimensions of discourse with its problematizing and privileging locations in the spacings of societal relations. It was not a concept or a program in finding spaces that were implicitly either oppressive or emancipatory since both views rest on the utopian compensations of their own imagination. Rather, it was an attempt by Foucault in articulating his approach to discourse at the point of its emergence out of societal anxieties and its ability to reshape the actual spatial relations of societal reality. It was not the inwardly confined search for an alternative space or a more truthful originating space but the attempt to view those imaginative links as spiraling outward, necessarily heterogeneous, overflowing their boundaries, allowing one to problematize the lines of other spaces, and thereby imaginatively practicing change.[74] Foucault of course never subsequently made use of the concept of heterotopia. Perhaps he felt it was too easily misread as an effort to find a compensating alternative space; perhaps he felt that it represented an effort that had not fully broken with either the compensations of finding the "enigmatic secret" of the interred other or its counterpart in suspecting the privileged coherence of an encompassing discourse. Whatever the case, genealogy would become the preferred term. But in the dilemmas of this short article one can see how it is important to view his subsequent treatments of discursive formations, their ability to create interred spaces, with a cautionary about their presumed compensations as well as our own in reflecting upon them. It is with this in mind that I now turn to his reflections on the discourse of liberal governmentality.

LIBERAL GOVERNMENTALITY AND ITS SACRED PROMISES

> It cannot be said, then, that liberalism is a utopia never realized. . . . It is not a dream that comes up against reality and fails to find a place within it.
>
> —Foucault[75]

Perhaps apocryphally, Foucault is said to have told the audience during his 1979 Collège de France lecture series that if they wanted to understand the "will not to be governed," they should study the work of F. A. Hayek.[76] Hayek of course was an economist and philosopher whose books *The Road to Serfdom* (1944) and *The Constitution of Liberty* (1960) defended the promise of laissez-faire liberalism and the autonomy of the market order as the best guarantee of liberty in the context of the Cold War and the increasing state interventionism of liberal democracies in the postwar years. And Foucault's 1979 lectures were the culmination of his developing reflections on modern governmentality begun in the mid-1970's.[77] Specifically, the 1979 lectures, titled "The Birth of Biopolitics," dealt with the rise of problems within governmental discourse and rationality in the nineteenth and twentieth centuries over questions associated with populations (e.g., issues of "health, sanitation, birthrate, longevity, race . . .") but became largely focused on an exploration of their emergent connections within the advent of a particular governmental rationality and practice, that of liberalism in the eighteenth century. Certainly, toward the end of the lecture series, Foucault and his coresearchers considered the work of Hayek among others, since they focused on the postwar rise of neoliberal currents in Germany and the United States. And in their analyses of these neoliberal currents, they saw the return of an enduring and recurrent form of liberal reflection on the "art" of limited government, one that was of course mutating into different technological practices of government but one that nevertheless retained something of a core problematic.

For Foucault, liberalism could be fruitfully accessed not as either a static set of ideas or a set of developing juridical arrangements but as a "tool for criticizing reality." Liberalism was therefore a specific kind of technological rationale involving an ethos and recurrent reflection on the limits of government. Refusing both juridical and abstract considerations of liberalism according to utopian principles of contractualism and the Marxist reduction of this ideological domain as a mere cover for the structural conditions of capitalism's development, Foucault sought to explore the specificity of liberalism's recurrent *problematic* within the interface between the two, taking seriously on the one hand the liberal principle that "government . . . cannot be its own end" and on the other the sanctified circumscribing of *homo economicus* as constituting the autonomous domain and limit through which human flourishing and governmental survival were both to be obtained. Hence, for Foucault, "actually existing liberalism" did not arise until the debates over political economy in the eighteenth century had matured into an internalized criticism of previous governmental reliance on "State reason." If the mercantilists still had as their objective the wealth and might of the sovereign and the physiocrats attempted to divine a formula through which such wealth could be maximized, it was not until classical political economy pronounced an inscrutable and totemic limit in the manipulation of commerce for governmental aims that liberalism as an art of "frugal government" was born.[78] Adam Smith is of course a pivotal figure here, making the question of the counterproductiveness of excessive government and the mysterious workings of an autonomous commercial *society* a recurrent liberal problematic, both as a form of skeptical, corrective governmental reflection of its own aims and as a technological incitement to know and nurture the preconditions of *homo economicus*.

Foucault believed that it was only in taking seriously this evolving liberal discourse over the limits of governmental practice and its privileged elevation of the "market" as the ultimate "test" and "locus" of human flourishing that one could explain and make sense of the paradoxical expansion of governmental power in the nineteenth and twentieth centuries along a biopolitical normalizing and disciplinary axis, whose rationale does not spring from a "totalized government" but one that seeks to economize on its own costs in the interest of maximizing the life and liberty of its population.[79] The liberal art of governing then is not so much about governing less "but about the continual injunction that politicians and rulers should govern cautiously, delicately, economically, modestly."[80] Foucault states:

> It is here that the question of liberalism comes up. It seems to me that at that very moment it became apparent that if one governed too much, one did not govern at all—that one provoked results contrary to those one desired. What was discovered at that time . . . was the idea of *society*. That is to say, that government not only has to deal with a territory, with a domain, and with its subjects, but that it also has to deal with a complex and independent reality that has its own laws and mechanisms of disturbance. This new reality is society. . . . One must take into account what it is. It becomes necessary to reflect upon it, upon its specific characteristics, its constants and its variables.[81]

Liberal political reason therefore establishes the historical condition and marks out a field of concerns in which civil society becomes the autonomous domicile of human nature and activity. For the ensuing development of the human sciences, such concerns "are as much *technical* as they are political and ideological."[82] For if social scientific knowledge cannot be reduced to the aims of government, it nevertheless serves as a crucial tool of criticism and correction of the limits of liberal governmentality from within its problematic, a limit that serves not as an absolute bar or barrier to its *techne* but instead as an incitement all the more to refine its aims and shape its outcomes through a mediated distance.[83] It is important therefore to see how Foucault's understanding of liberal political reason mediates and innovates upon the "pastoral power" he elaborated in earlier reflections on governmentality.[84] If Western governmentality inherited from Christian thought an individualizing, particularizing concern over tending to the well-being of one's flock, Foucault's reflections on liberal governmentality stress the imperative that such concern cannot come from above, cannot come directly through the aims of government but must come through the inculcation within the particulars of civil society of one's own self-discipline and normalized correction.

It should be remembered that Foucault's term is the neologism "governmentality" rather than government. Hence, his concern and interest lay in the discourse through which the space of government itself was recurrently given shape as well as those successively elaborated spaces posited as objects of govern*mental* concern and limit, in particular, those interiorized spaces through which liberal citizens learn to valorize/demonize as prime indicators of self-governance. The rationality and source of pastoral power come then not from government but must come from *society*, from within the "flock" as it were—or, more specifically, as one can begin to see, from a particular internment of the social that gives "birth to values." And as "society" comes to know itself, this propels two trajectories: on the one hand an inwardly driven concern for normalization and on the other the outward posited governmental concern toward the correction of pathological deviance. Here one can see a link drawn to the analysis of the crusading moralism so central to American political development in James Morone's *Hellfire Nation*.[85] Here also, one can see one of the central "dilemmas" of African American political discourse; that between struggles against governmental subjection and exclusion and its oft-present counterpart, the dilemmas of African American self-improvement, self-help, self-economizing. For perhaps nothing is more central to liberal governmentality than the critique of the corruptive failure and tyrannical perversions of past governmental aims, and yet always lurking subsequently is the question of the rededication of *society* toward its cherished values of freedom and autonomy. Such "pathologies" as race then become the ultimate catalyst for a feedback loop, propelling a progressive elaboration of the "problem" of race.

In their explorations of contemporary neoliberal currents, Foucault and his coresearchers attempted to explain both neoliberal's technical innovations as well as its return to an enduring liberal problematic. For them, American neoliberalism, associated with the Chicago school of the postwar years, developed in reaction to the "excessive government exhibited in its eyes . . . by the New Deal, war planning, and the great economic and social programs generally supported by postwar Democratic administrations."[86] But far more than a negative critique of the welfare state and economic interventionism, Foucault saw in these currents a radicalizing technical innovation. If classical laissez-faire liberalism attached a naturalism to civil society and *homo economicus* and the rise of the liberal welfare state attempted to ameliorate the margins of its outcomes while otherwise nurturing the capacities of economic autonomy, American neoliberalism exhibits a behavioral "constructivist" impulse to extend the dynamics of the market to other domains, including government itself.[87] It seeks to "extend the rationality of the market, the schemes of analysis it proposes, and the decisionmaking criteria it suggests to areas that are not exclusively or not primarily economic. For example the family and birth policy, or delinquency and penal policy."[88] Society itself is therefore deemed to be insufficient for a market order, and all human activity therefore is to be judged and understood within the purview of one's aptitude in economizing "purposive conduct entailing strategic choices between alternative paths, means, and instruments."[89] Positing a radical faculty of choice, the proper task of government is to thus train the values of seeing one's entire life as an enterprise of self-capitalization, and government itself becomes posited as a second-order market of goods and services whose regulatory functions, to the extent necessary, are geared toward this functionality.[90] For American neoliberalism, then, the sanctification of the market and its dynamics no longer marks a cautionary limit to governmental action nor even a privileged frame of reference for public policy but represents the fullest expression and ideal of its constructive objectives.

In focusing on the technological developments of liberal governmentality, Foucault's reflections thus seem to disclose an inexorable logic of the liberal mode of government, one where its ever-tightening chains of biopolitical knowledge and power yield ever increasing pressures for the extension of normalization and discipline into the capillaries of the body politic, whose strength and resilience come not through a totalizing power from above but, paradoxically, through the persuasiveness and innocuousness of its reflections on the limits of government with regard to maximizing human autonomy, freedom, and flourishing. Yet this would give the course of liberal regimes a coherence belying the heterogeneity of their historical trajectories, their historical particulars. In our own contemporary period, neoliberalism constitutes only one strand amid a variety of other interweaved discourses despite indications of its undeniable presence (e.g., notions of the stakeholder society, calls for reorienting government services according to "user fees," the privatization of governmental responsibilities from prisons and schools to the military). At best, they outline a general plan of research, as Foucault himself stated, whose benefits lie in refusing the static polarity between the utopian consolations of liberal abstract theorizing and the Marxist reduction of political development according to a determining ground of capitalist development. If liberalism is a dream that nevertheless finds a "place" in reality, it must not be forgotten that it is a "dream" whose compensations and reflections are propelled by particular understandings, particular internments of historically *heterogeneous* problems.

Foucault's work on governmentality was therefore geared toward illuminating an enduring if many-sided liberal *problematic*: that of the birth and rise of commercial society as possessing its own autonomous dynamics. Commercial society became a *question* for early liberal theorists, an emerging space enabling a dream of human freedom and autonomy *against* the direct intentions and grasp of sovereign monarchical power. But, in the process, commercial society became progressively sanctified as the privileged guarantor of human freedom and autonomy, an interred space inciting a need to refine a knowledge of its boundaries, an imagined object inviting biopolitical supplements to its magical properties, generating a manifold impulse to guard against, correct, and exclude those pathologies that jeopardize its promise.[91] Though Foucault did not develop this line of argument, liberalism's problematic of sanctifying commercial society and *homo economicus* could be inferred as its ultimate heterotopia of compensation. And if so, the task is not to trust or suspect the pervasiveness of its discourse or even its inevitable consequences but to show how they emerge from problems whose particular shape can be seen as "still more illusory."[92] It is in this spiraling that Foucault's contentions on governmentality and ethical freedom begin to make sense. For if the condition of possibility for ethical freedom lies in the ability to reflect upon one's problematic present, it consists not in the form of a utopian escape or in a binding resignation toward a problematic origin, but in sifting through and spiraling out the lines of prior illusory reflections. As Hartz, discussed in chapter 3, argued, the question of an enduring American liberal discourse should fall not on either a trust or suspicion of its pervasiveness or even on a rejection of its illusions, but on how something of its dream could be magnified and persist in the presence/absence of the "problem" of race and therefore the need to "read" and practice these paralyzed fractures differently.

THE EPIDEMIOLOGY OF RACE, POVERTY, AND ETHNICITY

> The object, then, was not the elimination of poverty but the discipline of the poor. . . . The answer to the problem . . . to separate dangerous free whites from dangerous slave blacks.
>
> —Edmund Morgan[93]

> What would need to be studied now, therefore, is the way in which the specific problems of life and population were raised within a technology of government which, without always having been liberal—far from it—was always haunted since the end of the eighteenth century by liberalism's question.
>
> —Michel Foucault[94]

In the introduction to *Coping: Essays on the Practice of Government*, Daniel Patrick Moynihan's 1972 edited collection of his reflections on the tumultuousness of the decade prior, Moynihan isolated what was for him something of the prime lesson he drew from his intimate involvement in the shifts of that period. For him, the lesson of his experience was that the "*crucial stage in solving a problem in government is that point where one defines what kind of problem it is* . . . the process of careful definition can have a quality of revelation, and the experience becomes all the more intense when it emerges that others cannot or will not follow" (original emphasis).[95] Of course, Moynihan's reflections are not of those of a philosopher from on high but are filled with layers of his own self-ironizing and pathos. After all, there was perhaps no other person as prominently engaged as Moynihan during the 1960s in uniting the domains of social scientific problem-solving and the crafting of public policy. Moynihan's reflections thus encompass an acknowledgment of his own hubris early on but also something of an accusation that others misunderstood him or, worse, proceeded upon a wrong or "ill-stated problem." The most intense backdrop for his reflections were of course the controversies over the Moynihan Report, *The Negro Family: The Case for National Action*, in which one witnessed both his exuberance at problem redescription and, in its fallout, the corrective lessons he learned through which one can identify him as a consummate liberal interlocutor in the Foucauldian sense. Indeed, in his essay "Liberalism and Knowledge," Moynihan offered himself "in a spirit not of apology, but merely of preface," as a lesson in navigating the dangerous waters between liberalism and knowledge, by which he meant the hubristic optimism placed in the "curious synthesis of statistics and opinion which has emerged from the breeding of truth with technology. In a word, to social science."[96] Of course, Moynihan's lesson was not simply a rejection of the promise of social scientific knowledge, naïve or otherwise, but a more cathected contextual confluence emerging out of the indictments of race, poverty, and ethnicity. What Moynihan objected to was the rise of the "professionalization of reform" from the mid-'60s on, spawned by the radicalizing of racial and class indictments, in which liberal reformers, pursuing an erroneous problem definition, were jeopardizing the promise of liberal limited government.

One can clearly see the irony of Moynihan's own involvement in elevating the promise of social scientific knowledge in his early work in the late 1950s and the mid–'60s on traffic safety. In essays such as "Epidemic on the Highways" and "Traffic Safety and the Body Politic," Moynihan sought a different approach to the increasing problem of traffic-related deaths.[97] What was clear to him was that a stalemate had been reached between legislative proposals that treated traffic safety as an issue of law-breaking—that is, invoking a kind of sovereign injunction against drivers—and those that saw traffic safety as an issue of profiteering—that is, penalizing the auto industry. Either instance became stalemated in a heavy-handed governmental approach to the problem. Instead, Moynihan proposed a different regulatory description of the problem, one that sought a social scientific approach to traffic safety in terms of public health and safety, one that treated traffic safety in terms of the language of epidemiology, one that therefore would avoid excessive governmental intrusion into the autonomy of drivers and automobile manufacturers, instead seeking gently to nudge corrective and preventive behavior. As he stated:

> The point is that traffic accidents are part of the general phenomenon of accidents, which have become the largest single cause of death between ages one and thirty-five for most of the industrial nations of the world. They are a particular aspect of our culture. . . . Just as classical forms of disease were in general treated by magic until perhaps two centuries ago, accidents have until this moment been thought of as somehow "wild" occurrences which do not conform to the sequential chain of causal events that define the way things in general take place . . . [but] the etiology of the accident . . . is, in fact, fundamentally similar to disease. . . .[98]

Moynihan thus sought to redefine the problem of auto safety in terms of public health and therefore as "a problem for scientists" that "could in the end produce less bureaucracy, less harassment, less regulation, less intimidation, insult, and coercion."[99] The promise of an epidemiological approach to social problems like auto safety thus lay in investigating "why disease and injury afflict some people more than others, and why they occur more frequently in some locations and times than at others . . . in the epidemiological approach to public health problems, 'the primary units of concern are *groups* of persons, not separate individuals' " (original emphasis).[100]

Of course, momentously, Moynihan did not restrict his epidemiological approach to the body politic in terms of the problem of traffic safety but also began to assert ethnicity as an epidemiological tool in the understanding of American political, social, and economic life, particularly in the urban North. Thus, his book *Beyond the Melting Pot*, coauthored with Nathan Glazer in 1963, attempted to illuminate the differential experiences and issues confronting *groups* of persons in New York City qua their ethnic cohesiveness.[101] But two things in particular stand out with regard to the aims of their book, undergirding the epidemiological social scientific perspective with which they approached the question of ethnicity. First, the assimilative approach to American social and political life ideologically obscured the actual pathways through which immigrant and racial groups had come to find their niche within the body politic, what we would now call their means of acculturation. In calling attention to ethnicity, then, the authors were only secondarily interested in making an ideological argument about cultural pluralism. Rather, their interest lay in yielding more insightful and thicker accounts explaining, say, the prevalence of Irish in the fading "machine governments" of many Northern cities or the special difficulties confronting Negroes and Puerto Ricans in taking advantage of the educational system or their concentration in lower-paying occupations. Calling their book "a beginning book," Moynihan and Glazer took an approach to ethnicity that was very much in the tradition of Robert Park. Ethnic culture was an object for them interesting in its motion, a set of intragroup relationships that shaped behavior, itself adapting to or finding difficulty in changing contextual circumstances. It was not ethnicity as a kind of indelible heritage or insular programming that made it interesting for them but rather that "as the groups were transformed by influences in American society, stripped of their original attributes, they were recreated as *something new*, but still as identifiable groups" (emphasis added).[102] It was therefore almost a meaningless aside to assert that the American social fabric would continue to be shaped by differences in ethnic-group adaptation. Of course it would. One need only look at how things worked in New York City to see how self-evident that maxim was.

Second, ethnic culture was a universal tool for assessing dynamic group behavior. Perhaps not all aspects of American social, political, or economic life could be saliently understood through ethnic group behavior—though in their more assertive moments the authors could claim that "ethnic identity is an element in all equations"[103]—but, since ethnic culture was for them a variable placeholder allowing a holistic approach to group location and mobility, it was likely never very far from the surface of such questions. Hence, for them all groups could be assessed in terms of their ethnic relational ties. Indeed, in New York, they considered ethnic groups to be a synonym for *interest group*:

> This is perhaps the single most important fact about ethnic groups in New York City. When one speaks of the Negroes and Puerto Ricans, one also means unorganized and unskilled workers, who hold poorly paying jobs in the laundries, hotels, restaurants, small factories or who are in relief. When one says Jews, one also means small shopkeepers, professionals, better-paid skilled workers in the garment industries. When one says Italians, one also means homeowners in Staten Island, the North Bronx, Brooklyn and Queens.[104]

Ian Haney Lopez makes much of this dimension of their argument, seeing it ominously as an early instance of the eventual evacuation of the specifically racial and structural claims of discrimination enacted through this ethnic interest group leveling. If all ethnic groups are merely interest groups, then the claims of a particular ethnic/racial group are merely those cited in pursuit of a specific group interest and therefore cannot possess any distinctiveness for governmental redress apart from the claims of other such interest groups. Certainly by the 1970s, ethnicity studies in general and Nathan Glazer's work in particular would bear out this line of argument in terms of the backlash against affirmative action.[105] But to read this ideological argument too strongly into their book at this point is to make too hasty a judgment. It would completely evacuate the special if ambivalent concern with which Moynihan would approach "the Negro problem" in his Report barely two years later. Indeed, why argue "The Case for National Action" at all if African Americans were just another interest group? Rather, the book's emphasis lies in presenting and testing what the authors considered to be a new, comprehensive tool in the understanding of the mobility (or lack thereof) of groups in American urban life. For Moynihan at least, there was a certain exuberance in treating ethnic culture as a new promising epidemiological instrument, one where the arguments and conclusions of their analyses of particular ethnic groups were clearly of secondary importance to the social scientific possibilities afforded by the concept itself. In other words, they did not conceive of ethnicity as a social scientific concept in order to advance a particular argument or hidden agenda, political or ideological, but saw ethnicity as a way to generate more insightful understandings of the dynamism of American life[106] and, for Moynihan, yield better approaches to social problems.

Still, Lopez's argument focuses on a consequential dimension of their conceptual universalism. For if all or most cultural group behavior could be placed under the sign of ethnicity, then race and racial cultural behavior were likewise placed on the same analytic continuum. One of the more startling results of their book was therefore their comparative treatment of Jews, Italians, blacks, and Puerto Ricans without a priori qualitative distinctions.[107]

In short, though differences in starting circumstances mattered a great deal, the significant conclusions to be found lay not for them in the past but in the dynamism of their present circumstances, that is to say, in the capacities of their ethnic cultural resilience to adapt and thrive within the American milieu. And clearly, qua their ethnic cultural identity and practices, Negroes and Puerto Ricans were judged lacking. Already, special emphasis was placed on family structure, both in the sense of extended family networks capable of serving a support capacity and in their supposed patriarchal or matriarchal orientation. For Negroes, "they did not develop the same kind of clannishness [as European immigrant groups], they did not have the same close family ties, that in other groups created little pools for ethnic businessmen and professionals to tap. . . . The Negro family was not strong enough to create those extended clans that elsewhere were most helpful for businessmen and professionals."[108] Further, "The experience of slavery left as its most serious heritage a steady weakness in the Negro family. There was no marriage in the slave family—husbands could be sold away from wives, children from parents. There was no possibility of taking responsibility for one's children, for one had in the end no power over them."[109]

Ultimately, despite such comparative reflections, Moynihan and Glazer did not concentrate on solutions; their aim was to depict a world of transitions, adaptations, obstacles. They were not as yet against governmental programs in support of racial and ethnic minority groups.[110] They did not deny larger structural factors that shape the outcome of ethnic cultural group behavior. Rather, their claims at this point were more modest if darkly anticipatory: whatever structural features and historical origins shaped the circumstances of these groups, they also lived and thrived and met frustrations and obstacles in accordance with the adaptive resilience of their cultural practices. If one can charge the authors with a hidden agenda, it lay in a sacred faith in and sympathy for the ability of ethnic groups to enact varying degrees of autonomy, to instantiate through their ethnic cultural practices the ultimate validation of American freedom and mobility—not through assimilating but through carving their own distinctive interred niche. And, just as the study of ethnic culture could allow a return to that promise of autonomous freedom, so it was also that racial groups qua their ethnic cultural practices would become problematized anew.[111]

Any attempt to contextualize the surrounding period of Lyndon Johnson's Howard University Speech on June 4, 1965, and Moynihan's Report, *The Negro Family: The Case for National Action*, written in the winter of 1964–1965 and released to the public later in 1965, must therefore grapple with what appears from the present vantage point to be an estranging sight: an ambivalent nation on the move wary of dark storm clouds gathering. The Kennedy administration had successfully instilled a certain youthful "can do" spirit in government. American wealth and prosperity had built up a confidence that no social problem lay beyond the reach of willed determination and the right expertise. Those in support of the civil rights movement could credulously believe that the nation was finally addressing what many saw as its greatest sin and blemish, the exclusion and subordination of African Americans. The 1964 Civil Rights Act had banned discrimination in schools, employment, and public accommodations. Lyndon Johnson, playing second fiddle to no one, would push through the Voting Rights Act the following year, promising much more. But ominous signs were also undeniable. Michael Harrington's *The Other America*, published in 1963, disclosed a shocking sight for those accustomed to seeing America as a land of affluence: tens of millions of people "existing at levels beneath those necessary for human decency."[112] The Vietnam War was increasingly becoming an unavoidable topic of contention. Kennedy's assassination itself could be read as a cryptic portent. The Watts riot in 1965 would hammer home the growing disaffection within the urban cities outside of the south.

Moynihan's involvement in both the Howard University speech and in his Report demonstrates this ambivalence, and the two need to be read of a piece. It is common to view the Howard University speech as emblematic of Johnson's Great Society, as representing liberalism's finest hour, while vilifying the Moynihan Report, but the two are nearly identical in their argumentative structure except perhaps in where they place their emphasis. After all, Johnson's speech was a public event, whereas the Moynihan Report was an internal document. Where Johnson's speech appeals to a moral determination for national action, downplaying the ominous necessity for action in the face of growing urban disorder, the Moynihan Report begins with that necessity, premising itself on a "new crisis in race relations" and the national security imperative of "carrying forward" the "Negro American Revolution."[113] But action with regard to what problem and what question? Certainly, both the speech and the Report signal a shift then occurring in the civil rights era as its consideration began to encompass the deprivations of the urban North. With juridical barriers to racial integration and equality increasingly tumbling down, the problem of racial inequality and discrimination had come by contagion to problematize other issues, other spaces, in particular the pervasive conditions of poverty and egregious economic and social inequality. In a land with rising expectations of affluence in the face of a growing acknowledgment of an "Other America," the gap between the two came visible at a critical time, on the international stage as well as domestically, jeopardizing the promise of American freedom at one of its moments of greatest assertion.[114] Johnson's Howard University speech therefore pitches itself in seeking to nobly rise to the occasion of those expectations, with words so hallowed we hardly even pay notice:

> *Beyond the law lay the land. . . .* Here, unlike any place yet known, all were to share the harvest. . . . Each could become whatever his qualities of mind and spirit would permit—to strive, to seek, and, if he could, to find happiness. This is American justice. . . . It is the glorious opportunity of this generation to end the one huge wrong of the American

> Nation and, in so doing, to find America for ourselves, with the same immense thrill of discovery which gripped those who first began to realize that here, at last was a home for freedom. [emphasis added][115]

No doubt Johnson's speech (and the words of Daniel Patrick Moynihan and Richard N. Goodwin, the primary writers) are inspiring. It is a rousing reaffirmation of American exceptionalism. For many liberals today, particularly those who appeal to a lost moment over a liberal governmental approach to racial deprivation and economic inequality, Johnson's speech epitomizes that promise. But note already the ironic tension and ambivalence in Johnson's words. In the context of arguing for renewed national action "to fulfill these rights," Johnson appeals to a liberal creed that bounds its promise in a space *beyond the law*. There is thus already a hedging, an ambivalence, over the extent to which national action can guarantee "equality as a fact and as a result," the extent to which governmental redress can go beyond its sacred limits.[116] This ambivalence, more clearly delineated in the Moynihan Report, therefore houses a particular liberal problematizing question over the problem of race, poverty, and economic deprivation and is therefore haunted as well by the bounds of that very question: those between equality of opportunity and equality of results.

Both the Moynihan Report and the Howard University speech make the distinction between equal opportunity and equal results the fulcrum of their arguments. Where Johnson forcefully argues for equality of results, thereby signaling a new frontier in seeking to realize the dream of American freedom, the Moynihan Report is more measured, engaging in a philosophical discussion of "Liberty and Equality" as sometimes incompatible "twin ideals of American democracy."[117] In particular, the Report rhetorically posits the *demand* for equality of results to blacks and then considers its radical implications, citing Nathan Glazer: "The demand for economic equality is now not the demand for equal opportunities for the equally qualified: it is now . . . a demand for equality of results, of outcomes."[118] No doubt the differences between Johnson's speech and the Report on this score goes a long way toward explaining their different receptions. The speech clearly avoids any blame or attribution to blacks, consistently placing responsibility in the hands of the nation. Even when the speech goes on to discuss the Negro family, it is couched in sympathetic, therapeutic tones. Still, the Moynihan Report shares its commitment to national action, although driven not so much by collective responsibility but by national security: "The principal challenge of the next phase of the Negro revolution is to make certain that equality of results will now follow. If we do not, there will be no social peace in the United States for generations."[119]

Perhaps more tellingly, however, is that both center this divide between equality of opportunity and equality of results on the issue of black unemployment, specifically black male unemployment. When in the draft outline to his Report, Moynihan rhetorically asked, "What are we trying to change?" he had already interred an answer in addressing the issue of black unemployment. In his own slightly different published version of the Report (separate from the leaked report and its subsequent governmental release) in *Daedalus* in the fall of 1965, he would state:

> From the very outset, the principal measure of progress toward equality will be that of employment. . . . For the Negro American it is already, and will continue to be, the master problem. It is the measure of white bona fides. It is the measure of Negro competence, and *also of the competence of American society*. Most importantly, the linkage between problems of employment and the range of social pathology that afflicts the Negro community is unmistakable. Unemployment not only controls the present for the Negro American; but in a most profound way, it is creating the future as well. [emphasis added][120]

Employment was thus already the magical talisman through which the Negro problem and the promise of American autonomy were fatefully twinned. But rather than politically problematize the nation's capacity to realize this promise, Moynihan set off the Negro problem as an exception, an exception specifically formulated in comparison to other ethnic group cultures.

According to Moynihan's sympathetic biographer, "Moynihan and his team made a discovery" around this time, a statistical anomaly revelatory in its capacity to redefine the Negro problem and no doubt at the center of his feelings of resentment over being misunderstood in the fallout of the Moynihan Report.[121] Dubbed "Moynihan's scissors" by his friend James Q. Wilson, what Moynihan discovered was the statistical correlation of two lines, one representing black male unemployment, the other showing the take-up of Aid to Families with Dependent Children (AFDC). According to their logic and in the postwar numbers, the two lines ran closely parallel. But crucially in 1963, the lines "crossed." Even when black male unemployment dipped down, the caseload for AFDC continued to rise. Certainly if the economic sphere is the ultimate guarantor of prosperity and freedom, those lines crossing problematize that promise. Employment should allow one to pursue the American dream. But rather than spiraling out the implications of this problem, Moynihan spiraled them in. He would go on to measure black male unemployment with a variety of other indices within the black family, notably, the rate of illegitimate births, the rate of juvenile delinquency, the anomalous proportion of black female employment to male employment, the number of black households with the father absent or divorced. What "Moynihan's scissors" revealed to him was that the problem of black unemployment had its roots elsewhere. Liberal compensatory efforts to increase black employment alone would be futile. The dimensions of the problem—"capable of perpetuating itself without assistance from the white world"—required a liberal cultural supplement/intervention into the family.

Foucault's biopolitical spiral was at work, moving out of the domain of work as it were. Explicitly drawing on psychoanalytic theory, Moynihan highlighted the importance of one's family upbringing, not so much in terms of mental health but, now, with regard to the building and nurturing of human capital. Slavery, systemic discrimination, segregation—all of these legacies were not denied but channeled with regard to their consequences for the ability of the black family structure to enable the pursuit of economic self-capitalization. But Moynihan is clear in rejecting any ahistorical notion of the family. Citing *Beyond the Melting Pot*, he states:

> . . . as with any other nation, Americans are producing a recognizable family system. But that process is not completed by any means. There are still, for example, important differences in family patterns surviving from the age of the great European migration to the United States, and these variations account for notable differences in the progress and assimilation of various ethnic and religious groups. A number of immigrant groups were characterized by unusually strong family bonds; these groups have characteristically progressed more rapidly than others.[122]

The focus on ethnic cultural family practices thus connected two spaces for Moynihan in the form of a therapeutic approach to the "Negro problem." Clearly, it allowed a rediscovery of racial pathology. Moynihan explicitly rejected genetic or biological explanations; racial pathology (paradigmatically, but not exclusively black pathology) was interred therapeutically and sympathetically into the cultural interiority of their special group origins and group practices. But what is not so clearly remarked upon is that the "discovery" of ethnic culture enabled the resanctification of the economic sphere as the ultimate guarantor of American freedom and progress. Other ethnic groups (by which he clearly meant white ethnic groups) were realizing that dream. They were not all the same, they had their own challenges, forms of adaptation, weaknesses and strengths. But a knowledge of their cultural forms and cultural practices *enhanced* the governmental understanding of the roots of human freedom and flourishing, roots that had their ultimate arena in the autonomous sphere of human commerce, capaciously appreciated—a sphere *beyond* the law. The problem of racial inequality could be an object of legitimate governmental interest and concern insofar as it jeopardized and deviated from this balance. Far from problematizing that balance, racial inequality via ethnic cultural practices was confined as a supplemental space, the proper knowledge of which could preserve and restore that balance.

Was ethnic culture then a heterotopia of compensation? Was it a supplemental space, able to relate other spaces, maintaining a perfect compensatory illusion in the face of a messy, jumbled problematic world? For Moynihan, the promise of ethnicity within the American liberal context seems to bear this out. Ethnicity enabled a logic of triage in a liberal governmental discourse over the scope, aims, and limits of governmental action, a discourse that, as I've tried to show, is propelled by the "hidden presence of the sacred," interred within the autonomous sphere of economic commerce, now supplemented with new technological knowledge about the propensities of one's cultural commerce.[123] But a discursive logic ought never to be mistaken for "reality." That, at any rate, is one of the central lessons I've tried to demonstrate through Foucault. Such "illusory" logics spring only from continual tension with a problematizing world, interred and bounded only in the face of anomalous resistance to its memorial reflections, nurtured only to the degree individuals accept the ethical implications of its consoling compensations. Moynihan alone, much less any "elite decision-maker" posited by Skrentny, can accomplish that in a vacuum. It is only in recovering the heterogeneity of that problematizing tension that one can see both what nurtures a discursive reflection and the possibility of living, conceiving those fractures differently. And for that, I briefly turn to the War on Poverty.

Few things in recent American political memory seem as contentious as the governmental initiative known as the War on Poverty during the mid- to late 1960s. It constitutes both the wildest ambition of Johnson's Great Society and for many its worst flaw. Begun with the Economic Opportunity Act of 1964, it was devised by the Johnson administration in the hope of ending once and for all the problem of poverty and persistent inequality. Inaugurating an array of programs and services such as Job Corps, Head Start, work-study, and the funding for neighborhood centers, the War on Poverty became collectively implemented through the ethos of Community Action Programs (or CAP) and through guidelines put forth by the Office of Economic Opportunity.[124] From the beginning, however, its conception seems to have been ideologically and strategically divided. Through Harrington's book and the prevailing currents then ascendant about mass society and alienation, poverty was seen as the outcome of pervasive disaffection and apathy. Rather than as an effect of poverty, such disaffection was seen as the cause.[125] The task was therefore to instill motivation and hope by encouraging the participation and community building of impoverished communities, that is, to instill a sense of collective and individual responsibility and investment in one's own life chances. This camp sought to model its efforts on the program known as the Henry Street Settlement, on the Lower East Side, funded by the Ford Foundation since 1957, which envisioned community building as its main ethos. According to Moynihan, however, there were those, including himself, who fought for more purely economic forms of relief, ranging from simple monetary relief to job training. In line with his thinking in the Moynihan Report, unemployment was the key, and reducing poverty ought to target the ability of the impoverished and the poor to find work. Ultimately, with the appointment of Sargent Shriver to resolve the dispute, "community action" became the centerpiece of Johnson's War on Poverty and "maximum feasible participation" its slogan, though it would remain a hybrid program encompassing both funding for participatory encouragement and more traditional funding for job training and specific forms of relief.

To hear Moynihan's side of the story and, increasingly, that of a large number of neoliberals, "maximum feasible participation" was a recipe for radical disaster. Indeed, Moynihan's book *Maximum Feasible Misunderstanding* cannot refrain from italicizing well nigh every mention of the phrase, as if the words themselves are incredulous, capable of critiquing itself. In his view, not only did the "community action" view diffuse and displace a real focus and concentration on the causes of poverty, but also it ran the risk of exacerbating the problem, first by reinforcing bureaucratic clientalism and therefore extending government into areas that were inappropriate; second, and somewhat contradictorily, because it was "the one portion of the program that would not be directly monitored from Washington";[126] and, finally, because it reflected a very "specific theory of social change" for radical elite liberals (whom he paradigmatically identified with the Ford Foundation) whose agenda seemed to involve a poisonous mixture of nihilistic messianism and racial guilt, whose "communitarian anarchism" and "Old Testament protest" "politicized juvenile delinquency [in the context of Mobilization for Youth programs]."[127] Hence, for Moynihan, these elite reformers were proceeding upon a disastrous understanding of the problem, constituting themselves as a professional class of radical bureaucrats who were less interested in the interests of the poor themselves than in their own vision of social change.[128] At the core of Moynihan's objection to CAP programs was that they *politicized* an economic issue, specifically the issue of employment, which, in the analysis presented here, held for him a certain talismanic status.

From a different angle, Barbara Cruikshank's *The Will to Empower: Democratic Citizens and Other Subjects* critiques the CAP focus of the War on Poverty, not because it politicized poverty but because it inaugurated the rhetoric of empowerment. Cruikshank's book is of particular interest for my argument because she seeks to apply a Foucauldian argument about governmental subjection to the language of empowerment that has become so diffused and pervasive in political life today, most notably for advocates of identity politics. In seeking to "empower" what were conceived as alienated subjects, the War on Poverty created a new technology of governance. Echoing some of the lines of Moynihan's critique but obviously for a different purpose, for Cruikshank the will to empower constitutes subjects by positing their interests, giving them identities for which they must be concerned, thereby extending biopolitics into new domains. Clearly, an application of Foucault's "repressive hypothesis," Cruikshank's argument is meant to highlight the processes and objects through which we've come to be concerned about our own self-governance. However, in my reading of her book and in the arguments advanced here about Foucault it is critical not to presume the coherence of these governmental discursive logics, to mistake their "dreams" for the reality of who we are. To do so leads only to suspicion, as the force of Cruikshank's book is clearly to cast suspicion on the language through which leftists have come to advance and envision the politics of marginalized groups. It is not enough to claim, as she advances, that the governmental logics through which we are made can be "unmade." Foucault, as I've tried to show, gives us a much more heterogeneous and cathected understanding of governmentality. The key to unmaking or living differently lies not just in realizing our own ethical freedom in the present to hold or withhold our allegiance to the governmental objects we've come to be concerned about. That path is vulnerable to the charge of solipsistic voluntarism that Stuart Hall attributed to Foucault in his foreclosure of psychoanalysis. Rather, one must *find* one's ethical freedom in the heterogeneity of problematics through which our own governmental discourses arose. One must return to those *events* in the spirit of genealogy, rather than escape into that ready-made compensation of the "will not to be governed," where the illusion of choice comes to be its own reward.

Still, Cruikshank's book captures an undeniable and important element of the puzzle—that in seeking the participation of the poor, liberal reformers conceptualized this "empowering participation" in particular *liberal* ways. Hence, it is not a question of choosing between Moynihan's dismissal of their politicizing efforts and embracing wholeheartedly their attempts to foster the political agency of the marginalized. The two were of a piece, encompassing a liberal crisis over and problematization of the investment of the poor and racial subjects in the sacred promise of American liberalism brought on by a critical mass of indictments over discrimination, inequality, and economic deprivation, the view that the ultimate compensation of their freedom and autonomy lay in the ability of the economic sphere to realize that autonomy. For the focus on alienation and motivation did not challenge or problematize the ability of the "system" to realize results. Though certainly some CAP advocates had a more radical agenda, the prevailing idea was that the problem of poverty was simply an instance of individuals becoming so discouraged that they no longer tried to participate, no longer had hope that they could realize economic mobility. Such disaffection caused a neglect of and a deficit in their civic productive skills. The idea was that if they were "empowered," they would help themselves and therefore restore confidence in that sacred promise. Whereas Moynihan believed this focus on community participation was unstable, displacing a focus on ameliorative measures within the economy with a politicization likely to radicalize the problem, both camps nevertheless held to the same assumption: that the ultimate vitiation of the problem of poverty and inequality lay within a largely untouched economic sphere.

Of course, of the two, Moynihan was the more prescient. Though both he and the CAP advocates sought to instill faith in economic opportunity, War on Poverty programs inaugurated an opportunity politics of a wholly different kind.[129] CAP neighborhood centers quickly became radicalized. Within a year of their implementation, urban mayors across the country were complaining about local CAP advocates contentiously challenging their authority. Urban riots increased in frequency and severity over the course of the rest of the decade. The CAP assumption that organizing and encouraging the participation of the poor and the marginalized would instill a normalized hope and confidence in the American promise fell flat on its face. Rather, in cities like Oakland, "community" and "grassroots" activists were using these programs to problematize other lines, other spaces, offering arguments about the "internal colonialism" of the cities in which they lived, the policies and politics through which their "ghettoes" were kept impoverished, subject to the disproportionate and racist hand of governmental power, for instance, in the form of police abuse or in the use of eminent domain for urban renewal projects and highway construction.[130] There is certainly an irony here connecting the origins of radical and militant grassroots calls for self-determination with the blind faith many Great Society liberals had in "encouraging" community participation. My point is not to romanticize these efforts but to show the heterogeneity in the depth of the problematizing indictments of this period, the many lines that were crossed, blurred and analogized. To be sure, Moynihan was right that the legacy of the War on Poverty exacerbated racial-ethnic conflict. Part of that had to do with the way CAP programs and funding were implemented within neighborhoods bounded by racial-ethnic borders, setting them momentously against one another. But surely Moynihan's evolving discourse played some role in this as well. Had he not argued that racial-cultural practices were pathologically deviant when compared with other ethnic groups? Had he not constituted ethnic groups as the real bearers realizing the promise of American mobility? Had he not restricted the economic inequality and grievances facing both (in different ways of course) to the interior and confined realm of the family and cultural adaptive practices—this in the service of sanctifying and insulating the promise held in the autonomy of the economic sphere—thereby foreclosing their cross-problematization?

In the fallout over the Moynihan Report[131] and in the overall radicalization of the country, in part through the War on Poverty, Moynihan began to associate with a new group of friends, primarily those former liberals now disillusioned with the delusions of their own former faith in what liberal government could do and who gathered in 1965 to start the journal *The Public Interest*. What linked them all was a distress over the "destructive and unpatriotic tenor of much of the new radicalism thrown up by the peace movement, the civil rights movement, and the campus upheavals."[132] "But," writes Moynihan's biographer, "there was always another key idea, which had to do with the claims of social science in relation to public policy. It was not a coincidence that virtually all of *The Public Interest* editors and writers they published were social scientists trained in one discipline or another. They had all watched social science being used and, as most of them thought, misused, as a guide to public policy and government action.

They shared a skepticism about the belief, which was a cornerstone of interventionist liberal thinking, that once social scientists identified a problem, it was the function of government to devise, fund and staff programs to deal with it, and the problem would duly disappear. Instead, says Seymour Martin Lipset, 'What was special about *The Public Interest* was skepticism.' "[133] For them, it was the crossing and comparisons of political lines that proved galvanizing, and their consequent radicalism was all the more egregious because they believed it had been nurtured by governmental elites of whom Moynihan was perhaps its paradigmatic recanting confessor. By the time of the Nixon administration, Moynihan was advising "benign neglect" of governmental intervention into racial issues, not because race, inequality, and poverty were no longer fundamental problems but because the scope of their runaway problematization was threatening the liberal order itself, in part fueled by the biopolitical extensions within which he himself had played such a large role.

But biopolitics was out of the bag, as it were. New social movements were springing up; second-wave feminism increasingly asserted itself; gay liberation was a watchword in certain cities. Still, if "Moynihan's experience rather accurately mirrored that of many other Americans . . . [if] more than almost anyone, Moynihan epitomized the changes that were taking place in many Americans' assumptions,"[134] it was because the lure of liberal *compensatory* government—that compensatory discourse that has its ultimate sanction in the autonomous workings of civil society beyond the limits of the law—was pendulously swinging back the other way. In the effort to redescribe the problem of racial inequality, the Moynihan Report had sought to bound a new cultural space as an object of governmental intervention. Put forth in the interest of insulating and rediscovering the promise of freedom held in the autonomy of civil-economic commerce, that racial-ethnic cultural space became problematized beyond its bounds. But amid the abyss of indictments, that biopolitical comparison between race and ethnicity became a fracture pointing the way to a reinscription of that compensatory promise, an outcome Moynihan had ambivalently hoped early on would be ameliorative of the "Negro problem" but whose contagion now threatened the promise itself. In addition to Nixon's Southern Strategy, Nixon would reach out to white ethnics speaking the language of a "silent majority" who did not protest, who quietly worked and found their own measure of freedom and autonomy. Foucault would have recognized a liberal "utopia" that found a new, if begrudged, place in reality. Perhaps, too, a new chapter needs to be added to Hartz's *The Liberal Tradition in America*, one where conservatives today kid themselves when they see themselves at war with liberalism, one also where one can admit with generosity the extent to which some New Deal and Great Society liberals, in pursuit of a faith so devout in the promise of American freedom and possibility, *almost* breached the bounds of liberalism's sacred limits.[135]

ETHNICITY AND THE SPACINGS OF MULTICULTURALISM

> It is *the spirit of this spiral* that keeps one in suspense, holding one's breath- and, thus, keeps one alive.
>
> —Jacques Derrida[136]

If racial-ethnic *culture* became prominent through a liberal governmental technology of compensation, then it must also be recognized how heterogeneously problematized that technology was from the moment of its advancement, beyond my own all-too-tidy narrative. Indeed, the liberal governmental "inclusion" of racial-ethnic culture sprang out of evolving problematizations whose roots preceded its governmental consideration.[137] As Thomas Sugrue and many others have made clear, postwar economic shifts, most prominently deindustrialization, exacerbated tensions and conditions that were channeled in racial ways well before the tumult of the 1960's. Part of Sugrue's effort is to counter neoliberal and neoconservative arguments that turn Great Society politics into both cause and effect, arguing that the urban riots and racial-ethnic conflicts of the '60s and '70s were the result of the radicalizing racial attention of Great Society liberals and their corresponding neglect of working-class white ethnics. But, through attention to key figures like Moynihan and Nathan Glazer, this charge is disingenuous, to say the least. From the perspective of the arguments advanced here, both the evolving neoliberal/conservative shift and the ideas we identify with Great Society liberalism were part of the same governmental discourse. Both sprang out of the growing crisis of race, poverty, and inequality in which the biopolitics of racial-ethnic *culture* became a form of problem redescription driven by a shared assumption that the promise of freedom and autonomy lay in the largely untouched and unquestioned domain of economic and civil commerce. And with regard to that magical object of compensation, race and ethnicity were differentiated in the form of a triage over their propensities in rediscovering that promise of compensation. Racial culture became a special problem, where its origins in slavery, discrimination, and segregation were not denied but situated in a distant past, on a sliding scale where the pressing questions lay not in that past but in emphasizing their deviance in the present—a deviance with regard to its abilities to generate normalized, self-capitalizing citizens propelling a whole index of issues of life and population "haunted by liberalism's question." Ethnicity was likewise reincorporated with regard to this specter, the knowledge and recognition of which could rediscover the promise of a land beyond the law, a freedom realized and built with ungoverned hands.

It is tempting to dismiss the governmental discourses of this period as so much ideological fodder and to concentrate on the economic structural problems and shifts of this period. And rather than accept the specular illusion of an economic sphere able to vitiate all problems, one could invert the image and attribute all problems to the shifts in capital accumulation during this period. But that too would still spur compensatory illusions, nurturing with suspicion rather than trust the utopian consolations of its shared desires. Govermentality, governmental reason and discourse, questions of self-governance, are discourses one must participate in, if only to counter that compensatory illusion of a sphere that need not be governed or of problematic, deviant spaces that must be absolutely governed. And within these discourses, one must set one's illusions and dreams alongside the "realities" from which they spring, not in the sense of escaping from those problematizing relations or in being determined by them but in working *through* those relations to see how they are heterogeneous, how they can be seen as still more illusory.

Certainly in our inclusionary multicultural age, the "inclusion" of race and ethnicity encrypts these civil-rights-era fractures. There is without doubt the hope and desire to treat race as a form of ethnicity, as other than pathological/deviant, even as questions of power, discrimination, and inequality spiral in to rupture those dreams. Ethnicity itself has become a fully accepted form of expression and activity, as Jacobson and Halter both show in different ways. But, as Halter's conclusion signals, there is a haunted residue for white immigrant ethnics. Even as ethnicity is accepted as a valuable rite of passage on the path to autonomous freedom, it is evacuated of its costs, encrypting a narrative of class origins that can only melancholically symbolize the real and imagined grievances of its (R)ocky incorporation. For Halter the focus on cultural difference lay at the hands of racial minorities. Yet Jacobson's book shows just how much that melancholic symbolization of ethnicity nurtured an active and world-building resentment over the perceived preferential treatment of race. For Jacobson, the problem lay in white ethnics who problematically felt left out and excluded by the attention to race. In quite different ways, then, both speak to the underlying perverted contagions between race and ethnicity underlying their surface forms. Indeed, we've come to see race and ethnicity as fundamentally opposed and the focus on cultural difference as the main culprit for their contagious confusions.

But, significantly, the logic of their comparisons and disjuncture was part of an encompassing governmental discourse over a liberal problem of compensation. By the time of the Ethnic Heritage Studies Act of 1972, these fractures between race and ethnicity had taken full multicultural shape. Ethnicity for white ethnics would be the subject of recognition and study, of appreciation for its contributions to the diversity of the American tapestry. But is it significant that those who came to testify during the hearings on the act were predominantly leaders of white ethnic organizations, people like Monsignor Geno Baroni, longtime black civil rights activist and Catholic leader of the National Center for Urban Ethnic Affairs, who spoke of the need for attention to working-class ethnics? Is it significant that the rediscovery of ethnicity for white ethnics is inevitably tinged in its narratives with a sense of loss? Is it entirely credulous to collapse all these uncanny bodily remains into an all-encompassing racial resentment or a pregiven class interest? In all of these questions, what kind of slippages and substitutions were involved? Rather than immediately spiraling in the efforts of such white ethnic organizations during the late '60s and '70s as reactive and resentful of race, perhaps we need to return to those nascent cross-problematizations, attend to how those problematizations indicted the promise of American freedom before they were folded back into a resentful defense of that dream.[138] Perhaps they did receive a raw deal, not because their problems were equivalent to race or certainly because racial minorities received any kind of "fair" deal but because certain heterogeneous questions were raised alike during this period, problematizing the compensatory edifice of American liberalism.

In short, if the multicultural landscape of racial-ethnic cultural inclusion remains tied to a problem of memory and memorializing over the fractures of certain civil-rights-era crypts, those fractures can be dissolved not through a suspicion or trust of our origins in it but in spiraling out the heterogeneous questions it raised, in refusing the compensatory consolations of an interest-group politics, in questioning and breaching that sanctified space wherein all political dreams find their limit and all political desires express their fealty, and, most important of all, in anticipating and analogizing those questions so that new problematizations can occur where one can begin to practice those paralyzed fractures differently.

NOTES

1. Nicholas Abraham and Maria Torok, *The Shell and the Kernel* (Chicago: University of Chicago Press, 1994), 141–142.
2. Of course, the concept of ethnicity is not itself new, but neither has it been uniform. See Werner Sollors, ed., *The Invention of Ethnicity* (Oxford: Oxford University Press, 1991).
3. Matthew Frye Jacobson, *Roots Too: White Ethnic Revival in Post-Civil Rights America* (Cambridge: Harvard University Press, 2006), and Marilyn Halter, *Shopping for Identity* (New York: Schocken, 2000).
4. Jacobson, *Roots Too*, 465.
5. Ibid., 6.
6. Halter, *Shopping for Identity*, 10–11. Basing her findings on the 1990 census, she reports that this correlation was most pronounced for white ethnics but was also present for racial minorities.
7. Ibid., 198, 69. For ethnicity as a form of cultural capital, see also Richard Alba's *Ethnic Identity: Transformation of White America* (New Haven: Yale University Press, 1990).
8. Halter, *Shopping for Identity*, 198.
9. Ibid., 3–4.
10. Ibid.
11. Ibid., 4–5.
12. Jacobson, *Roots Too*, 19. For Jacobson, the starting point of his text is thus how this "contagious idiom of group identity and group rights" mutated in the hands of white ethnics.

13. John Skrentny, *The Minority Rights Revolution* (Cambridge: Belknap, 2002).
14. Ibid., v.
15. Ibid., 7. Skrentny's claim to show "how weak groups often win big" thus seems to be valenced with an underlying claim (resentment) that there should be a strict correspondence between political demand and political compensation. But how then would this warp the perspective on ending black discrimination? That it was justifiable only once blacks themselves began to mobilize and agitate? And, further, that mobilization's only purpose is to gain the attention of elites? In its sinews, Skrentny's underlying theory of politics embraces a quite paternalistic approach.
16. My thinking on Skrentny's book has been much enriched by Victoria Hattam's comment "The 1964 Civil Rights Act: Narrating the Past, Authorizing the Future," *Studies in American Political Development* 18 (Spring 2004): 60–69.
17. Skrentny, *The Minority Rights Revolution*, vi.
18. Much rhetorical force is expended on the inclusion of nonblack racial minorities in affirmative action mandates by elites when such groups expressed little demand for them while white ethnic groups explicitly sent appeals to elite leaders to be included yet were denied. This need not be interpreted in the arbitrary manner Skrentny believes. Rather, it was very likely the case that many nonblack minorities were radicalized during this time (late 1960s) and purposely chose not to couch their politics in terms of appeals to "the Man" while white ethnic groups held more readily to this interest-group form of politics.
19. Mary Waters, *Ethnic Options: Choosing Identities in America* (Berkeley: University of California Press, 1990).
20. Wendy Brown, *States of Injury* (Princeton: Princeton University Press, 1995).
21. For Nietzsche, the memory necessary for promising as well as the origins of guilt have their basis in a contractual relationship whose ultimate guarantor for payment is the "recompense" of the debtor's body. "An equivalence is provided by the creditor's receiving, in place of a literal compensation for an injury, a recompense in the form of a kind of pleasure—the pleasure of being allowed to vent his power freely upon one who is powerless. . . ." Friedrich Nietzsche, *On the Genealogy of Morals*, trans. Walter Kaufmann and R. J. Hollingdale (New York: Vintage, 1989), 64–65.
22. The phrase comes from Foucault in his lifelong efforts to provide genealogical explorations of the present.
23. See for example, Nancy Fraser, "Foucault on Modern Power: Empirical Insights and Normative Confusions,"*Praxis International* 1 (Oct. 1981): 272–287, and Charles Taylor, "Foucault on Freedom and Truth," in *Foucault: A Critical Reader*, ed. David Hoy (Oxford: Blackwell, 1986), 69–102.
24. For a similar approach to the cohesiveness of Foucault's work, see Thomas L. Dumm's *Michel Foucault and the Politics of Freedom* (Walnut Creek: AltaMira Press, 2000).
25. I mean antitheoretical in the sense of refusing to erect a theory as *counter* to the present, as a compensating blueprint or moralizing guide against our reality—paradoxical because Foucault's interviews display a strange dance between theoretical flair and a desire to efface himself. One could argue that, especially in his earlier works, Foucault did not always consistently negotiate his own will to power and will to know, that is, one could find in his voice the occasional desire for a sacrosanct compensation, for example, the desire to recover and speak *from* the subjectivity of madness in the original preface to *Histoire de la folie* or of prophesizing the *coming* dissolution of the concept of man in the human sciences.

26. "I would like to say something about the function of any diagnosis concerning what today is. It does not consist in a simple characterization of what we are but, instead—by following lines of fragility in the present—in managing to grasp why and how that which is might no longer be that which is." Michel Foucault, "Structuralism and Post-Structuralism," in *The Essential Foucault*, ed. Paul Rabinow and Nickolas Rose (New York: New Press, 2003), 94.
27. "We shall not return to the state anterior to discourse—in which nothing has yet been said, and in which things are only just beginning to emerge out of the grey light; and we shall not pass beyond discourse in order to rediscover the forms that it has created and left behind it. . . ." Michel Foucault, *The Archaeology of Knowledge* (New York: Pantheon, 1972), 48.
28. See for example, "Polemics, Politics, and Problematizations" and "Technologies of the Self," in *The Essential Foucault*, ed. Paul Rabinow and Nikolas Rose (New York: New Press, 2003),18–24 and 145–169, respectively.
29. I further explore Foucault's relationship with psychoanalysis later on.
30. Here I confess not to recognize Foucault in Brown's *States of Injury*, particularly in her influential chapter "Wounded Attachments." Though this chapter shares many of her concerns over the melancholic and resentful propensities of identity in the post-'60s era, she builds her argument out of a paradoxical rejection of Foucault, claiming an elision of Nietzsche in his work, particularly the "removal of the 'will to power' from Nietzsche's complex psychology" and "his utter neglect . . . of the culture of modernity as the triumph of 'slave morality' " (63–64). Yet how else to understand Foucault's genealogical method if not to untangle the will to power from the will to know? How else to assess his critiques of the disciplinary consequences of the rise of the human sciences if they are not forms of moralizing ascetism that gave birth to values binding individuals internally and exacting cruelties on their bodies? To be sure, Foucault sparingly mentions Nietzsche in his corpus, but when he does, the discussion always involves pivotal moments in his own theorizing. See for example Hans Sluga, "Foucault's Encounter with Heidegger and Nietzsche" in *The Cambridge Companion to Foucault*, ed. Gary Gutting (Cambridge: Cambridge University Press, 2005), 210–239. It would be more accurate to say that Foucault took seriously Nietzsche's admonition to go beyond him, particularly in Nietzsche's own aristocratic moralizing tendencies and in refusing the utopian desire to recover a will to power completely free of *ressentiment*. And, in this regard, Brown's own conflicted moralism in this essay, her call for a recovery of desire "prior to its wounding," and her appeal to a democratic *discourse* (rather than practice) that can "adjudicate desires" and "forge an alternative future" seem themselves to be problematic appeals to a sovereign compensation or an untainted origin. *States of Injury*, 75–76.
31. Indeed, Skrentny himself traces the conceptualization of "anticipatory politics" to Daniel Patrick Moynihan in his article "The Professionalization of Reform," *Public Interest* 1 (1965): 6–16; see Skrentny, *Minority Rights Revolution*, 9, n19. Interestingly, however, although both Skrentny and Moynihan call attention to and problematize the emergence of elite reformers as a class, Moynihan's article embodies his ambivalence over the community action programs of the War on Poverty, which were designed ideally to *increase* participation of the poor in reform efforts. This clearly complicates Skrentny's overall argument that the anticipatory politics of the period disregarded the actual needs of the poor and the discriminated against. Moynihan's ambivalence was an ideological one based on the politically radical delusions of liberal reform. Skrentny's use thereby obliterates the ideological crisis going on during this period, turning a struggle over the *political* scope of inequality and discrimination into the arbitrariness of elite policymakers.

32. Derived from the French word *trier*, meaning to pick or to cull, "triage" is generally used to refer to the process of assigning treatment to injured persons in moments of crisis. James Kyun-Jin Lee's *Urban Triage: Race and the Fictions of Multiculturalism* (Minneapolis: University of Minn. Press, 2004) makes an interesting use of the word as a metaphor for understanding the multicultural literature of the 1980s in its connections to the urban crises of that period.
33. Nathan Glazer and Daniel P. Moynihan, *Beyond the Melting Pot* (Cambridge: MIT Press, 1963).
34. For instance, Moynihan had a long interest in studying auto safety through the lens of epidemiology, authoring "Epidemic on the Highways" in 1959 and the highly regarded "Traffic Safety and the Body Politic" in 1966. See, respectively, *The Reporter* 20, no. 9 (April 30, 1959): 16–23, and *The Public Interest* 3 (Spring 1966): 10–26.
35. Godfrey Hodgson, *The Gentleman from New York: Daniel Patrick Moynihan* (New York: Houghton Mifflin, 2000), 96.
36. U.S. Department of Labor, Office of Policy Planning and Research, *The Negro Family: The Case for National Action* (Washington, D.C.: Government Printing Office, 1965), 5.
37. Daniel P. Moynihan, *Maximum Feasible Misunderstanding: Community Action in the War on Poverty* (New York: Free Press, 1969). The title refers to the slogan of community action initiatives, "maximum feasible participation."
38. *The Public Interest* was founded in 1965; Moynihan was a frequent contributor.
39. See, for example, Nathan Glazer, "Daniel P. Moynihan on Ethnicity," and Seymour Martin Lipset, "The Prescient Politician," both in *Daniel Patrick Moynihan: The Intellectual in Public Life*, ed. Robert A. Katzmann (Washington, D.C.: Woodrow Wilson Center Press, 1998), 15–25, 26–43.
40. "Interpretive analytics" is the term Hubert Dreyfus and Paul Rabinow utilize for Foucault's methodological propensities in their *Michel Foucault: Beyond Structuralism and Hermeneutics* (Chicago: University of Chicago Press, 1982).
41. Indeed, the critique of ethnicity as a tool for preserving the racial status quo is both long standing and of more recent date. Yet nearly all such critiques elide the *liberal* and ideological dimensions of the problem, either leaving the question of motivation unexplored or ultimately attributing the animus toward ethnicity to a fundamental bedrock of racist investment or the preservation of class interest. For a sampling of this literature, see Alexander Saxton, "Nathan Glazer, Daniel Moynihan, and the Cult of Ethnicity," *Amerasia Journal* 4, no. 2 (Fall 1977): 141–150; Robert Blauner, *Racial Oppression in America* (New York: Harper and Row, 1972); Stephen Steinberg, *The Ethnic Myth* (Boston: Beacon, 1981); David Roediger, *Working toward Whiteness: How America's Immigrants Became White* (New York: Basic Books, 2005); Ian Haney Lopez, "'A Nation of Minorities': Race, Ethnicity, and Reactionary Colorblindness," *Stanford Law Review* 59 (Feb. 2007): 985–1063.
42. Or, as Nietzsche argued, for modern man caught "between an interior which fails to correspond to any exterior and an exterior which fails to correspond to any interior . . . Knowledge . . . now no longer acts as an agent for transforming the outside world but remains concealed within a chaotic inner world which modern man describes with a curious pride as his uniquely characteristic inwardness." Friedrich Nietzche, *Untimely Meditations* (Cambridge: Cambridge University Press, 1997), 78.
43. Michel Foucault, *The Use of Pleasure* (New York: Vintage, 1990), 8.
44. Michel Foucault, *Mental Illness and Psychology* (Berkeley: University of California Press, 1987), 56.
45. "The Ethics of the Concern of the Self as a Practice of Freedom," in *The Essential Foucault*, ed. Paul Rabinow and Nikolas Rose (New York: New Press, 2003), 41. This interview was originally conducted on January 20, 1984.

46. Stuart Hall, "Introduction: Who Needs Identity?," in Hall, *Questions of Cultural Identity* (London: Sage, 1996), 1–17.
47. Ibid., 14.
48. I refer here to his later lectures at the Collège de France and his last two completed volumes of *The History of Sexuality*. For *askesis*, see *The Use of Pleasure; The History of Sexuality, Volume 2* (New York: Vintage, 1990), 72–77; and "Technologies of the Self," in *The Essential Foucault*, ed. Paul Rabinow and Nikolas Rose (New York: New Press, 2003), 158–159. For Foucault, the arts of *askesis* in antiquity were a form of mental reflection, exercise, and training, "not a disclosure of a secret self but a remembering . . . not renunciation but the progressive consideration of the self" (158).
49. Jacques Derrida, "To Do Justice to Freud," in *The Work of Mourning*, ed. Pascale-Anne Brault and Michael Naas (Chicago: University of Chicago Press, 2001), 77–90.
50. Joel Whitebook, "Against Interiority: Foucault's Struggle with Psychoanalysis," in *The Cambridge Companion to Foucault*, ed. Gary Gutting (Cambridge: Cambridge University Press, 2005), 312–347.
51. See, for example, Didier Eribon's biography, *Michel Foucault* (Cambridge: Harvard University Press, 1991).
52. For a helpful analysis of the significance of these moves, see Hubert Dreyfus's "Foreword to the California Edition" in Foucault, *Mental Illness and Psychology*.
53. Foucault, "Preface to *The History of Sexuality, Volume Two*," in *The Essential Foucault*, ed. Paul Rabinow and Nikolas Rose (New York: New Press, 2003), 58–63.
54. For Foucault's "discovery" of Nietzsche, see Eribon, *Foucault*, 62, and Sluga, "Foucault's Encounter," 214.
55. Even in this, however, Foucault's characterization of psychoanalysis was always much more complex. See, for example, his discussion of psychoanalysis along with ethnology as countersciences at the very end of *The Order of Things* (New York: Vintage, 1994), 373–386.
56. See for example, his introduction, "Dream, Imagination, and Existence," to Ludwig Binswanger's *Dream and Existence,* originally published in 1954, reprinted in *Review of Existential Psychology and Psychiatry* 19 (1984–85): 29–78. In this impulse, one can also see Foucault's debts to Heidegger, the other main interlocutor for Foucault throughout his life. Indeed, one needs to see his late concern over the *care* of the self as always disclosing a larger world, rather than through a confining inwardness.
57. It might be argued that Nietzsche allowed Foucault to break from his early psychoanalytic impasse, freeing him to position psychoanalysis as one configuration in a network of subjecting power relations. But would Foucault have once again returned to psychoanalysis in his final updating of *The History of Sexuality*? After all, the three volumes he published narrate the structure of a genealogical return.
58. Foucault, "Dream, Imagination, and Existence," 64; Sluga, "Foucault's Encounter," 218.
59. Michel Foucault, *The Archaeology of Knowledge* (New York: Pantheon, 1972), 211.
60. Roy Boyne's *Foucault and Derrida: The Other Side of Reason* (New York: Routledge, 1990) makes the provocative case that Derrida's critique of *Madness and Civilization*, "Cogito and the History of Madness," was tacitly internalized by Foucault. From then on, Foucault never entertained any more illusions about liberating the interred other *from* its confining discourse, speaking increasingly about liberation as a practice *within* such discourses.
61. Michel Foucault, "Of Other Spaces," *Diacritics* 16 (1986): 22–27, and "Different Spaces," in *Aesthetics: The Essential Works of Michel Foucault*, ed. J. Faubion (London: Allen Lane, 1998), 175–85.

62. For a detailed analysis of the various uses and commentaries on the article, see Peter Johnson, "Unravelling Foucault's 'Different Spaces,'" *History of the Human Sciences* 19 (2006): 75–90. For another good discussion of the article, see Dumm, "Freedom and Space," in Dumm, *Michel Foucault and the Politics of Freedom*, 29–68.
63. Foucault, "Of Other Spaces," 23.
64. Ibid.
65. Ibid.
66. Ibid., 24.
67. Ibid.
68. Ibid.
69. Ibid., 25.
70. Ibid.
71. An interesting juxtaposing parallel can be drawn to Robert O. Self's study of race, place, and labor in the struggles of postwar Oakland in his *American Babylon* (Princeton: Princeton University Press, 2003). Self discusses the aesthetic campaigns for "industrial gardens" in the immediate postwar era of housing expansion in Oakland for industrial (largely) unionized labor. But Self situates these campaigns as housing something of a lost tragic vision, before the onset of struggles over racial integration, deindustrialization, and urban flight.
72. Foucault, "Of Other Spaces," 27.
73. Ibid.
74. Hence the moral neutrality with which he sometimes treated the prison, the asylum, the colony. Such central sites were heterotopias, in that they served to enable certain discursive dreams and illusions. He did not fault them for their illusory capacities; rather, the dilemma lay in the way their dreams spiraled in, cutting off their possible reimagination, constructing certain utopic visions as natural, and thereby confining those other spaces and bodies that problematize those visions.
75. Michel Foucault, "The Birth of Biopolitics," in *The Essential Foucault*, ed. Paul Rabinow and Nickolas Rose (New York: New Press, 2003), 204.
76. "Post-modernism Is the New Black," *The Economist*, Dec. 19, 2006, accessed July 9, 2007, www.economist.com/world/displaystory.cfm?story_id=8401159. A special report on "Shopping and Philosophy," this article is interesting in its own right, arguing that postmodern philosophers such as Foucault were unknowingly converging upon the revaluation of capitalism as the best resource for emancipating the individual and therefore contributing to the "postmodern" ascendance of consumerism in the 1980s and 1990s.
77. For synoptic accounts of Foucault's lectures on governmentality, see Colin Gordon, "Governmental Rationality: An Introduction," in Graham Burchell, Colin Gordon, and Peter Miller, eds., *The Foucault Effect* (Chicago: University of Chicago Press, 1991), 1–51, and Andrew Barry, Thomas Osborne, and Nikolas Rose, "Introduction" to Andrew Barry, Thomas Osborne, and Nikolas Rose, eds., *Foucault and Political Reason* (Chicago: University of Chicago Press, 1996), 1–17.
78. See, for example, Foucault, "The Birth of Biopolitics" and "Governmentality," in *The Essential Foucault*, ed. Paul Rabinow and Nickolas Rose (New York: New Press, 2003), 204–205, 233–40, respectively.
79. This cannot be overstressed. It is common to utilize Foucault as a theorist of the totalizing power of the state, but this is quite wrong. As will be clear later, it both overestimates and underestimates the sources of biopolitics, conflating a *discourse* of governmentality with government itself.
80. Barry et al., "Introduction," 8.
81. Michel Foucault, "Space, Knowledge and Power," in Sylvere Lotringer, ed., *Foucault Live* (New York: Semiotext(e), 1996), 337.

82. Barry et al., *Foucault and Political Reason*, 9.
83. And hence, propelling a quest for social scientific knowledge. Therefore, the question of liberalism's history of exclusion and its theories of inclusion betray an ongoing dynamism beyond a simple problematic incongruence or even a specific focus on its particular historical origins. See Uday Mehta's "Liberal Strategies of Exclusion," in *Tensions of Empire*, ed. Frederick Cooper and Ann Laura Stoler (Berkeley: University of California Press, 1997), 59–86. In particular, for Mehta, "liberal theory and liberal history are [not] ships passing in the night spurred on by unrelated imperatives and destinations." Indeed, informing this chapter is something of Mehta's parting question: "whether the development and consolidation of nineteenth-century social science can be understood as a *compensatory* response to the anthropological neglect that seventeenth-century Lockean liberalism encouraged" (emphasis added), 59, 80.
84. For pastoral power, see, for example, Michel Foucault, "'*Omnes et Singulatim*': Toward a Critique of Political Reason," in *The Essential Foucault*, ed. Paul Rabinow and Nickolas Rose (New York: New Press, 2003), 180–201.
85. James Morone, *Hellfire Nation: The Politics of Sin in American History* (New Haven: Yale University Press, 2003).
86. Foucault, "The Birth of Biopolitics," 206–207.
87. Ibid., 207. See also Barry et al., *Foucault and Political Reason*, 10–11, and Burchell et al., *The Foucault Effect*, 42–44.
88. Foucault, "The Birth of Biopolitics," 207.
89. Burchell et al., *The Foucault Effect*, 43.
90. Certainly the clearest example of the permeation of this shift lies in welfare policy, where the overriding imperative now is to normalize an economizing behavior among recipients. But the priority of market instrumentalism and functionalism subtly permeates many other domains. For example, Robert C. Post's subtle and complex study of antidiscrimination law in *Prejudicial Appearances: The Logic of American Antidiscrimination Law* (Durham: Duke University Press, 2001), makes the case that the functional logic of antidiscrimination law lies in the elevation of an abstract instrumental economizing rationale as the deciding factor in whether or not instances of discrimination are acceptable. And certainly we have seen how diversity rationales within affirmative action debates have concentrated on the benefits of diversity for one's own self-capitalization or on the needs for a cosmopolitan managerial class. The degrees of treatment for and toleration of cultural difference increasingly lie in the question of its benefits and perversions of individual and social capitalization as the ultimate instantiation of human freedom and autonomy.
91. And here one can see the special resonance of a "will not to be governed." As many liberal critics have asserted, suspected, and argued, liberalism's promise of negative liberty has always interred a very particular though shifting space of positive liberty.
92. For instance, historically contextualist approaches to Adam Smith and others of the Scottish Enlightenment reveal the hybridity within their various understandings of the phenomena of commercial society and therefore the fallacy of drawing a seamless line of development between their understandings and our own contemporary notions of "the market." See, for example, Istvan Hont and Michael Ignatieff, eds., *Wealth and Virtue: The Shaping of Political Economy in the Scottish Enlightenment* (Cambridge: Cambridge University Press, 1983).
93. Edmund Morgan, *American Slavery, American Freedom* (New York: Norton, 1975), 324, 328.
94. Foucault, "The Birth of Biopolitics," 207.
95. Daniel Patrick Moynihan, *Coping: Essays on the Practice of Government* (New York: Random House, 1972), 12.

96. Daniel Patrick Moynihan, "Liberalism and Knowledge," in *Coping: Essays on the Practice of Government*, 260.
97. Moynihan, "Epidemic on the Highways" and "Traffic Safety and the Body Politic," in Moynihan, *Coping: Essays on the Practice of Government*, 79–99.
98. Moynihan, "Traffic Safety and the Body Politic," 98.
99. Ibid., 99.
100. Nicholas Eberstadt, "Daniel Patrick Moynihan, Epidemiologist," in Katzmann, ed. *Daniel Patrick Moynihan: The Intellectual in Public Life*, 44–45.
101. For a critique of the book and its later consequences, see Lopez, " 'A Nation of Minorities.' " Though much of my argument parallels Lopez's regarding the evolving investment in ethnicity during this period, what distinguishes my approach is the need to see this investment as a problematic question rather than merely an ideological maneuver and, concomitantly, the possibility that its question could have been raised differently.
102. Glazer and Moynihan, *Beyond the Melting Pot*, 13.
103. Ibid., 6.
104. Ibid., 17.
105. Of course, Glazer has his own distinctive ambivalence regarding the treatment of African American discrimination. In 1975, he published *Affirmative Discrimination: Ethnic Inequality and Public Policy*, thus placing himself at the forefront of arguments against affirmative action. More recently, he has thrown his support for affirmative action as long as it is confined to African Americans.
106. Certainly, this primacy placed on the dynamism of American life can be itself ideological, and ultimately my reading of Moynihan argues this. Still, it is an ideological a priori quite different from the volitional or strategic maneuvering Lopez attributes to it.
107. Comparative reflections on European immigrants and race were not inaugurated at this time; indeed, Moynihan and Glazer reactivated a comparative problematic that had its endemic roots in Progressive-era immigration. But clearly, in the context of the waning of Americanization movements and the ascendance of the civil rights movement, that comparative problematic gained new significance in their hands. See Victoria Hattam, "Ethnicity: An American Genealogy," in *Not Just Black and White: Historical and Contemporary Perspectives on Immigration, Race, and Ethnicity in the United States*, eds. Nancy Foner and George Fredrickson (New York: Russell Sage Foundation, 2004) and *In the Shadow of Race: Jews, Latinos, and Immigrant Politics in the United States* (Chicago: University of Chicago Press, 2007).
108. Glazer and Moynihan, *Beyond the Melting Pot*, 33.
109. Ibid., 52.
110. Indeed, one can read them generously as supporting the various programs already in effect in New York City. In their role as prophets, they could argue that they had already seen the future of large-scale government support and that it was not enough, that it could not solve all the problems confronting particular ethnic-racial groups.
111. Of course, they did not originate the analysis of postslavery black family structure; it had already been explored in the work of E. Franklin Frazier, Kenneth B. Clark, and Stanley Elkins, among others. Directly influenced by these social scientists, all writing from the late 1930s to the 1950s, Moynihan and Glazer drew from them the language of a "culture" or "tangle of pathology." The distinctiveness of Glazer and Moynihan's use, however, lies in their making their theories of the government's interest in fostering an intervention into a contemporary problem.

112. Michael Harrington, *The Other America* (New York: Penguin, 1963), 1–2. Indeed, Harrington's book would be one of the direct causes of Kennedy's initial forays into the issue of poverty, subsequently taken up by Lyndon Johnson.
113. U.S. Department of Labor, Office of Policy Planning and Research, *The Negro Family: The Case for National Action* (Washington, D.C.: Government Printing Office, 1965), 1.
114. Reminiscent of Samuel Huntington's "Gap" theory of "third-world modernization," this problematic also speaks to the increasing connections drawn by antiracists critics with other "third-world" anticolonial liberation currents, from Malcolm X's appeal to the UN to the "third-world" strikes for ethnic studies departments toward the end of the decade.
115. Lyndon B. Johnson, "To Fulfill These Rights," in Lee Rainwater and William L. Yancey, eds., *The Moynihan Report and the Politics of Controversy* (Cambridge: MIT Press, 1967), 132.
116. To his credit, Johnson did not emphasize those limits, thus allowing others to imagine the implications of his words any number of ways. But as we will see in our analysis of its shared focus with the Moynihan Report on interiorizing reflections on the Negro family and the psychological roots of unemployment, those limits were being reinscribed in more subtle ways.
117. Rainwater and Yancey, *The Moynihan Report and the Politics of Controversy*, 48.
118. Ibid., 49.
119. Ibid.
120. Moynihan, "Employment, Income, and the Ordeal of the Negro Family," *Daedalus* 94 (Fall 1965): 747. The *Daedalus* volume published papers presented at a special conference on "The Negro American" sponsored by *Daedalus* and the American Academy of Arts and Sciences in April 1964. Other notable participants included Daniel Bell, Eric H. Erikson, Clifford Geertz, Oscar Handlin, and Talcott Parsons.
121. Hodgson, *The Gentleman from New York*, 92–94.
122. U.S. Department of Labor, *The Negro Family: The Case for National Action*, 5.
123. To see how this "dream" has nevertheless found a "place" in reality, consider the following recent passage: "While immigrants need specific rights and programmatic benefits, these would be of greatest help if provided within the context of communal and institutional settings providing the structure and guidance that we all need to make intelligent use of the choices—whether as consumers or as citizens—that material resources and rights afford us." Peter Skerry, "Citizenship Begins at Home: A New Approach to the Civic Integration of Immigrants," *The Responsive Community: Rights and Responsibilities* 14 (Winter 2003/2004): 27. In effect, one's training as a consumer citizen "begins at home."
124. For treatments of the Community Action Programs, see Peter Marris and Martin Rein, *Dilemmas of Social Reform: Poverty and Community Action in the United States, Second Edition* (Chicago: Aldine, 1967); John C. Donovan, *The Politics of Poverty* (New York: Pegasus, 1967); Marvin E. Gettleman and David Mermelstein, eds., *The Great Society Reader: The Failure of American Liberalism* (New York: Vintage Books, 1987). For differing critical approaches to the War on Poverty, see Frances Fox Piven and Richard A. Cloward, *Poor People's Movements: Why They Succeed and How They Fail* (New York: Vintage Books, 1979); Barbara Cruikshank, *The Will to Empower: Democratic Citizens and Other Subjects* (Ithaca: Cornell University Press, 1999); Charles Murray, *Losing Ground: American Social Policy, 1950–1980* (New York: Basic Books, 1984); James Morone, *The Democratic Wish: Popular*

Participation and the Limits of American Government (New Haven: Yale University Press, 1998); Moynihan, *Maximum Feasible Misunderstanding*; and Jill Quadagno, *The Color of Welfare: How Racism Undermined the War on Poverty* (Oxford: Oxford University Press, 1994).

125. Here one thinks of Nietzsche and the question of to what this need to confuse cause and effect (to posit a doer behind the deed) responds.
126. Moynihan, *Maximum Feasible Misunderstanding*, 87.
127. Ibid., 42, 18.
128. See Moynihan's "The Professionalization of Reform," *Public Interest* 1 (1965): 6–16, and "The Professors and the Poor" *Commentary* 46 (August 1968): 19–28. And here we see the origins of Skrentny's argument about the "arbitrary" "anticipatory politics" of policymakers during this period. Again, what Skrentny illuminates is really only one side of an ideological struggle waged during this period.
129. See, for example, Robert O. Self's rich account of the struggle in Oakland over the scope and direction of War on Poverty programs in his chapter "Opportunity Politics" in *American Babylon*.
130. The eventual radicalization of the civil rights movement in the form of Black Power and, later, the rise of the Black Panthers illustrates an important point with regard to Cruikshank's Foucauldian argument. For if the language of empowerment was inaugurated by a governmental discourse concerned with liberal normalization and self-investment/governance, clearly that language became a point of heterogeneous contention/resistance. Hence the language itself is neither oppressive nor emancipatory. And just as the space it carved could be interred as a deviation in restoring the promise of American liberalism, so also could it be imagined differently with regard to its own compensations. Certainly, in the hands of many Black Power advocates, the recovery of the space of black identity could be assumed/interred as the possibility of compensating for a problem of masculinity. But, just as well, that space could lead to the imagination of different spatial relationships as in the Black Panthers' reconceptualization of community in their "Ten-Point Program" and in the nascent communal services they provided. See, for example, Toni Morrison, ed., *To Die for the People: The Writings of Huey P. Newton* (New York: Writers and Readers Publishing, 1995), and Nikhil Pal Singh, *Black Is a Country* (Cambridge: Harvard University Press, 2004). At stake, of course, is whether such spaces are imagined as spiraling in or spiraling out, whether they lead to a reaffirmation of a specular compensation or propel problematizations that see their "reality" as capable of change, as "still more illusory."
131. For a detailed account of the Report's impact and reception, see Lee Rainwater and William L. Yancey's *The Moynihan Report and the Politics of Controversy*.
132. Hodgson, *The Gentleman from New York*, 124.
133. Ibid.
134. Ibid., 125.
135. With time, perhaps, we will begin to estrange that species of "liberalism" from the New Deal to the present with other than melancholic eyes. For a tentative but valuable attempt, see Laura Kalman, *The Strange Career of Legal Liberalism* (New Haven: Yale University Press, 1996).
136. Brault and Naas, *The Work of Mourning*, 90.
137. See, for example, Thomas Sugrue's *The Origins of the Urban Crisis: Race and Inequality in Postwar Detroit* (Princeton: Princeton University Press, 1996).
138. On the heterogeneity within the "white ethnic mobilization" during this period, see Perry L. Weed, *The White Ethnic Movement and Ethnic Politics* (New York: Praeger, 1973).

6 Conclusion
Remembering the Remains of Race

> In order to take history for memory, we have been obliged to turn from the dictatorship of the flesh to a thoughtful election of our pasts.
>
> —Anne Norton[1]

In the beginning of Raymond Williams's 1970 essay "A Hundred Years of Culture and Anarchy," Williams engages his readers in a curious historical bait and switch.[2] Speaking of the late '60s and its conflicts over "demonstrations and public order, about education and its expansion," Williams delays a bit before revealing that he is in actuality referring to the 1860s in England and the struggles during that time over the extension of the franchise to working-class men rather than to the 1960s, as most readers might have assumed. In particular, he concentrates on the events of July 1866 when "some sixty thousand workers" converged on Hyde Park, only to clash with police barriers over the right to demonstrate. Why did he play upon the contemporary assumptions of his readers? As Williams would explain, partisans in the conflicts of the 1960s often "invoked" the spirit of Matthew Arnold's *Culture and Anarchy*,[3] and Williams wanted his readers to remember the actual backdrop for Arnold's own defense of culture as the repository of "the best that has been thought and said" as against the threat of anarchy, disorder, and the phrase Arnold would popularize: philistinism. Williams argued, "Arnold's emphasis on culture—his kind of emphasis—was a direct response to the social crisis of those years, and what he saw as opposed to culture was *anarchy*, in a sense very similar to many recent public descriptions of demonstrations and the protest movement. He did not see or present himself as a reactionary, but as a guardian of excellence and of humane values. That, then as now was the strength of his appeal" (original emphasis).[4]

Williams's call to "remember Hyde Park" has deep resonance within the scope of this book's analysis of liberal multicultural discourse. Certainly in the shift toward cosmopolitanism, liberal multicultural commentators channeled something of the spirit of Matthew Arnold. Any worthy conception of culture, they argued, would not dwell on difference but open itself to the best that the world had produced in fostering citizens of the world. Philosophers like Kwame Anthony Appiah and Martha Nussbaum made this notion of cosmopolitanism the central axis of their engagement with cultural pluralism. And certainly contributors to multicultural discourse engaged in polemics over our own contemporary forms of philistinism. The last section of Charles Taylor's "The Politics of Recognition" engages the question of a "presumption of equal worth" for cultures that, in the words of Saul Bellow, had yet to produce a "Zulu Tolstoy." Indeed, we have also encountered this anxiety already with David Hollinger, who spoke of the "will to descend" for racial groups, citing Martin Bernal's controversial *Black Athena*.

But, beyond these uncanny similarities, this book has also engaged in the project of remembering the "Hyde Parks" of liberal multicultural discourse. Of course, there is no singular event that lies interred at the base of liberal multiculturalism. Instead, it is of central significance that the remains of race as they are appropriated in multicultural discourse call forth many associations with the past. But what is consistent across liberal multicultural discourse is the manner in which race is remembered, the patterns over which a racially exclusive past is laundered, appropriated, and newly disavowed. After all, as Williams himself articulates, Hyde Park has become an "immemorial" part of our democratic tradition, which is to say that it has become appropriated in a way that confirms rather than challenges the historicist hegemony of a liberal democratic tradition. His call to remember Hyde Park therefore involves not its literal recall but of how we might remember it, of what is absent in its archived memorialization. Similarly, racial discrimination and exclusion have consistently been invoked in liberal multicultural discourse as a driving force, but in ways that straitjacket its memory in the service of a hegemonic appropriation that disavows its own alterity.

My focus on the role of race in liberal multicultural discourse has thus revolved around the politics of memorialization surrounding that constitutive residue. From the moment race became a symbol for revaluing a static cultural difference, its constitutive challenge within liberal norms was already severed and effaced. It was inevitable therefore that, upon deeper reflection, liberal commentators would find that revaluation a threat to liberal norms, thereby "shortcircuiting," in Williams's words, the memory of the challenge their own Hyde Parks raised. Hence, liberal multicultural discourse certainly memorialized race, but in ways that short-circuited its deictic or indexical resonances. Rather than a residue of the conflicts and alterity in which the presence of the liberal tradition or the presence of American exceptionalism were given shape, meaning, and scope, race was reconfirmed as an abject presence either invariably static across its own memorial narratives or synonymously associated with every fear and anxiety haunting the boundaries of contemporary Western liberal democracies. When Susan

Moller Okin raised the threat of cultural difference to the rights of women, what drove her account was the fear that the gains made for women's rights had not been sufficiently memorialized in liberal societies. But, rather than engage the ongoing politics of that struggle within liberal societies, that is to say, rather than probe the continuing indexical tremulousness of that struggle, she memorialized those struggles as a consolidating force for a liberal hegemony. She herself had evacuated the challenge and alterity that feminist struggle had posed for Western liberal democracies. She, like many commentators engaged in liberal multicultural discourse, was involved in consolidating the historicist hegemony of liberalism by displacing its own conflicted alterity onto a specter cast out from liberalism's own time.

To remember the Hyde Parks of race is therefore to recall the cultural and political scenes wherein the meaning and presence of race and liberal democracies were constitutively twinned and challenged. But if we are to do justice to these scenes or, better, create our own time from them, it is imperative that they not become timeless object lessons for an authoritative historicism but instead index the time-knots of its and our own lived contexts. This calls for negotiating between Fredric Jameson's imperative to "always historicize" and Spivak's caution that this will always involve the mediation of our own "power, desire, and interest." What might bridge the two is the recognition of our own desire for presence in the contexts we inhabit rather than the displacements and disavowals of those ascriptive desires onto the residual and emergent presences of others. Williams's reinvocation of Arnold was not simply to chart a seamless timeline between the reactionaries of the past and reactionaries of his present. Rather, he seemed to retain some sympathy for Arnold because Arnold did not try to mask his own reactions to the conflicts of that time, unlike the contemporary invocations of Arnold, who, for Williams, appropriated Arnold's claims by forgetting Hyde Park. Of the many stories that the residues of race in America might foretell, it is imperative that we index and probe the contexts of our own use instead of crafting a hegemonic narrative that admits no constitutive alterity. This is paradigmatically true for the appropriative use of race in consolidating American liberalism's own timeless narrative.

Louis Hartz was a foreteller of the relentless hegemony liberalism exerted on the American political imaginary. He therefore provides a prophetic caution in more ways than one when we consider the increasing hegemony the American exceptionalist version of liberalism has exerted on the comparative fate of multiculturalism. Recall that, rather than question how an assumptive Americanism could exert such a colonizing force on American history and political thought, he retold that narrative from the standpoint of its historicist trappings. Consequently, it is no surprise that the indexes on race would be so scant and insignificant. What connects the two is that a deeper engagement with race would directly expose the constitutive challenges and alterity in the hegemonic formation of that assumptive Americanism. It would show how race was repeatedly invoked as the container for the nation's own tremulous and disavowed ascriptions of itself. Resigned to the power of liberal hegemony, Hartz could look only outside the nation's borders for resources that might break the spell of that dissimulation. He hoped that the increasing contact with the outside world would shatter its own insular liberal fragment. At the end of his life, Hartz in more ways than one left America in search of these possibilities. He was, one could say, an advocate of multiculturalism *avant la lettre*.

But if his own study is any indication, a multicultural or cosmopolitan embrace of global cultural difference by a historicist and hegemonic American exceptionalism will likely be the occasion for the continued appropriation and exorcism of its own shadows. We have already seen Will Kymlicka complain about the colonizing export of an American view of racism cloud the possibilities of his own version of multicultural citizenship. If one has already foreclosed the historical difference contained in American liberal norms, its hegemony on a comparative or global multiculturalism will ever be a reconsolidation of its own historicism, the illusion of a worldwide end of history, submerging not just the residues of race in the American context but also the residues of colonialism and the subaltern remains of the world. Fortunately, the emperor has no clothes; it has no power except through those institutional presences acquiesced and built by the "power, desire, and interest" of its shifting adherents. Clearly, the power of this investment in liberal historicism is formidable. But there have always been Hyde Parks that remain to spur the alterity of our own political investments, resources that enliven our own untimeliness to our political time, confronting each of us with the challenge of articulating the historical difference of our own "power, desire, and interest" without folding them back into a harried historicism that disavows the residues of the past just as much as the emergent possibilities of the present.

In recalling the remains of race in liberal multicultural discourse, this book implicitly calls for a continuing investment in the emergent possibilities of multiculturalism. Despite the evolving hegemony of an American liberal historicist exceptionalism, that discourse remains fundamentally no better or worse than any other emergent discourse in our own time. The key argument of this book involves how one might memorialize our emergent claims through it and the appropriations of its residues. Like Williams, I would argue that its emphasis on culture could provide a window that intensifies our apprehension of the conflicts and signposts in which the corporeality of American exceptionalism is constituted and forged. But this depends on contesting the politics of memorialization in which the presences of cultural difference are taken to be timeless and static, of possible novel political significance but not the constitutive residues in and of themselves of past political struggles. Certainly, before its appropriation in liberal political discourse, before the entire animus over its normative basis, multiculturalism was a loose, contradictory catchword for insurgent political struggles that challenged the meaning and materiality of an American liberal disavowal of race across many different contexts. If it posed no cross coherence of its own, if it remained on the level of untimely resentments and attachments in the form of identity politics, it nevertheless attempted to expose the problematic presence of a liberal hegemony that dissimulated its own racial basis. If multiculturalism's value lies not in formulating a distinct oppositional politics, it nevertheless called attention to and problematized the alterity of American exceptionalism. The eruptions of identity politics indicted the disavowed dissimulations that seemed central to this exceptionalism: its disavowal of its own cultural presencing, the continuing but shifting exclusion and marginalization of women and racial groups, its appropriation of the remains of race by eviscerating their possibility as a resource for countermemory and counterpolitics. The chief value of multiculturalism in my view was that, rather than leave these resources behind, safely in the past, it forced one to return to them as haunting presences of our own timeliness, of "what we are" on the path toward the possibilities of what we could have and can be.

To remember Hyde Park was for Williams a call to linger on the crises and contingencies through which the right of the franchise was not foretold but struggled over and contested in its embodied and material meaning. In the context of multiculturalism, the call to remember the remains of race should likewise not be an exorcism of a distant and cast-off past but an invitation to linger on what it might foretell to us about the emergent problematizations of race lived in our own time. We might then recall our own recent multicultural conflicts and debates over "demonstrations and public order, about education and its expansion" not as the anxious sign of a "dictatorship of the flesh" beckoning the renewed hegemony of an American exceptionalist idea of freedom but all the more a spur for embracing the democratic "election of our pasts."

It might then be fitting to conclude by returning to where we began, with the figure of President Barack Obama, who has served more than any other in recent times as the screen for our residual and emergent fears and hopes. This of course has been both the source of his appeal and the dread he evokes. The idea that he can accommodate all aspects of the American story, that in showing himself as the product of diverse and contrary strands in the American narrative—that he might allay the political stalemates of the past and build a newly reflective consensus—has fostered not a sense of hope and change but instead a sense of resignation and an uncritical embrace of American exceptionalism. That is to say, the specular political investments placed in the mere presence of President Obama have predictably reinforced a sense of politics as spectacle. Still, it must be said that President Obama has tried to pluralize and widen the terms by which we might memorialize the American exceptionalist canon, thereby injecting hints of dissonance and alterity that, if he does not dwell upon them, may nevertheless spur us to reconsider. One of the distinctive hallmarks of his rhetorical stance has been precisely the pronounced effort to juxtapose contrary and unconventional

American portraits—combining the common resentments of both whites and blacks, showcasing the inspiration and sacrifice drawn across racial lines,[5] or highlighting an unconventional cast of American exemplars from a disabled Asian American female veteran of the Iraq War to a 102-year-old Haitian woman and recent U.S. citizen.[6] On the one hand such efforts provoke challenges to the assumptions of the American story; on the other hand they have just as well reinforced a confidence in American exceptionalism.

Consider for instance, President Obama's Second Inaugural Address.[7] Perhaps the line that will be remembered most from the address is the rhythmic litany "Seneca Falls, Selma, and Stonewall":

> We, the people, declare today that the most evident of truths—that all of us are created equal—is the star that guides us still; just as it guided our forebears through Seneca Falls, and Selma, and Stonewall. . . . It is now our generation's task to carry on what those pioneers began.

Here is a prime example of how President Obama has rhetorically attempted to scramble our conventional understandings of the narrative of American exceptionalism. By recasting these primal events in struggles over the rights of women, blacks, and gays as the efforts of "pioneers" and our "forebears," he both included them within the archives of American exceptionalism and also drained them of any untimely dissonance in their own right. It might surprise the individuals involved in Seneca Falls, Selma, and Stonewall to be considered pioneers and forebears, and they most certainly would have viewed with ambivalence if not outright disdain the idea that they were upholding a self-evident truth laid down before them, merely following a script set down in advance. The very act of including them has eviscerated any sense that they were forging something new and revolutionary, of any sense that to do so, they had to challenge and reinvent the terms that had occluded them.

Obama's juxtaposition also drains from us the ability to reconsider these events in ways that might instill in us the possibility for action and reinvention. It eviscerates for us, in the very act of remembrance, any fissure of alterity that might connect us to them and open up newly emergent ways of seizing our present. They have become mere footnotes in an historicist exceptionalist frame, just as "our generation's task" will likely be so consigned. So why bother? Did not Obama himself conclude that these "self-evident" truths were vouchsafed as our "lasting birthright"? To be sure, the overarching theme of the address was to differentiate self-evident from "self-executing" ideals. But if what we are proposed to execute is merely an "allegiance to an idea articulated in a declaration made more than two centuries ago," then we will likely be complacent, arrogant, or, worse, search for scapegoats for what forestalls the realization of this allegiance.

Swearing on the bibles of Martin Luther King Jr. and Abraham Lincoln, peppering his address with references to Lincoln's own Second Inaugural, perhaps President Obama should have pursued more deeply those allusions. Lincoln's Second Inaugural directly challenged the triumphalism and assurance expected on the eve of the end of the Civil War, castigating both North and South for believing God was on their side, even as both sought to "avert" the real "cause" of the war, not just the "peculiar and powerful interest" in slavery but God's judgment of its offense:

> If we shall suppose that American slavery is one of those offenses which, in the providence of God, must needs come . . . that He gives to both North and South this terrible war as the woe due to those by whom the offense came, shall we discern therein any departure from those divine attributes which the believers in a living God always ascribe to Him? . . . Yet, if God wills that it continue until all the wealth piled by the bondman's two hundred and fifty years of unrequited toil shall be sunk, and until every drop of blood drawn with the lash shall be paid by another drawn with the sword . . . so still it must be said "the judgments of the Lord are true and righteous altogether."[8]

Lincoln's Second Inaugural is an indictment on the eve of triumph. It is a submission to the will of God's judgment over the monstrous evasion of the crime of slavery. It is a humble admission of human fallibility stretching all the way down to our founders and forebears. Perhaps, then, President Obama should have returned to that night on March 18, 2008, when he chastised his former pastor for the "profound mistake" of speaking "as if our society was static; as if no progress has been made." Returning to that crypt, he might have juxtaposed the controversial sermon of Reverend Jeremiah Wright, "Confusing God and Government,"[9] with that of Lincoln's Second Inaugural. He might have recovered how Reverend Wright's sermon was not about how there had been no change or progress but about how governments constantly change—for better or worse. He might have recovered how Reverend Wright recounted the uneven progress and backwards slide the government had shown to people of color across American history. He might have recovered the central theme of Reverend Wright's sermon: that governments are fallible, that "governments fail." Set against the faith that only "God does not fail," that only "God does not change," Reverend Wright's sermon directly indicted the hubris of American providentialism. So when the U.S government "wants us to sing 'God Bless America,' no no no, not 'God Bless America,' God Damn America . . . as long as she tries to act like she is God and she is Supreme." Perhaps if Obama had done so, we might have considered that, like Lincoln before him, Reverend Wright was indicting our complacency that God and providence are on our side, guaranteeing our "lasting birthright." We might at the very least have considered far more seriously that not only do self-evident truths require our execution of them but that they are fragile and not so self-evident to us after all.

NOTES

1. Anne Norton, "The Virtues of Multiculturalism," in *Multiculturalism and American Democracy*, eds. Arthur M. Meltzer, Jerry Weinberger, and M. Richard Zinman, (Lawrence: University Press of Kansas, 1998), 131.
2. Raymond Williams, "A Hundred Years of Culture and Anarchy," in *Problems in Materialism and Culture* (London: Verso, 1980), 3–8.
3. Matthew Arnold, *Culture and Anarchy and Other Writings* (Cambridge: Cambridge University Press, 1993).
4. Williams, "A Hundred Years of Culture and Anarchy," 3.
5. At the conclusion of his "A More Perfect Union" speech, Obama highlighted the dedication of a young white woman, Ashley, to helping other families get sufficient health care despite her own struggles with a mother stricken with cancer and ends with the story of an elderly black man who states that he has joined the campaign simply because of people like Ashley.
6. Tammy Duckworth and Desiline Victor, respectively.
7. "Inaugural Address by President Barack Obama," January 21, 2103, accessed January 31, 2014, www.whitehouse.gov/the-press-office/2013/01/21/inaugural-address-president-barack-obama.
8. "Abraham Lincoln's Second Inaugural Address," March 4, 1865, accessed January 31, 2014, www.loc.gov/rr/program/bib/ourdocs/Lincoln2nd.html.
9. Jeremiah Wright, "Confusing God and Government," April 13, 2003, accessed January 31, 2014, www.sluggy.net/forum/viewtopic.php?p=315691&sid=4b3e97ace4ee8cee02bd6850e52f50b7.

Bibliography

Abbott, Philip. "Still Louis Hartz after All These Years: A Defense of the Liberal Society Thesis." *Perspectives on Politics* 3, no. 1 (March 2005): 93–109.

Abraham, Nicholas, and Maria Torok. *The Shell and the Kernel*. Chicago: University of Chicago Press, 1994.

Alba, Richard. *Ethnic Identity: Transformation of White America*. New Haven: Yale University Press, 1990.

Anderson, Benedict. *Imagined Communities*. London: Verso, 1983.

Anzaldua, Gloria. *Borderlands/La Frontera: The New Mestiza*. San Francisco: Aunt Lute Books, 1987.

Appiah, Kwame Anthony. *Cosmopolitanism: Ethics in a World of Strangers*. New York: Norton, 2007.

———. *The Ethics of Identity*. Princeton: Princeton University Press, 2005.

———. *In My Father's House: Africa in the Philosophy of Culture*. Oxford: Oxford University Press, 1993.

Arendt, Hannah. *Between Past and Future*. New York: Penguin, 1977.

———. *The Human Condition*. Chicago: University of Chicago Press, 1958.

Arnold, Matthew. *Culture and Anarchy and Other Writings*. Cambridge: Cambridge University Press, 1993.

Baldwin, James. *The Fire Next Time*. New York: Vintage, 1963.

Balfour, Lawrie. *The Evidence of Things Not Said; James Baldwin and the Promise of American Democracy*. Ithaca: Cornell University Press, 2001.

Balibar, Etienne, and Immanuel Wallerstein. *Race, Nation, Class: Ambiguous Identities*. New York: Verso, 1991.

Barkan, Elazan. *The Guilt of Nations*. New York: Norton, 2000.

Barry, Andrew, Thomas Osborne, and Nikolas Rose, eds. *Foucault and Political Reason*. Chicago: University of Chicago Press, 1996.

Barry, Brian. *Culture and Equality*. Cambridge: Harvard University Press, 2001.

Beltrán, Cristina. *The Trouble with Unity: Latino Politics and the Creation of Identity*. New York: Oxford University Press, 2010.

Benjamin, Jessica. *The Bonds of Love*. New York: Pantheon, 1988.

———. *Like Subjects, Love Objects*. New Haven: Yale University Press, 1995.

Bercovitch, Sacvan. *The American Jeremiad*. Madison: University of Wisconsin Press, 1978.

———. *Puritan Origins of the American Self*. New Haven: Yale University Press, 1975.

Bhabha, Homi. *The Location of Culture*. New York: Routledge, 1994.

Blauner, Robert. *Racial Oppression in America*. New York: Harper and Row, 1972.

Blight, David W. *Race and Reunion*. Cambridge: Belknap Press, 2001.

Bloom, Allan. *The Closing of the American Mind*. New York: Simon & Schuster, 1987.

Bourne, Randolph. "Transnational America." *Atlantic Monthly*, July 1916, 86–97.
Boyne, Roy. *Foucault and Derrida: The Other Side of Reason*. New York: Routledge, 1990.
Branch, Taylor. *Pillar of Fire; America in the King Years, 1963–65*. New York: Simon & Schuster, 1998.
Brault, Pascale-Anne, and Michael Naas, eds. *The Work of Mourning*. Chicago: University of Chicago Press, 2001.
Brown, Michael K. *Race, Money, and the American Welfare State*. Ithaca: Cornell University Press, 1999.
Brown, Wendy. *Regulating Aversion; Tolerance in the Age of Identity and Empire*. Princeton: Princeton University Press, 2006.
———. *States of Injury*. Princeton: Princeton University Press, 1995.
Bruyneel, Kevin. *The Third Space of Sovereignty; The Postcolonial Politics of U.S.-Indigenous Relations*. Minneapolis: University of Minnesota Press, 2007.
Burchell, Graham, Colin Gordon, and Peter Miller, eds. *The Foucault Effect*. Chicago: University of Chicago Press, 1991.
Butler, Judith. *Bodies That Matter*. New York: Routledge, 1993.
———. *Excitable Speech: A Politics of the Performative*. New York: Routledge, 1997.
——— and Joan W. Scott, eds. *Feminists Theorize the Political*. New York: Routledge, 1992.
Butler, Paul. "Racially Based Jury Nullification: Black Power in the Criminal Justice System." *Yale Law Journal* 105, no. 3 (Dec. 1995): 677–725.
Carens, Joseph. *Culture, Citizenship, and Community*. Oxford: Oxford University Press, 2000.
Carmichael, Stokely, and Charles V. Hamilton. *Black Power*. New York: Random House, 1967.
Carr, E.H. *What Is History?* New York: Vintage, 1961.
Caruth, Cathy. *Unclaimed Experience; Trauma, Narrative, and History*. Baltimore: Johns Hopkins University Press, 1996.
Chakrabarty, Dipesh. *Provincializing Europe: Postcolonial Thought and Historical Difference*. Princeton: Princeton University Press, 2000.
Cheah, Pheng, and Bruce Robbins, eds. *Cosmopolitics: Thinking and Feeling beyond the Nation*. Minneapolis: University of Minnesota Press, 1998.
Cheng, Anne Anlin. *The Melancholy of Race*. Oxford: Oxford University Press, 2001.
Cohen, Joshua, ed. *For the Love of Country: Debating the Limits of Multiculturalism*. Boston: Beacon, 1996.
Conley, Dalton. *Being Black, Living in the Red: Race, Wealth, and Social Policy in America*. Berkeley: University of California Press, 1999.
Connolly, William E. *The Ethos of Pluralization*. Minneapolis: University of Minnesota Press, 1995.
———. *Identity/Difference: Democratic Negotiations of Political Paradox*. Ithaca: Cornell University Press, 1991.
Cooper, Frederick, and Ann Laura Stoler, eds. *Tensions of Empire*. Berkeley: University of California Press, 1997.
Crenshaw, Kimberle, Neil Gotanda, Gary Peller, and Kendall Thomas, eds. *Critical Race Theory: The Key Writings that Formed the Movement*. New York: New Press, 1995.
Cruikshank, Barbara. *The Will to Empower: Democratic Citizens and Other Subjects*. Ithaca: Cornell University Press, 1999.
Darder, Antonia, and Rodolfo D. Torres. *After Race: Racism after Multiculturalism*. New York: New York University Press, 2004.
Dawson, Michael C. *Black Visions: The Roots of Contemporary African-American Political Ideologies*. Chicago: University of Chicago Press, 2003.

Deleuze, Gilles, and Felix Guattari. *Anti-Oedipus; Capitalism and Schizophrenia.* Minneapolis: University of Minnesota Press, 1983.
Derrida, Jacques. *Archive Fever; A Freudian Impression.* Chicago: University of Chicago Press, 1996.
———. "Force of Law: The 'Mystical Foundation of Authority.'" In *Deconstruction and the Possibility of Justice*, edited by Drucilla Cornell, Michel Rosenfeld, and David Gray Carlson, 3–67. New York: Routledge, 1992.
———. *Of Grammatology.* Baltimore: Johns Hopkins University Press, 1976.
———. *Writing and Difference.* Chicago: University of Chicago Press, 1978.
Dillard, Angela. *Guess Who's Coming to Dinner Now? Multicultural Conservatism in America.* New York: New York University Press, 2001.
Donovan, John C. *The Politics of Poverty.* New York: Pegasus, 1967.
Dreyfus, Hubert, and Paul Rabinow. *Michel Foucault: Beyond Structuralism and Hermeneutics.* Chicago: University of Chicago Press, 1982.
Du Bois, W. E. B. *The Souls of Black Folk.* New York: Penguin Books, 1989.
Dudziak, Mary. *Cold War Civil Rights: Race and the Image of American Democracy.* Princeton: Princeton University Press, 2002.
Dumm, Thomas L. *Michel Foucault and the Politics of Freedom.* Walnut Creek: AltaMira Press, 2000.
Edsall, Thomas Byrne, and Mary D. Edsall. *Chain Reaction.* New York: Norton, 1992.
Ellison, Ralph. *Shadow and Act.* New York: Random House, 1953.
Eng, David, and David Kazanjian, eds. *Loss; The Politics of Mourning.* Berkeley: University of California Press, 2003.
Eribon, Didier. *Michel Foucault.* Cambridge: Harvard University Press, 1991.
Ericson, David F., and Louisa Bertch Green. *The Liberal Tradition in American Politics.* New York: Routledge, 1999.
Esquith, Stephen L. *Intimacy and Spectacle: Liberal Theory as Political Education.* Ithaca: Cornell University Press, 1994.
Euben, J. Peter. *Platonic Noise.* Princeton: Princeton University Press, 2003.
Faubion, J., ed. *Aesthetics: The Essential Works of Michel Foucault.* London: Allen Lane, 1998.
Felman, Shoshana. *The Juridical Unconscious; Trials and Traumas in the Twentieth Century.* Cambridge: Harvard University Press, 2002.
Foner, Nancy, and George Fredrickson, eds. *Not Just Black and White: Historical and Contemporary Perspectives on Immigration, Race, and Ethnicity in the United States.* New York: Russell Sage Foundation, 2004.
Foucault, Michel. *The Archaeology of Knowledge.* New York: Pantheon, 1972.
———. *The Care of the Self.* New York: Vintage, 1988.
———. *Discipline and Punish.* New York: Vintage, 1977.
———. "Dream, Imagination, and Existence." *Review of Existential Psychology and Psychiatry* 19 (1984–85): 29–78.
———. *The History of Sexuality, Volume 1.* New York: Vintage, 1990.
———. *Madness and Civilization: A History of Insanity in the Age of Reason.* New York: Vintage, 1965.
———. *Mental Illness and Psychology.* Berkeley: University of California Press, 1987.
———. *The Order of Things.* New York: Vintage, 1994.
———. "Of Other Spaces." *Diacritics* 16 (1986): 22–27.
———. *The Use of Pleasure.* New York: Vintage, 1990.
Fraser, Nancy. "Foucault on Modern Power: Empirical Insights and Normative Confusions." *Praxis International* 1 (Oct. 1981): 272–287.
———. *Justice Interruptus; Critical Reflections on the "Postsocialist" Condition.* New York: Routledge, 1997.
Fuchs, Lawrence H. *Hawaii Pono: A Social History.* New York: Harcourt Brace, 1961.

Gadamer, Hans-Georg. *Philosophical Hermeneutics*. Berkeley: University of California Press, 1976.
———. *Truth and Method*. New York: Continuum, 1999.
Gates Jr., Henry Louis, ed. *"Race," Writing, and Difference*. Chicago: University of Chicago Press, 1986.
Genovese, Eugene D. *Roll, Jordan, Roll: The World the Slaves Made*. New York: Vintage, 1976.
Gerstle, Gary. *American Crucible: Race and Nation in the Twentieth Century*. Princeton: Princeton University Press, 2001.
———. "Liberty, Coercion, and the Making of Americans." *American Historical Review* 99: 4 (1994): 524–558.
———. "Race and the Myth of the Liberal Consensus." *Journal of American History* (September 1995): 579–586.
Gettleman, Marvin E., and David Mermelstein, eds. *The Great Society Reader: The Failure of American Liberalism*. New York: Vintage Books, 1987.
Gillman, Susan. "'Dementia Americana': Mark Twain, 'Wapping Alice' and the Henry K. Shaw Trial." *Critical Inquiry* 14, no. 2 (Winter 1988): 296–314.
Gilroy, Paul. *Against Race; Imagining Political Culture beyond the Color Line*. Cambridge: Belknap Press, 2000.
———. *The Black Atlantic*. Cambridge: Harvard University Press, 1993.
———. *Postcolonial Melancholia*. New York: Columbia University Press, 2005.
Gitlin, Todd. *Twilight of Our Common Dreams: Why America Is Wracked by Culture Wars*. New York: Metropolitan Books, 1995.
Glazer, Nathan. *Affirmative Discrimination: Ethnic Inequality and Public Policy*. New York: Basic, 1975.
———. *Ethnic Dilemmas, 1964–1982*. Cambridge: Harvard University Press, 1983.
———. *We Are All Multiculturalists Now*. Cambridge: Harvard University Press, 1998.
——— and Daniel Patrick Moynihan. *Beyond the Melting Pot*. Cambridge: MIT Press, 1963.
Goldberg, David Theo, ed. *Anatomy of Racism*. Minneapolis: University of Minnesota Press, 1990.
———. *Racist Culture*. Cambridge: Blackwell, 1993.
———, ed. *Multiculturalism: A Critical Reader*. Cambridge: Blackwell, 1994.
Gordon, Avery F. *Ghostly Matters: Haunting and the Sociological Imagination*. Minneapolis: University of Minnesota Press, 1997.
——— and Christopher Newfield, eds. *Mapping Multiculturalism*. Minneapolis: University of Minnesota Press, 1996.
Gooding-Williams, Robert. *In the Shadow of Du Bois: Afro-Modern Political Thought in America*. Cambridge: Harvard University Press, 2009.
———. *Look, a Negro!: Philosophical Essays on Race, Culture, and Politics*. New York: Routledge, 2006.
Graham, Hugh Davis. *Collision Course: The Strange Convergence of Affirmative Action and Immigration Policy in America*. New York: Oxford University Press, 2002.
Greenstone, J. David. *The Lincoln Persuasion*. Princeton: Princeton University Press, 1993.
Gutmann, Amy, ed. *Multiculturalism: Examining the Politics of Recognition*. Princeton: Princeton University Press, 1994.
Gutting, Gary, ed. *The Cambridge Companion to Foucault*. Cambridge: Cambridge University Press, 2005.
Habermas, Jurgen. *The Structural Transformation of the Public Sphere*. Cambridge: MIT Press, 1991.
Hall, Stuart, ed. *Questions of Cultural Identity*. London: Sage, 1996.
Halter, Marilyn. *Shopping for Identity*. New York: Schocken, 2000.

Harrington, Michael. *The Other America*. New York: Penguin, 1963.
Harris, Cheryl. "Whiteness as Property." *Harvard Law Review* 106, no. 8 (1993): 1709–1791.
Harris, Paul. *Black Rage Confronts the Law*. New York: New York University Press, 1997.
Hartog, Hendrik. "Lawyering, Husband's Rights, and the 'Unwritten Law' in Nineteenth-Century America." *Journal of American History* 84, no. 1 (June 1997): 67–96.
Hartman, Saidiya V. *Scenes of Subjection: Terror, Slavery, and Self-Making in Nineteenth Century America*. Oxford: Oxford University Press, 1997.
Hartz, Louis. *The Founding of New Societies*. New York: Harcourt, Brace, 1964.
———. *The Liberal Tradition in America*. New York: Harcourt, Brace, 1955.
———. *The Necessity of Choice*. New Brunswick: Transaction, 1990.
Hattam, Victoria. "History, Agency, and Political Change." *Polity* 32, no. 3 (Spring 2000): 333–338.
———. *In the Shadow of Race: Jews, Latinos, and Immigrant Politics in the United States*. Chicago: University of Chicago Press, 2007.
———. "The 1964 Civil Rights Act: Narrating the Past, Authorizing the Future." *Studies in American Political Development* 18 (Spring 2004): 60–69.
Heidegger, Martin. *Basic Writings*. New York: HarperCollins, 1993.
———. *Being and Time*. Albany: SUNY Press, 1996.
Higham, John. "Multiculturalism and Universalism: A History and Critique." *American Quarterly* 45 (June 1993): 195–219.
Hirschman, Albert O. *The Passions and the Interests*. Princeton: Princeton University Press, 1977.
Hochschild, Jennifer. *Facing Up to the American Dream: Race, Class, and the Soul of the Nation*. Princeton: Princeton University Press, 1995.
Hodgson, Godfrey. *The Gentleman from New York: Daniel Patrick Moynihan*. New York: Houghton Mifflin, 2000.
———. *The Myth of American Exceptionalism*. New Haven: Yale University Press, 2009.
Hofstadter, Richard. *The American Political Tradition*. New York: Knopf, 1996.
Hollinger, David. "Authority, Solidarity, and the Political Economy of Identity: The Case of the United States." *Diacritics* 29, no. 4 (Winter 1999).
———. *In the American Province*. Baltimore: Johns Hopkins University Press, 1985.
———. "National Culture and Communities of Descent." *Reviews in American History* 26, no. 1 (1998): 312–313.
———. "National Solidarity at the End of the Twentieth Century: Reflections on the United States and Liberal Nationalism." *Journal of American History* 84 (Sept. 1997).
———. "Not Universalists, Not Pluralists: The New Cosmopolitans Find Their Own Way." *Constellations* 8, no. 2 (2001): 236–248.
———. "Not What We Had in Mind, But . . ." *Reviews in American History* 30 (2002): 346–354.
———. *Postethnic America: Beyond Multiculturalism*. New York: Basic Books, 1995.
———. *Science, Jews, and Secular Culture; Studies in Mid-Twentieth Century American Intellectual History*. Princeton: Princeton University Press, 1996.
Honig, Bonnie. "Declarations of Independence: Arendt and Derrida on the Problem of Founding a Republic." In *Rhetorical Republic; Governing Representations in American Politics*, edited by Frederick M. Dolan and Thomas L. Dumm, 201–225. Amherst: University of Massachusetts Press, 1993.
———. *Democracy and the Foreigner*. Princeton: Princeton University Press, 2003.
Honneth, Axel. *The Struggle for Recognition*. Cambridge: MIT Press, 1996.
Hont, Istvan, and Michael Ignatieff, eds. *Wealth and Virtue: The Shaping of Political Economy in the Scottish Enlightenment*. Cambridge: Cambridge University Press, 1983.

hooks, bell. *Ain't I a Woman? Black Women and Feminism*. Boston: South End Press, 1999.

———. *Yearnings: Race, Gender, and Cultural Politics*. Boston: South End Press, 1990.

Hoy, David, ed. *Foucault: A Critical Reader*. Oxford: Blackwell, 1986.

Hull, Gloria T., Patricia Bell Scott, and Barbara Smith, eds. *All the Women Are White, All the Blacks Are Men: But Some of Us Are Brave*. New York: The Feminist Press, 1993.

Ignatiev, Noel. *How the Irish Became White*. New York: Routledge, 1995.

Ingram, David. *Group Rights; Reconciling Equality and Difference*. Lawrence: University Press of Kansas, 2000.

Ireland, Robert M. "Insanity and the Unwritten Law." *American Journal of Legal History* 32, no. 2 (April 1988): 157–172.

———. "The Libertine Must Die: Sexual Dishonor and the Unwritten Law in the Nineteenth-Century United States." *Journal of Social History* 23, no. 1 (April 1987): 26–44.

Iton, Richard. "The Sound of Silence." *Perspectives on Politics* 3, no. 1 (March 2005): 111–115.

Jacobson, Matthew Frye. *Roots Too: White Ethnic Revival in Post-Civil Rights America*. Cambridge: Harvard University Press, 2006.

———. *Whiteness of a Different Color: European Immigrants and the Alchemy of Race*. Cambridge: Harvard University Press, 1998.

Johnson, Peter. "Unravelling Foucault's 'Different Spaces.'" *History of the Human Sciences* 19 (2006): 75–90.

Kallen, Horace. *Culture and Democracy in the United States*. New York: Boni & Liveright, 1924.

Kalman, Laura. *The Strange Career of Legal Liberalism*. New Haven: Yale University Press, 1996.

Kammen, Michael. *Contrapuntal Civilization; Essays toward a New Understanding of the American Experience*. New York: Thomas Y. Crowell, 1971.

Kaplan, Sidney. *American Studies in Black and White*. Amherst: University of Massachusetts Press, 1991.

Katzmann, Robert A., ed. *Daniel Patrick Moynihan: The Intellectual in Public Life*. Washington, D.C.: Woodrow Wilson Center Press, 1998.

Katznelson, Ira. "Civic Ideals: Conflicting Visions of Citizenship in U.S. History." *Political Theory* 27, no. 4 (Aug. 1994): 565–570.

———. *Liberalism's Crooked Circle*. Princeton: Princeton University Press, 1996.

———. *When Affirmative Action Was White*. New York: Norton, 2005.

King, Desmond. *Making Americans: Immigration, Race, and the Origins of Diverse Democracy*. Cambridge: Harvard University Press, 2000.

——— and Rogers M. Smith. "Racial Orders in American Political Development." *American Political Science Review* 99(2005): 75–88.

King Jr., Martin Luther. *A Testament of Hope: The Essential Writings of Martin Luther King*, edited by James M. Washington. New York: HarperCollins, 1986.

Koptiuch, Kristin. "'Cultural Defense' and Criminological Displacements: Gender, Race, and (Trans)Nation in the Legal Surveillance of U.S. Diaspora Asians." In *Displacement, Diaspora, and Geographies of Identity*, edited by Smadar Lavie and Ted Swedenburg, 215–233. Durham: Duke University Press, 1996.

Kymlicka, Will. "American Multiculturalism in the International Arena." *Dissent* (Fall 1998): 73–79.

———. *Liberalism, Community, and Culture*. Oxford: Oxford University Press, 1989.

———. *Multicultural Citizenship: A Liberal Theory of Minority Rights*. Oxford: Oxford University Press. 1995.

———. *The Rights of Minority Cultures*. Oxford: Oxford University Press, 1995.

Lacan, Jacques. *Ecrits*. New York: Norton, 2006.

Laclau, Ernesto. *Emancipation(s)*. London: Verso, 1996.

——— and Chantal Mouffe. *Hegemony and Socialist Strategy*. London: Verso, 1985.

Lebovics, Herman. "The Uses of America in Locke's Second Treatise of Government." *Journal of the History of Ideas* 47, no. 4 (1986): 567–581.

Lee, James Kyun-Jin. *Urban Triage: Race and the Fictions of Multiculturalism*. Minneapolis: University of Minnesota Press, 2004.

Lee, Sharon M. "Racial Classification in the U.S. Census, 1890–1990." *Ethnic and Racial Studies* 16, no. 1 (1993): 75–94.

Levin, Daniel Lessard. *Representing Popular Sovereignty: The Constitution in American Political Culture*. Albany: SUNY Press, 1999.

Lipsitz, George. *The Possesive Investment in Whiteness: How White People Benefit from Identity Politics*. Philadelphia: Temple University Press, 1998.

Lopez, Ian Haney. " 'A Nation of Minorities': Race, Ethnicity, and Reactionary Colorblindness." *Stanford Law Review* 59 (Feb. 2007): 985–1063.

———. *White by Law: The Legal Construction of Race*. New York: New York University Press, 1996.

Lorde, Audre. *Sister Outsider*. Freedom, CA: The Crossing Press, 1984.

Lotringer, Sylvere, ed. *Foucault Live*. New York: Semiotext(e), 1996.

Lowe, Lisa. *Immigrant Acts*. Durham: Duke University Press, 1996.

Lowndes, Joseph. *From the New Deal to the New Right: Race and the Southern Origins of Modern Conservatism*. New Haven: Yale University Press, 2008.

———, Julie Novkov, and Dorian T. Warren, eds. *Race and American Political Development*. New York: Routledge, 2008.

Lukes, Steven. *Liberals and Cannibals: The Implications of Diversity*. London: Verso, 2003.

Machen, Lewis H. "Should the Unwritten Law Be Written?" *Virginia Law Register* 13, no. 2 (June 1907): 107–113.

MacIntyre, Alasdair. *After Virtue: A Study in Moral Theory*. London: Duckworth, 1981.

Maguigan, Holly. "Cultural Evidence and Male Violence: Are Feminist and Multicultural Reformers on a Collision Course in Criminal Courts?" *New York University Law Review* 70, no. 36 (1995).

Markell, Patchen. *Bound by Recognition*. Princeton: Princeton University. Press, 2003.

———. "The Recognition of Politics: A Comment on Emcke and Tully." *Constellations* 7, no. 4 (2000): 496–506.

Marris, Peter, and Martin Rein. *Dilemmas of Social Reform: Poverty and Community Action in the United States, Second Edition*. Chicago: Aldine, 1967.

Marshall, Steen H. *The City on the Hill from Below: The Crisis of Prophetic Black Politics*. Philadelphia: Temple University Press, 2011.

Marx, Anthony W. *Making Race and Nation*. Cambridge: Cambridge University Press, 1998.

Mehta, Uday S. *The Anxiety of Freedom: Imagination and Individuality in Locke's Political Thought*. Ithaca: Cornell University Press, 1992.

———. *Liberalism and Empire*. Chicago: University of Chicago Press, 1999.

———. "Liberal Strategies of Exclusion." *Politics and Society* 18, no. 4 (1990): 427–454.

Melzer, Arthur M., Jerry Weinberger, and M. Richard Zinman, eds. *Multiculturalism and American Democracy*. Lawrence: University Press of Kansas, 1998.

Michaels, Walter Benn. *Our America: Nativism, Modernism, and Pluralism*. Durham: Duke University Press, 1995.

Minnow, Martha, Michael Ryan, and Austin Sarat, eds. *Narrative, Violence, and the Law; The Essays of Robert Cover*. Ann Arbor: University of Michigan Press, 1992.

Mizruchi, Susan L. *The Rise of Multicultural America: Economy and Print Culture, 1865–1915*. Chapel Hill: University of North Carolina Press, 2008.
Modood, Tariq. "Anti-essentialism, Multiculturalism, and the 'Recognition' of Religious Groups." In *Citizenship in Diverse Societies*, edited by Will Kymlicka and Wayne Norman, 175–189. Oxford: Oxford University Press, 2000.
Moraga, Cherrie L., and Gloria Anzaldua. *This Bridge Called My Back: Writings by Radical Women of Color*. Watertown: Persephone Press, 1981.
More, Sir Thomas. *Utopia*. New York: Norton, 1992.
Morgan, Edmund. *American Slavery, American Freedom*. New York: Norton, 1975.
Morone, James A., Eldon Eisenach, Wilson Carey McWilliams, and Rogers M. Smith. "Symposium on *Civic Ideals*." *Studies in American Political Development* 13 (Spring 1999): 184–244.
Morrison, Toni. *Playing in the Dark; Whiteness and the Literary Imagination*. Cambridge: Harvard University Press, 1992.
———, ed. *Race-ing Justice, En-gendering Power*. New York: Pantheon, 1992.
———, ed. *To Die for the People: The Writings of Huey P. Newton*. New York: Writers and Readers Publishing, 1995.
——— and Claudia Brodsky Lacour, eds. *Birth of a Nation'hood; Gaze, Script, and Spectacle in the O.J. Simpson Case*. New York: Pantheon, 1997.
Moynihan, Daniel Patrick. *Coping: Essays on the Practice of Government*. New York: Random House, 1972.
———. "Employment, Income, and the Ordeal of the Negro Family." *Daedalus* 94 (Fall 1965): 771–814.
———."Epidemic on the Highways." *The Reporter* 20, no. 9 (April 30, 1959): 16–23.
———. *Maximum Feasible Misunderstanding: Community Action in the War on Poverty*. New York: Free Press, 1969.
———. "The Professionalization of Reform." *Public Interest* 1 (1965): 6–16.
———. "Traffic Safety and the Body Politic." *The Public Interest* 3 (Spring 1966): 10–26.
Murray, Charles. *Losing Ground: American Social Policy, 1950–1980*. New York: Basic Books, 1984.
Myrdal, Gunnar. *An American Dilemma*. New York: Transaction Publishers, 1995.
Nelson, Cary, and Lawrence Grossberg, eds. *Marxism and the Interpretation of Culture*. Chicago: University of Illinois, 1988.
Nepo, Mark, ed. *Deepening the American Dream*. San Francisco: Jossey-Bass, 2005.
Ngai, Mae M. *Impossible Subjects: Illegal Aliens and the Making of Modern America*. Princeton: Princeton University Press, 2004.
Nietzsche, Friedrich. *On the Genealogy of Morals*. Translated by Walter Kaufmann and R. J. Hollingdale. New York: Vintage, 1989.
———. *Untimely Meditations*. Cambridge: Cambridge University Press, 1997.
Noble, David W. *Death of a Nation: American Culture and the End of Exceptionalism*. Minneapolis: University of Minnesota Press, 2002.
Nobles, Melissa. *Shades of Citizenship; Race and the Census in Modern Politics*. Stanford: Stanford University Press, 2000.
Norgren, Jill, and Serena Nanda. *American Cultural Pluralism and Law*. Westport: Praeger, 1996.
Norton, Anne. *Alternative Americas: A Reading of Antebellum Political Culture*. Chicago: University of Chicago Press, 1986.
———. *Bloodrites of the Post-Structuralists*. New York: Routledge, 2002.
———. "Engendering Another American Identity." In *Rhetorical Republic: Governing Representations in American Politics*, edited by Frederick M. Dolan and Thomas L. Dumm, 125–142. Amherst: University of Massachusetts Press, 1993.
———. *Republic of Signs*. Chicago: University of Chicago Press, 1993.
Note. "The Cultural Defense in the Criminal Law." *Harvard Law Review* 99 (1986): 1293–1311.

Note. "Recognition of the Honor Defense under the Insanity Plea." *Yale Law Journal* 43 (1934): 809–814.

Novkov, Julie. *Racial Union: Law, Intimacy, and the White State in Alabama, 1865–1954*. Ann Arbor: University of Michigan Press, 2008.

Nussbaum, Martha C. *Cultivating Humanity*. Cambridge: Harvard University Press, 1997.

Okihiro, Gary Y. *Cane Fires: The Anti-Japanese Movement in Hawai'i, 1865–1945*. Philadelphia: Temple University Press, 1991.

Okin, Susan Moller. "Is Multiculturalism Bad for Women?" In *Is Multiculturalism Bad for Women?*, edited by Joshua Cohen, Matthew Howard, and Martha Nussbaum, 9–24. Princeton: Princeton University Press, 1999.

Oliver, Melvin L., and Thomas Shapiro. *Black Wealth, White Wealth: A New Perspective on Racial Inequality*. New York: Routledge, 1997.

Omi, Michael, and Howard Winant. *Racial Formation in the United States*. New York: Routledge, 1994.

Orren, Karen, and Stephen Skowronek. *The Search for American Political Development*. Cambridge: Cambridge University Press, 2004.

———. "Structure, Sequence, and Subordination in American Political Culture: What's Traditions Got to Do with It?" *Journal of Policy History* 8, no. 4 (1996): 470–494.

Parekh, Bhikhu. *Rethinking Multiculturalism*. Cambridge: Harvard University Press, 2000.

Pasquale, Santo de. "Provocation and the Homosexual Advance Defence: The Deployment of Culture as a Defence Strategy." *Melbourne University Law Review* 26 (2002): 110–143.

Pateman, Carol. *The Sexual Contract*. Stanford: Stanford University Press, 1988.

Pattell, Cyrus R.K."Comparative American Studies: Hybridity and Beyond." *American Literary History* (Spring 1999): 166–186.

Phillips, Anne. *Multiculturalism without Culture*. Princeton: Princeton University Press, 2009.

———. *The Politics of Presence*. Oxford: Oxford University Press, 1995.

Piven, Frances Fox, and Richard A. Cloward. *Poor People's Movements: Why They Succeed and How They Fail*. New York: Vintage Books, 1979.

Plotke, David. *Building a Democratic Political Order*. Cambridge: Cambridge University Press, 1996.

Pocock, J.G.A.*The Machiavellian Moment: Florentine Political Thought and the Atlantic Republican Tradition*. Princeton: Princeton University Press, 1975.

———. *Politics, Language, and Time: Essays on Political Thought and History*. Chicago: University of Chicago Press, 1989.

Portes, Alejandro, and Ruben G. Rimbaut. *Immigrant America: A Portrait*. Berkeley: University of California Press, 1996.

Povinelli, Elizabeth A. *The Cunning of Recognition: Indigenous Alterities and the Making of Australian Multiculturalism*. Durham: Duke University Press, 2002.

Post, Robert C. *Prejudicial Appearances; The Logic of American Antidiscrimination Law*. Durham: Duke University Press, 2001.

Quadagno, Jill. *The Color of Welfare: How Racism Undermined the War on Poverty*. New York: Oxford University Press, 1996.

Rabinow, Paul, and Nikolas Rose, eds. *The Essential Foucault*. New York: New Press, 2003.

Rainwater, Lee, and William L. Yancey, eds. *The Moynihan Report and the Politics of Controversy*. Cambridge: MIT Press, 1967.

Ranciere, Jacques. *Dis-agreement*. Minneapolis: University of Minnesota, 1999.

———. *The Names of History*. Minneapolis: University of Minnesota Press, 1994.

Rao, Vijayrendra, and Michael Walton, eds. *Culture and Public Action*. Stanford: Stanford University Press, 2004.

Rawls, John. *Political Liberalism*. New York: Columbia University Press, 1993.
Raz, Joseph. *Ethics in the Public Domain: Essays in the Morality of Law and Politics*. Oxford: Oxford University Press, 1994.
———. *The Morality of Freedom*. Oxford: Oxford University Press, 1988.
Reed Jr., Adolph L. *W.E.B. DuBois and American Political Thought*. Oxford: Oxford University Press, 1997.
Reinecke, John. *Language and Dialect in Hawaii: A Sociolinguistic History to 1935*. Honolulu: University of Hawaii Press, 1969.
Renteln, Alison Dundes. *The Cultural Defense*. Oxford: Oxford University Press, 2004.
Ricoeur, Paul. *Hermeneutics and the Human Sciences*. Cambridge: Cambridge University Press, 1981.
———. *Time and Narrative*. Vol. 3. Chicago: University of Chicago Press, 1993.
Rimonte, Nilda. "A Question of Culture: Cultural Approval of Violence against Women in the Pacific-Asian Community and the Cultural Defense." *Stanford Law Review* 43 (July 1991): 1311–1327.
Roediger, David. *Towards the Abolition of Whiteness*. London: Verso 1994.
———. *The Wages of Whiteness*. London: Verso, 2007.
———. *Working toward Whiteness: How America's Immigrants Became White*. New York: Basic Books, 2005.
Rogin, Michael. *Blackface, White Noise*. Berkeley: University of California Press, 1996.
———. "'Make My Day!': Spectacle as Amnesia in Imperial Politics." *Representations* 29 (Winter 1990): 99–123.
———. *Ronald Reagan, the Movie: And Other Episodes in Political Demonology*. Berkeley: University of California Press, 1987.
Said, Edward. *Culture and Imperialism*. New York: Vintage, 1994.
———. *Orientalism*. New York: Vintage, 1979.
Sandel, Michael. *Liberalism and the Limits of Justice*. Cambridge: Cambridge University Press, 1982.
Saxton, Alexander. "Nathan Glazer, Daniel Moynihan, and the Cult of Ethnicity." *Amerasia Journal* 4, no. 2 (Fall 1977): 141–150.
Schlesinger Jr., Arthur M. *The Disuniting of America: Reflections on a Multicultural Society*. New York: Norton, 1992.
Scott, Joan. *Gender and the Politics of History*. New York: Columbia University Press, 1999.
Self, Robert O. *American Babylon*. Princeton: Princeton University Press, 2003.
Shachar, Ayelet. *Multicultural Jurisdictions: Cultural Differences and Women's Rights*. Cambridge: Cambridge University Press, 2001.
Shulman, George. "American Political Culture, Prophetic Narration, and Toni Morrison's *Beloved*." *Political Theory* 24, no. 2 (May 1996): 295–314.
———. *American Prophecy: Race and Redemption in American Political Culture*. Minneapolis: University of Minnesota Press, 2008.
———."Hope and American Politics." *Raritan* 21: 3 (2002): 1–19.
———. "The Pastoral Idyll of *Democracy*." *Democracy* 3 (Fall 1983): 43–54.
Silverman, Hugh J., ed. *Gadamer and Hermeneutics*. New York: Routledge, 1991.
Sing, James. "Toward a Synthetic View of Provocation and Culture in the Criminal Law." *Yale Law Journal* 108, no. 7 (May 1999): 1845–1884.
Singh, Nikhil Pal. *Black Is a Country*. Cambridge: Harvard University Press, 2004.
Skerry, Peter. *Mexican Americans: The Ambivalent Minority*. Cambridge: Harvard University Press, 1993.
Skinner, Quentin. *Visions of Politics*. Cambridge: Cambridge University Press, 2002.
Skowronek, Stephen. "The Reassociation of Ideas and Purposes: Racism, Liberalism, and the American Political Tradition." *American Political Science Review* 100, no. 3 (2006): 385–401.
Skrentny, John. *The Minority Rights Revolution*. Cambridge: Belknap Press, 2002.

Sleeper, Jim. *The Closest of Strangers: Liberalism and the Politics of Race in New York*. New York: Norton, 1990.
———. *Liberal Racism: How Fixating on Race Subverts the American Dream*. New York: Penguin Books, 1997.
Smith, Nicholas H. *Strong Hermeneutics; Contingency and Moral Identity*. New York: Routledge, 1997.
Smith, Rogers M. "Beyond Tocqueville, Myrdal, and Hartz: The Multiple Traditions in America." *American Political Science Review* 87, no. 3 (Sept. 1993): 549–566.
———. *Civic Ideals: Conflicting Visions of Citizenship in U.S. History*. New Haven: Yale University Press, 1997.
———. *Stories of Peoplehood*. Cambridge: Cambridge University Press, 2003.
———, Desmond King, and Philip A. Klinkner. "Challenging History: Barack Obama and American Racial Politics." *Daedalus* 140 (2011): 1–15.
——— and Phillip A. Klinkner. *The Unsteady March: The Rise and Decline of Racial Equality in America*. Chicago: University of Chicago, 2002.
Sneirson, Judd F. "Black Rage and the Criminal Law: A Principled Approach to a Polarized Debate." *University of Pennsylvania Law Review* 143, no. 6 (June 1995): 2251–2288.
Sollors, Werner. *Beyond Ethnicity*. Oxford: Oxford University Press, 1986.
Song, Sarah. *Justice, Gender, and the Politics of Multiculturalism*. Cambridge University Press, 2007.
Spinner-Halev, Jeff. *Boundaries of Citizenship: Race, Ethnicity and Nationality in the Liberal State*. Baltimore: Johns Hopkins University Press, 1994.
———. *Surviving Diversity: Religion and Democratic Citizenship*. Baltimore: Johns Hopkins University Press, 2000.
Spivak, Gayatri Chakravorty. *In Other Worlds*. New York: Routledge, 1988.
Stannard, David E. *Honor Killing: How the Infamous 'Massie Affair' Transformed Hawai'i*. New York: Viking, 2005.
Steinberg, Stephen. *The Ethnic Myth*. Boston: Beacon, 1981.
Stevens, Jacqueline. "Beyond Tocqueville, Please!" *American Political Science Review* 89, no. 4 (Dec. 1995): 987–995.
Stoler, Ann Laura. *Race and the Education of Desire*. Durham: Duke, 1995.
Sugrue, Thomas. *The Origins of the Urban Crisis: Race and Inequality in Postwar Detroit*. Princeton: Princeton University Press, 1996.
Takaki, Ronald. *A Different Mirror: A History of Multicultural America*. Boston: Little, Brown, 1993.
Taylor, Charles. *The Ethics of Authenticity*. Cambridge: Harvard University Press, 1991.
———. *Human Agency and Language: Philosophical Papers*. Vol. 1. Cambridge: Cambridge University Press, 1985.
Tocqueville, Alexis de. *Democracy in America*. New York: Harper Perennial, 1988.
Todorov, Tvetan. *The Conquest of America*. New York: Harper & Row, 1984.
Tomasky, Michael. *Left for Dead: The Life, Death and Possible Resurrection of Progressive Politics in America*. New York: Free Press, 1996.
Trilling, Lionel. *The Liberal Imagination*. New York: Doubleday Anchor, 1950.
Tucker, Robert C., ed. *The Marx-Engels Reader*. New York: Norton, 1972.
Tully, James, ed. *Philosophy in an Age of Pluralism; The Philosophy of Charles Taylor in Question*. Cambridge: Cambridge University Press, 1994.
———. *Strange Multiplicity; Constitutionalism in an Age of Diversity*. Cambridge: Cambridge University Press, 1995.
Umphrey, Martha Merrill. "The Dialogics of Legal Meaning: Spectacular Trials, the Unwritten Law, and the Narratives of Criminal Responsibility." *Law and Society Review* 33, no. 2 (1999): 393–423.
U.S. Department of Labor, Office of Policy Planning and Research. *The Negro Family: The Case for National Action*. Washington, D.C.: Government Printing Office, 1965.

Vance, Rupert B., and Waller Wynne Jr. "Folk Rationalizations in the 'Unwritten Law.'" *American Journal of Sociology* 39, no. 4 (Jan. 1934): 483–492.
Viswanathan, Gauri, ed. *Power, Politics, and Culture; Interviews with Edward Said*. New York: Pantheon, 2001.
Volpp, Leti. "Feminism versus Multiculturalism." *Columbia Law Review* 101, no. 5 (June 2001): 1181–1218.
———, and Mary L. Dudziak, eds. *Legal Borderlands: Law and the Construction of American Borders*. Baltimore: Johns Hopkins University Press, 2006.
———. "(Mis)identifying Culture: Asian Women and the 'Cultural Defense.'" *Harvard Women's Law Journal* 17 (1994): 57–101.
———. "Talking 'Culture': Gender, Race, Nation, and the Politics of Multiculturalism." *Columbia Law Review* 96 (1996): 1573–1617.
Waldron, Jeremy. "Minority Cultures and the Cosmopolitan Alternative." *University of Michigan Journal of Law Reform* 25, no. 3: 751–93.
Walzer, Michael. *Exodus and Revolution*. New York: Basic, 1986.
———. *Interpretation and Social Criticism*. Cambridge: Harvard University Press, 1987.
———. *On Toleration*. New Haven: Yale University Press, 1997.
———. *Spheres of Justice: A Defense of Pluralism and Equality*. Oxford: Blackwell, 1983.
———. "What Does It Mean to Be an 'American'?" *Social Research* 57, no. 3 (1990): 591–614.
Warner, Michael. *The Trouble with Normal*. Cambridge: Harvard University Press, 1999.
Waters, Mary C. *Ethnic Options: Choosing Identities in America*. Berkeley: University of California Press, 1990.
Weed, Perry L. *The White Ethnic Movement and Ethnic Politics*. New York: Praeger, 1973.
Weinberg, Arthur. *Attorney for the Damned: Clarence Darrow in the Courtroom*. Chicago: University of Chicago Press, 1989.
Weinstock, Daniel M. "The Political Theory of Strong Evaluation." In *Philosophy in an Age of Pluralism: The Philosophy of Charles Taylor in Question*, edited by James Tully, 171–193. Cambridge: Cambridge University Press, 1994.
West, Cornel. *Prophetic Reflections*. Monroe: Common Courage Press, 1993.
———. *Race Matters*. New York: Vintage, 1994.
Wilentz, Sean. "Uses of *The Liberal Tradition*." *Perspectives on Politics* 3, no. 1 (March 2005): 117–120.
Willett, Cynthia, ed. *Theorizing Multiculturalism; A Guide to the Current Debate*. Malden: Blackwell, 1998.
Williams, Patricia J. *The Alchemy of Race and Rights*. Cambridge: Harvard University Press, 1991.
Williams, Raymond. *Problems in Materialism and Culture*. London: Verso, 1980.
Wilson, Woodrow. *The Papers of Woodrow Wilson*, edited by Arthur S. Link. Princeton: Princeton University Press, 1978.
Wolfenstein, Eugene Victor. *Inside/Outside Nietzsche: Psychoanalytic Explorations*. Ithaca: Cornell University Press, 2000.
———. *Psychoanalytic-Marxism: Groundwork*. London: Free Association Books, 1993.
———. *The Victims of Democracy: Malcolm X and the Black Revolution*. New York: Guilford Press, 1993.
Wolin, Sheldon. *Politics and Vision*. Princeton: Princeton University Press, 2006.
———. *The Presence of the Past*. Baltimore: Johns Hopkins University Press, 1989.
Woo, Deborah. "The People v. Fumiko Kimura: But Which People?" *International Journal of the Sociology of Law* 17 (1989).
Yamin, Priscilla. *American Marriage: A Political Institution*. Philadelphia: University of Pennsylvania Press, 2012.
Young, Iris Marion. *Justice and the Politics of Difference*. Princeton: Princeton University Press, 1990.

Index

Page numbers followed by n indicate notes.